IN TIME OF WAR

By
Susan Zerlaut King

In Time of War by Susan Zerlaut King

ISBN: 978-1-7637149-9-1

Copyright © Susan Zerlaut King 2025

All rights reserved. Other than for the purposes and subject to the conditions prescribed under the Copyright Act, no part of this publication may be reproduced, stored in a retrieval system, or transmitted in any form or by any means, electronic, mechanical, photocopying, recording or otherwise, without the prior permission of the publisher.

This edition first published in 2025 by immortalise
www.immortalise.com.au - info@immortalise.com.au

Typesetting and cover layout by Ben Morton

Cover photo: Authors' father Harold Willius Zerlaut, Aviation Corps.

IN TIME OF WAR

By

Susan Zerlaut King

Contents

Author's note ix

Introduction 1

Part One   9

Preparing for War 1917 11

Home Front Newaygo County, 1917 18

Letters and Related Articles 1917 35

Part Two   83

War Continues 1918 85

Home Front Newaygo County, 1918 97

Letters and Related Articles 1918 111

Part Three   339

Victory Achieved 1919-1921 341

Home Front Newaygo County, 1919-1921 348

Letters and Related Articles 1919-1921 353

Note of Thanks 376

Bibliography 378

Unattributed Sources 380

For the Fallen

And a glory that shines upon our tears.
They went with songs to the battle, they were young,
Straight of limb, the true of eye, steady and aglow.
They were staunch to the end against odds uncounted;
They fell with their faces to the foe.
They shall grow not old, as are that we left grow old;
Age shall not weary them, nor the years condemn.
At the going down of the sun and in the morning,
We will remember them.

Laurance Binyon

Study the past, if you would divine the future.

Confucius

Dedicated to our servicemen and women,

past and present,

and to those who support them.

In memory of my father, Harold Willius Zerlaut, WWI Aviation Corp,

287th Aero Squadron, 1917-1919.

Author's note

In Time of War is not meant to be a history of World War I. The reader will not find details of battles fought or strategies of army against army. Rather, it's the story of the people who lived through the Great War, the soldiers who served from Newaygo County, Michigan, and the people back home who loved them. It investigates the hardships the soldiers faced, many in France who had never been outside Newaygo County before the war began. It details the challenges those on the home front faced from the many shortages, the difficulties caused from losing working family members to the draft, or the stresses caused by having to prove one's loyalty to the United States.

My interest in World War I began early in my life. My father enlisted in the Aviation Corps, a division of the Signal Corps. He was attached to the 287th Aero Squadron as an airplane mechanic. He dreamed of becoming a pilot and was about to fulfill that dream when the Armistice was signed. He returned home with a collection of World War items that has fascinated me for years. Among them were his heavy, wool great coat, wide brimmed hat, and much worn, leather boots. I remember sleeping under a dark brown army blanket surrounded by the weighty smell of wool. When he died, a box of photos from his time in the service surfaced, adding to my curiosity of all things World War I.

A few years ago, while doing microfilm research of articles in the *Fremont Times Indicator* for another book, I came across a letter written home by a WWI soldier. I learned it was the practice of the newspaper to print all letters brought to them by families of those serving in the war. This letter led me on a journey of great discovery and deep involvement in the lives of those who lived through the Great War.

I kept my eye out for other letters and soon had a folder full of them, including two letters written by my father that I never knew existed. Later the letters were printed in a booklet called *Letters Home* by the Terry Wantz Historical Research Center in Fremont, Michigan. Then I dutifully placed them back in the folder and for the next few years involved myself in other writing projects.

But the letters continued to beckon me every time I heard mention of the war. I always felt there was more that should be done with them and that these men must not be forgotten. So, I returned years later to microfilm to look for letters and articles which I might have missed, and, as it turned out, I had missed a lot! Eventually I had a collection of over one hundred letters from ninety-plus servicemen. Besides the letters, there were articles describing promotions, servicemen returning home, information about those missing in action, and sadly, obituaries.

The letters presented here were highly censored until the Armistice was signed, whereupon they grew in length and detail. They are printed exactly as they were written with no correction of spelling or grammar, except for the express purpose of readability, so that readers may experience them exactly as they were first read by their families.

To give background information and to put the letters into perspective the book has been divided into three parts. A section each has been created for 1917, 1918, and 1919-1921. Each section begins with the world view of the war, followed by the events taking place on the home front. The letters and articles conclude each section by telling the rest of the story in the servicemen's own words.

Many more men served from Newaygo County than are represented here. Sadly, I know there are other servicemen whose experiences we may never know. It is my hope that those recognized in this book will stand in good stead for every soldier, no matter his rank or duties, as brave men who loved their country.

In Time of War
Servicemen Recognized

Darrel Alton	Dick Deur
Richard Ashford	Donald M. Dickinson
Mason Bacon	Bill Dobben
Charles Baker	Emen Doud
Ray E. Bassett	Bryan Dragoo
Merrit Beisel	Harry Dursema
Ralph Beisel	Darrel H. Eppele
Mason Brace	Carl H. Felber
John Brookhuis	Henry Felber
Ford Brooks	John G. Frens
Edwin Brown	Henry C. Fox
George Burns	Roy C. Gardenour
Charles Coburn	Henry Geerds
James C. Coburn	Dan F. Gerber
S. A. Colman	Ward Giddings
David E. Crabb	Warren Giddings
Lynn Crawford	Len Gilbert
Russell Crawford	Vernon Gilbert
Dallas Darling	Frank B. Henry
Will Dawe	Lawrence B. Henry
Gerritt Deters	Juell J. Hewitt

Ralph L. Hilton
Howard Hines
Fred Hoad
David T. Hopkins
Frank Jackson
Milan Jackson
Joe Jewell
Bert Jones
Harold B. Kempf
Merrit Kimbell
James J. Kuypers
Benjamin Lambers
J. M. Leslie
John M. Lewis
Ralph R. Lewis
Renard Looyengoed
Clarence L. Misner
Stanley Morrison
Dewey S. O'Neal
Austin Olney
Roy Parker
Harold A. Rasey
Frank H. Raymond

Frederick Paul Reber
Harry C. Reddy
Walter Robbins
Charles J. Sanborn
Howard J. Schoolmastser
Herman Schuiteman
John Scott
Albert Siems
J. B. (Bart) Simmonds
Glen Smith
Griffin H. Smith
Lee A. Sommers
Paul E. Steffe
John R. Stone
Glenn Taylor
James Tiesinga
Floyd Tinney
Kay W. Towne
C. C. Upton
Oscar Vickstrom
Chauncy Warren
Charles Wise
Harold Zerlaut

Introduction

On June 28, 1914, Sarajevo, part of the Balkan province of Bosnia and Herzegovina, became the center of conflict which ignited the Great War.

Archduke Franz Ferdinand of Austria, nephew of Emperor Franz Joseph, had been inspecting the army of Sarajevo with his wife Archduchess Sophie. In Austria, Ferdinand was especially disliked by the Austrian people because of his hot temper and violence. Ferdinand was also despised by Emperor Franz Joseph, whose son had committed suicide, leaving Ferdinand next in line to the imperial throne of the thousand-year-old Hapsburg Empire. Franz Joseph had been against the marriage of Ferdinand and Sophie from the beginning, only allowing it under pressure from Pope Leo XIII. Even so, the marriage came with numerous restrictions. Sophie was not allowed to become Empress of Austria, nor could their children be in line to the throne. Sophie was also excluded from all public ceremonies.

The trip to Sarajevo had infuriated Franz Joseph. Ferdinand had been espousing ideas suggesting Austria, Hungry, and the Slavs should all have their own governments; ideas which Franz Joseph feared would cause him and others to lose power. Even though the Balkan Wars of 1912-1913 had created high anti-Austrian sentiment, making such a trip very risky, Ferdinand persevered with his plans against all advice.

In Time of War

This time his plans included his wife, Sophie. In Sarajevo they would celebrate their fourteenth wedding anniversary where they could act as they pleased allowing Sophie to ride by Ferdinand's side in an open car.

As Ferdinand and Sophie traveled through Sarajevo streets, six terrorists from a revolutionary group threw a bomb injuring several in their party. The couple was left mostly unharmed. The Archduke asked General Oskar Potrorick, the military governor, for more security, but none was given.

An hour later the party moved on. The Archduke expressed his desire to go to the hospital where the victims of the bombing had been taken. In doing so, the driver took a wrong turn. The assassins had mostly dispersed thinking they had lost their chance, but one young Bosnian named Gavelo Princip found himself suddenly close to the royal couple as the vehicle stopped to turn around. The chance to shoot the Archduke was all he had needed. He took aim, shot twice, and killed both the Archduke and Duchess.

In Sarajevo riots followed the murders, but back in Austria the public and relatives of Ferdinand had a much milder response. Even at the royal funeral for Ferdinand, no foreign dignitaries had been invited. Emperor Franz Joseph intervened to allow the Archduchess' coffin to be placed next to the Archduke, but set at a lower level than his. She was not allowed to be buried in the plots for Hapsburg royalty, so both were buried in crypts beneath the chapel of the Artstetten Castle.

Introduction

For Austria this was the opening they had been preparing for in their plan to spread military and political power throughout the center of Europe, squashing those in their way with brute force if necessary. Retribution was the only option on the table as far as Austria and Germany were concerned. It began in a letter to Serbia with a clear attempt to provoke war. Serbia was given a list of ten impossible demands, including complete surrender of its sovereignty which put Austria in charge. Serbian subjects were to be tried and punished by Austrian tribunals. Serbia was given forty-eight hours to comply, while Austria made itself scarce and unavailable. England, France, and Russia made every effort to intervene to no avail. As the clock ticked away the hours and minutes, war became a reality.

At that time most of the European countries were monarchies, their leaders related to each other. They had large standing armies, fully armed. It soon became a house of cards as country after country was drawn into the conflict, duty bound by treaties. Germany declared war on France which was duty bound to aid Russia. When neutral Belgium refused to let German troops pass through to France, Germany declared war on Belgium. Great Britain then came to the aid of Belgium along with its territories of Australia and Canada.

Through it all the United States under President Woodrow Wilson remained neutral. Though many politicians of the time, including Theodore Roosevelt and others who were part of the Preparedness Movement, pushed the United States to build up an army and prepare for war, President Wilson turned to diplomacy as a means to settle the conflict. In 1916, President Wilson was re-elected under the slogan, "He kept us out of the war," though by that time he was personally moving towards intervention.

Many Americans had no taste for war and did not want to get involved in what they considered Europe's problems. The country was already in a state of unrest. There were ongoing clashes between labor and the unions. The prohibition movement led by the Women's Christian Temperance Union, Anti-Saloon League and others were pushing hard against anti-prohibition supporters in the fight over the 18th amendment. Suffragettes in their battle for the 19th amendment were ramping up their rallies with protests for voting rights for women. In many cases the turmoil and outrage these disagreements caused led the public to violence.

And then there was Pancho Villa.

The United States was already contending with the possibilities of war, but it was a war with Mexico, not Germany. In 1916, the U.S. was involved in a serious conflict along the Texas border between Pancho Villa and U.S. backed Venustrano Carrinza. The U. S. recognized Carrinza as the head of Mexico's government in October 1915, and in doing so provided rail transportation for Carrinza's forces from Eagle Pass to Douglas, Arizona to engage in battle with Villa, now known as the Battle of Aqua Prieta. The great losses

Introduction

taken by Villa caused him to retaliate by attacking U. S. mining executives on January 9, 1916. Next, the border town of Columbus, Mexico was raided resulting in the deaths of eighteen Americans.

The killing prompted the creation of the Mexican Expedition against Pancho Villa in March 1916. The Expeditionary forces were led by General "Black Jack" Pershing. Thousands of U.S. soldiers searched northern Mexico for Villa. Though Villa had many enemies, he also had many supporters and was able to avoid capture. The conflict was eventually settled diplomatically, though the U.S. decidedly left troops along the border to continue their lookout for Pancho Villa.

Meanwhile, the war overseas continued. The brutality brought against neutral Belgium by Germany turned world opinion against them. The Belgians tenacious resistance astounded Germany, who thought they could virtually walk through Belgium on their way to France. Later Germany retaliated against their resistance by killing hundreds of men, women, and children and burning their villages.

Both Germany and Britain needed raw materials to support their war effort. On February 4, 1915, Germany proclaimed the North Sea, the area between Britain, Germany and Belgium, a war zone. They followed with a blockade of Britain to keep it from receiving vital imports. Germany warned that all merchant ships, even those from neutral countries, were subject to sinking without warning.

May 5, 1915, the Lusitania was sunk, killing 1000 people; of them, 128 were Americans. There was outrage from the American people. The United States protests caused Germany to agree to cut back on submarine warfare, but they resumed doing so again February 1, 1917, taking the risk that such actions might cause the U. S. to enter the war. The U.S. then broke off all relations with Germany.

Germany still did not back down. While it was returning to England from the United States, the RMS Laconia was torpedoed and sunk February 25, 1917. Several passengers were killed, including more Americans. The account of the sinking was read to both U.S. Houses of government with calls to declare war.

Unknown to the United States near the end of the Mexican Expeditionary to Mexico, British intelligence chirographers had deciphered information gathered from Germany. They received this information in January, but not wanting to reveal their decoding skills to Germany, kept the information secret until finally in March they shared the intelligence with President Wilson. The decoded message was a telegram from German Foreign Minister Zimmerman to the ambassador from Mexico, Heinrich von Ecklandt, proposing an alliance between Germany and Mexico. In their effort to exploit the Mexican crisis, Germany offered Mexico the return of territories in Arizona, Texas, and California if they were victorious in their war, in exchange for Mexico joining Germany's cause. Soon

Introduction

after the telegram was printed in the newspapers there were more U-boat attacks on American ships.

Congress declared war on Germany April 6, 1917.

In Time of War

PART ONE

In Time of War

Preparing for War
1917

Food and supplies and the attrition of fighting men dangerously jeopardized the successful end of the war for France and the Allies. War-torn France was jubilant when the U. S. entered the war. But help was far from immediate. The United States had been on the verge of war for months, yet it was woefully unprepared. General John J. Pershing from the Mexican Expedition was appointed commander of the American Expedition Force. In June 1917, he reached France with the First Division and was joined by the 42nd Rainbow Division of the National Guard, so named by Colonel Douglas MacArthur because it was made up of units that stretched from one end of the country to the other just like a rainbow. However, it wasn't until early 1918 that enough trained troops reached France to engage in battle.

After realizing a volunteer army would not succeed, a conscripted army had to be established, trained, and outfitted almost from scratch. The United States had a strong navy, but in 1917 with a population of approximately 100 million it had only an army of about 125,000. In contrast, Germany began the war with 4.5 million troops and was mobilizing more. On May 18, 1917, the Selective Service Act was signed by President Wilson. The act required all men twenty-one to thirty to register for the draft. In 1918 this act was expanded to men ages eighteen to forty-five. By war's end twenty-two million men had registered, with five million being drafted. Another 1.5 million volunteered and 500,000 had signed up for the Navy or Marines. But building an army took valuable time as the Allies fought valiantly, wondering if they could hold on long enough for the Americans to arrive.

After the declaration of war everything the U.S. needed for war had to be moved in large quantities and quickly. The United States had been manufacturing guns and ammunition and other supplies for the Allies but had vastly under supplied itself. The U.S. was also obligated to continue sending food overseas yet needed to feed its own army at the same time. The army needed barracks, training areas, hospitals, uniforms, rifles, munitions, and equipment, and they needed them NOW. Supplies were often bottle-necked due to the lack of fuel to transport them, creating chaos that had to be tamed or there would be utter failure. To that end the government took control of the railroad industry and shipping yards, regulating everything from traffic to wages. Federal agencies also oversaw the production and use of fuel and food supplies.

To gear up for war took money---lots of it. The U.S. banks had already given credit to the Allies to purchase goods. To lose the war meant to lose repayment of those debts. An income tax hike failed to procure enough money. Finally, the government issued the sale of Liberty Bonds. These bonds had attractive interest rates and were highly promoted by patriotic propaganda campaigns. When entering the war the country was divided; it was hoped the patriotic messaging would bring unity. In all, after four drives, more than $17 billion was raised.

It was this patriotic pressure, however, to buy war bonds that created the fervor that contributed to a very ugly side of the United States during WWI. The propaganda machine had to keep the pro-American sentiment going to support the war effort, ultimately convincing people to volunteer for the army, the Red Cross and other organizations, to voluntarily follow rationing, and provide money through buying Liberty Bonds. Posters, newspapers, and hate films chastised the American people to not let the Huns win, to do their part in stomping out the Kaiser. To not buy Liberty Bonds meant you were anti-war and un-American.

When the U.S. went to war, a quarter of the population was German-born or of German descent. Portraying the people of German descent as un-American and disloyal to the country gave "patriotic" license to use these people as a scapegoat for all the wrath and anger other citizens were feeling about the war.

After casting immigrants as anti-American, people began seeing spies around every corner. So overzealous was the general public that German Americans began living in fear. Some stopped speaking German in public. Others changed their names or the names of their businesses to more American sounding names. Still many German Americans lost their jobs and livelihood. The public became so programmed with German phobia they would tolerate nothing less than 100% American. Books by German authors were removed from the libraries. Music written by German composters was ripped from music books. And at the extreme, common names of many items were changed. Sauerkraut became Liberty Cabbage, Frankfurters were Liberty Dogs and German measles, of course, were Liberty measles. It did not help that German saboteurs *were* found in some manufacturing factories.

In some of the most flagrant violations of our constitution's free speech protection, the Espionage Act 1917 and The Sedition Act of 1918 were passed to quash any dissent. Any "disloyal, profane, scurrilous, or abusive language" about the U.S., its government, the war, military, draft, or the flag could lead to $10,000 in fines and up to 20 years in prison.

In November 1917, alien (non-citizen) immigrants were required to register as Alien enemies. Registrants were made to complete a four-page document providing family information, details of immigration, physical description, a photograph, and fingerprints. This was also required of American born women married to German immigrants. They were barred from owning firearms, or residing and working in restricted zones. Those who showed cause to aid the enemy were placed in military camps. Thus, many dissenters, alien or otherwise, who criticized the war in any form, were frightened into silence.

Preparing for War 1917

Other propaganda campaigns were taking place as well to address the many shortages that were surfacing. Supplies and food were being diverted to the Allies and the U.S. Army. People were told that self-rationing was akin to patriotism. Fuel holidays encouraged motorists not to drive on Sundays. There were Wheatless Mondays and Wednesdays, and Meatless Tuesdays, Thursdays, and Saturdays, allowing more food to be used for the war. Coal was to be conserved by volunteering for Heatless Mondays, and awful bread called Liberty Bread was substituted for white flour bread.

Finally, it was the ultimate shortage of men of working age for manufacturing jobs, farm work, teachers and other jobs that presented opportunities for women 'to do their bit.'

Now Americans who believed the ocean would keep them safe from war, watched their troops yet unhardened by war, leave to cross 3000 miles of open sea, through rough waters and under threat of enemy submarines, to a future no one could predict.

In Time of War

But There's No One Busted Yet

by
William Herschell

When I hear some folks complainin'
"Bout the burdens they must bear
Just to keep our soldiers fightin'
In the trenches "over there,"
Then I want to show a picture,
One I saw the other day,
Of a little Belgian youn'un
An' her granny, old an' gray.
In each face was tears and terror,
Born of Teuton greed and lust,
An' I pledged my all to Freedom,
If to give my all I must.
Then a new song woke within me.
A refrain I can't forget;
"we'll all go broke if we haf t'---
But there's no one busted yet!"

    Buy Your Bonds—Load Your Guns;
    Buying Early Halts the Huns.

    Buy Your Bonds Now
    And "save your face."
    Delay and dodging
    Mean disgrace.

Warning to German Alien Enemies!

April 19, 1917

Fremont Times-Indicator

To all United States Attorneys and Marshals:

Dear Sir:--

You are hereby directed to give full publicity to the following statement:

No German alien enemy in this county, who has not hitherto been implicated in plots against the interests of the United States, need have any fear of action by the Department of Justice so long as he observes the following warning:

OBEY THE LAW
KEEP YOUR MOUTH SHUT.

Respectfully,
T. W. GREGORY,
U. S. Attorney General.

Home Front
Newaygo County, 1917

After the declaration of war on, April 6, 1917, emotions ran high. Enthusiasm abounded as people were assured they would win the war. Parades with lots of flag waving were followed by speeches and patriotic singing. In Newaygo County in the city of Fremont a patriotic demonstration was planned for April 27. Its purpose, as stated in the April 19 *Fremont Times-Indicator,* was to "stir this community to its very depths and arouse every citizen to a true sense of his obligation to his county during the great national crisis."

The plans for the demonstration were: "...a civic parade in which the pupils of the public schools will play an important part. Not only will the public school children be in line to march but the city officials. The members of the Board of Trade and many others will take part in the parade....The parade will end at the school house where appropriate exercises will take place. It is expected the new 50 foot steel flag pole will be erected on the school ground by that time and the flag will be raised with appropriate ceremony. Exercises by the school children and an address by a prominent speaker will make up a remainder of the program.

In the evening a monster patriotic mass meeting will be held in the Auditorium at which some of Michigan's most prominent orators will speak...This is a community affair and every loyal American is expected to participate."

In case anyone planned to skip the demonstration, the day before the event the newspaper proclaimed, "Patriotism Will Run Rampant Tomorrow". It reminded readers that "Men, women, and children of Fremont and western Newaygo County will show their loyalty to the Stars and Stripes in a patriotic demonstration which is expected to surpass anything ever held in this county. This will be a loyalty celebration and every red-blooded American citizen who is loyal to the flag is expected to take an active part in this event...If you have a flag, bring it with you."

The day of the event businesses closed early as did the canning factory. The loyalty parade had 1800 participants and that evening the auditorium was filled to capacity.

A few days later Paul D. Merrifield, principal of Fremont High School, went to Grand Rapids and enlisted in the Officers Reserve Training Corps of the U.S. Army. This was soon followed by twenty-four young men answering the call for the Army, Navy, National Guard, and officer Reserve Training Corps. However, volunteers did not make a large enough army and a draft was enacted May 18, 1917. Beginning in August the *Fremont Times-Indicator* began listing the names of those drafted from Newaygo County and continued to do so until all quotas were met.

The men who left for service were given a community send-off. *The Hesperia Union*, November 23, 1917, details the grand farewell for their soldier boys.

"Monday evening the Berean Sunday School class and the State Bank of Hesperia gave a public supper in honor of the boys who left this week for their training at Camp Custer.

The people of the nearby community were all invited to be at the I.O.O.F. hall at 6:30 o'clock, where, through the generosity of the State Bank in furnishing a bountiful supply of oysters and crackers, and the ladies who furnished sandwiches, pickles and cakes, a very appetizing oyster supper was served to about two hundred people, at the tables tastefully decorated with little flags.

After the supper the Presbyterian orchestra gave several selections after which Rev. Wylie gave a few remarks explaining the purpose of the gathering which was to bid God speed to the young men who have been chosen to represent us on the battle front. Miss Isabelle Becker spoke of our duty to the boys who have been called to make the supreme sacrifice for our liberty. The boys at the front are called to endure great hardships and perhaps give their life to relieve us of this oppression, while we should consider it an opportunity to give our money for the comfort of these boys."

Governor Sleeper designated a Patriotic Day when "all the people of Michigan may show by their participation in public meetings and demonstrators that they stand ready to furnish financial sinew of the war which their sons and brothers will wage overseas. I am asking that a meeting be held in each of the 8000 schools of the state the evening of October 15 with a program suitable for the occasion...Let us put a light in the windows of every one of the schoolhouses of Michigan on that evening, that all may see and know how our state meets its obligations in the support of American's fighting men on the battlefield."

On November 21, the *Fremont Times-Indicator* detailed the patriotic mass meeting held in Fremont at an auditorium filled to capacity in order to pay respect to those selected from the second draft call. "Many unable to get seats stood through the entire program, while a large number of people could not gain admission to the hall."

The Home Guard made their first public appearance at this event which gave an air of the military to the proceedings. Records show Fremont, like other small communities, created its own Home Guard. The duties of the Guard were to "maintain civic order and discipline, to complement the nation's armed forces, and to defend their homes, if necessary." By fall fifty-two men began training to prepare against German threats.

The men met once a week for drills. Sometimes men home on furlough would take over the drills as did Lt. Selah W. Reber and his brother Fritz. The guards had to equip themselves with khaki-colored uniforms at the cost of twenty dollars each. Guns were provided by Home Guard headquarters in Lansing.

Two other organizations would come to play an important role during the war. In July the Fremont branch of the Red Cross had increased its numbers to 325 members and was hoping to reach a membership goal of one thousand. They developed classes to train members in making surgical dressings. Those who passed rigid exams were then licensed for this work.

Another department of the Red Cross became known as the sewing circle. They met in a vacant department store. No special training or certification was needed for these tasks. They turned out bed sheets, pillowcases, towels, table napkins, handkerchiefs, gowns, hospital shirts, pajama suits, bathrobes, bed socks and more. Another department was being developed as a knitting department for making socks. Several other communities including Newaygo, Sitka, and Grant became Red Cross Auxiliaries. As these items were completed, they were shipped to Chicago and then forwarded to Washington for dispersal.

Just before Christmas, December 20, 1917, Governor Sleeper sent out a plea for the Red Cross.

"It is a privilege to call your attention to the Christmas Membership Campaign by the Red Cross...There are five million members of the Red Cross in our country—it needs fifteen million to carry out its work... (I) call upon all our people to lend their assistance thereto by becoming members or renewing their memberships and enrolling others in their organization."

Members of the Red Cross would often meet trains of soldiers as they crisscrossed the country, handing out oranges, cigarettes, hot coffee, and sandwiches. The servicemen were anxious for news from home so they were given newspapers, and stamped postcards which the Red Cross would later mail for them.

Another organization came to mean a lot to servicemen, and that was the Y.M.C.A. Members would ride the trains along with the servicemen raising the spirits of the soldiers by singing or just spending time talking with them. Once overseas they provided entertainment, a speaker on Sundays, and gave soldiers paper, envelopes, books, magazines and newspapers.

It wasn't long before shortages caused by the war mounted until the community began to feel the pinch. First numerous rumors needed to be addressed, the most common being that home-canned goods were going to be confiscated by the government to help feed the army. The truth was the Food Administration was encouraging housewives to can fruits and vegetables in order to have enough food for their families as shortages of many foods would probably get worse.

Another problem arose when it was time to dig potatoes. The shortage of manpower endangered the crops as thousands of bushels of potatoes were about to be destroyed by frost. The overwhelming response of the community saved the crops as people hurried to various rural potato fields and began digging. Many businesses closed for the day to make more helpers available.

As production of wheat became more and more deficient in feeding soldiers *and* the American people, hackles rose on consumer's backs. Some blamed farmers calling them "slackers" for not doing enough, accusing them of not purchasing their share of Liberty Bonds, and withholding grain to increase the price. Both accusations were false.

The Food Administration issued an order in December that stated, "Not only is the conservation of wheat for human food a high patriotic duty at this time, but both the letter and spirit of the Food Control Act forbids the use of wheat for feeding animals." Millers were notified "not to sell any consumer more than his actual requirements for 30 days."

In a Times-Indicator article December 20, the seriousness of the fuel shortage was explained to its readers. More use of wood instead of costly coal for fuel was desperately needed. It even suggested people "having stumps, rail fences or timber that could be used for fuel should 'do their bit' for humanity and the government." Railroads were allowed to confiscate coal from dealers as needed. Fremont Lumber and Fuel Co. lost two out of four of its car consignments of coal for railroad use.

December saw the culmination of the propaganda people had been subject to for several months when vigilance turned to

Home Front Newaygo County, 1917

vigilantism by self-appointed individuals who took to task many others in the county for supposed acts of disloyalty. People were forced to make public loyalty statements which were printed in the newspaper as was that of Henry Deters on December 5, 1917.

To My Fellow American Citizens:

I feel I have made wrong statements relative to the present situation as to the American and German trouble, and I take this way of publicly apologizing for any and all such expressions. I wish to say that in the future I shall do my very best to be a true citizen of our United States.

I can see the folly of the past. I have a brother in the war service and should necessity require, I am ready to serve my country as a soldier.

Henry Deters
In the presence of
Henry McCarty and Henry Keegstra.

This was followed by the forced apology of Ben Kunnen on December 13, under the title "Fremont No Place For Pro-Germans".

"Indignation over continued expression of Pro-German sentiment in this community reached fever heat last

Wednesday night when Ben Kunnen, who is said to have made unpatriotic statements, was forced to sign an apology to the public for his alleged Pro-German attitude and kiss the flag as a token of humility and of submission to the United States government.

Mr. Kunnen was taken from his home on Dayton St. to a cottage at Fremont Lake and here a pre-arranged program was carried out. Being unable to secure an iron cross from the Kaiser in time for the ceremony, a symbol of the sacred emblem was clipped upon the head of the victim with barber's clippers, and the word "Hun" was printed upon his forehead with iodine. As evidence of future loyalty to the flag and the great nation which it represents, Mr. Kunnen kissed the Stars and Stripes and subscribed to the following apology:

'To Loyal Citizens of the United States:

In spirit of utter humility and supplication, I, Ben Kunnen, having come to realize my unfitness and unworthiness to share the protection of the United States Government, hereby beg of the citizens of the United States the privilege of withdrawing, retracting, and recalling, and apologizing for, each and every remark and inference I have made concerning the President or the United States Government which lacks the proper esteem and respect due from a person enjoying the protection of this Flag; and I further beseech the people for forgiveness and mercy for my hitherto grossly insulting and unpatriotic remarks concerning the President of the United States and the

Government. If I am allowed the privilege of remaining longer under the protection of this Flag, I solemnly swear that I shall never again mention or in any manner refer to the President or the Flag or the Government of the United States, or of any of her Allies, except in the upmost respectable manner, and in a tone of deepest respect. I further solemnly swear that I shall never again mention or in any manner refer to Germany or her Allies, or anything appertaining thereto, except in the proper tone of disgust and disapproval.'"

The Pastor of the Second Christian Reformed Church answered his critics on December 13.

"To the Citizens of Fremont:

Inasmuch as my loyalty seems to be questioned by some people of this locality, I wish to take this means of letting you know just where I stand in respect to the government and the war. Before this country had severed relations with Germany, I was a pacifist, a believer in the stand and policy of our ex-Secretary of State, Hon. Wm. Jennings Bryan. Since war has been declared and pacifism seemed no longer tenable, I have cast my lot with the government and do what I can to bring this war to a successful issue.

In respect to the article printed in the Grand Rapids Press under date of Dec. 10th, stating that I had called upon the ministers of this city to hold an "indignation meeting" and furthermore that I had signed a pledge of loyalty, it is false. As a minister of the gospel and as president of the Minister's Conference, I felt it my duty to pulse their sentiments as regards the methods employed of late in this city for the purpose of stamping out Pro-Germanism and see if we ought not to voice our disapproval in the local paper of such methods. I was actuated to do this only by the highest motives. While I admired the zeal of these patriots, I question their methods. I stood with the President, who in commenting upon the Ohio affair, (the lynching of a German American coal miner) urged upon all citizens to have the law take its course. As we could not come to a unanimous agreement, we decided to drop the matter. This is the so-called "indignation meeting" to which the Press correspondent referred. Finally, I signed no pledge of loyalty. No one has ever requested me to do so. If the proper authorities feel the need of this I will gladly do so. What actuated the correspondent of the Press to write this I am not able to state. However being a follower of my Master who when He was reviled, reviled not again but gave it over unto Him who judgeth rightly, I shall not press said person for an apology.

In conclusion let me add that I bear no ill will toward any of the citizens of Fremont but only have their welfare at heart.

Hoping this will clarify the situation and thanking you, Mr. Editor, for the space you so kindly allotted me.

      I am yours for America, Rev. Wm. Kuipers"

The methods used by citizens to stamp out Pro-Germanism was questioned in a letter to the *Grand Rapids Press* and reprinted by the *Fremont Times-Indicator* on December 20.

"Dear Editor of the Press:

What is the sentiment of the people in regard to an occurrence which took place in Fremont last week? I allude to the torturing of a man for alleged pro-German statements. Before I go further I wish you to understand that I am a thoroughly patriotic American citizen.

The man I refer to was taken from his home at night, taken to Fremont Lake and tortured so that he has been confined to his bed since.

Now I believe a person who favors the enemy should be punished by law, but when have the laws of civilized America allowed certain people to mete out justice as they see it? Let the man be taken to court and given a chance to prove innocence or guilt. In the instance I referred to it is a question as to whether the man was guilty or not.

The procedure looks very much to me as a band of Austro-Germans torturing their enemy instead of "law-abiding patriotic American citizens" as they class themselves.

A Patriotic Irish-American" Fremont, Mich.

Charles B. Magennis took issue with above letter which was reprinted in the Fremont paper:

"Editor of the Press:

In the Press of Dec. 13, Patriotic Irish-American from Fremont asks the sentiment of the people in regard to the recent unpleasant jobs of teaching lukewarm citizens up that way the value of either shouting for Uncle Sam or keeping their mouths shut. That patriotic Irish-American asks and deserves an answer.

In the first place simple, unadorned and unhyphenated Patriotic American should be ample signature to a communication of this nature unless you have the courage to sign your name.

Regarding the Fremont cases the writer of the article in question is mistaken. Under the guise of "freedom of speech" persons may make speeches which actually border on treason and there is no law to punish them. Until legal provision is made in such cases—and it will be made—must the men and women who have sent boys to fight, maybe never to return, listen to propaganda calculated and intended in many cases to aid the heathen those boys go to fight? No. Then perhaps just such little lessons as the recent Fremont jobs and others will tend to keep the cool German-sympathizing citizens where they belong until such laws are passed as will make their near treasonable chatter illegal. Because the law is extremely democratic and allows freedom of speech does it follow that real Americans shall allow this freedom to be used to hold up America (I use the word advisedly, meaning the United States and Canada) to the advantage of her enemies?

You say "let the man be taken to court and prove his innocence or guilt." A good many have been taken to court and proved their "innocence"—because there was no law to cover their cases. And then they swagger up the street with their tongue in their cheek, laughing in their sleeves, which encourages their brothers to go and do likewise. The time is past when pro-Germanism will pay big dividends in this country and the sooner this is well understood the better.

Charles B. Magennis"

The year ended with a call from the American Defense League for action. Published in the Times-Indicator December 27, the article was a long rambling message of anti-German propaganda and urging of *all* residents to be classified by their amount of loyalty. The article in part states:

Mayor Senf, of this city, today made public a request received from Richard M. Hurd, Chairman of the Board of Trustees of the American Defense Society, urging citizens here to organize a local vigilance corps, for the purpose of aiding the Government in putting an end to German propaganda and enemy activity which has been responsible for fires, ammunition plant explosions, sabotage, food scares and other attempts to damage the morale of the American people.

Recent events in this country make it plain that the German method of propaganda, which has been so effective in Russia and Italy, is now being attempted in this country with an alarming degree of success...The far reaching need of the local Vigilance Corps can be seen when it is known that in this country alone there are today several million alien enemies representing Germany, Austria, Bulgaria, Turkey, and other countries sympathetic or allied with the Prussian autocracy... The plan of organization undertaken by the society and recommended to loyal Americans provides for the enrollment of a small American Vigilance Corps in every city and town which shall classify all residents under the following terms:

1. Loyal
2. Disloyal
3. Doubtful
4. Unknown.

Following the general classification of citizens the committee is urged to make further designation of the following list:

1. Alien enemy
2. Pro-German
3. Anti-Government

...At the earliest possible moment when you have made your classification of alien enemies, pro-Germans, and those opposed to the government in this war, send this list to the Police Department, the local representative of the Department of Justice and to whatever representatives of the army or any intelligence bureaus there are in your community.

Proof that this request was ever carried out has not been found by the author.

In Time of War

Letters and Related Articles
1917

In Time of War

**Merritt Kimbell
Written from Texas
May 24, 1917**

Since coming here I have been practicing in foot drill most of the time, until recently we were given our horses. At first were given a short mounted drill, mostly to learn how to mount and dismount and how to handle the reins. There is a lot of slow trot to it with the feet out of the stirrups. We are drilling about eight hours a day with about two or three hours of mounted drill.

The saddles are new and stiff and most of the men get pretty sore. I take a bath every night and use the Government soap which is good for soreness.

The horses are old at it and seem to know what to do. My horse isn't much for looks but she certainly knows what to do and is easy to manage. The following is our schedule. We get up at 6:15. That is the first call. At 6:25 we are dressed, have folded our blankets and sheets and put them under the pillow and have swept around our cots. Then at 6:30 is roll call after which we wash and get ready for breakfast. At about 7:30 we start to drill; that lasts about an hour. We then go to the gymnasium for some exercises. After this we don our overalls and shirt, go to the stable to curry the horses, spending another hour. Each man is furnished a curry comb, cloth and brush. The horses are then turned loose in the corral. We are back at quarters at 10:30, have an aiming or sighting drill until dinner time. At 1:30 we either drill mounted or dismounted until about 4:30 when the horses are put in the stalls. After supper, "retreat" about 6:30, then we do as we please but must be in bed at 11:00.

Sundays there is no afternoon drill and we don't get up until 7:00. We expect to go to the field range in a few days and will be gone a month perhaps.

It has been pretty warm here. Corn is in the tassel and they have just finished the onions.

I receive a copy of your paper every week and the news in it sounds good to me.

Merritt Kimbell
U.S. Cavalry, Laredo, Texas
May 25, 1917

It hasn't rained here for some time and tonight at 6:45 it was 101 degrees. That is pretty warm, but not for this country. I suppose we will notice it in July and August.

I went swimming in the Rio Grande. The river is only about a block wide, deep near the shore and shallow in the middle. The water is not very clear but is warm. We can look across from our drill grounds and see the Mexicans working.

With the exception of one day, I have led the bunch in mounted drills, think it must be on account of the horse I have. Everyone is getting to like the mounted work now as they have become used to the saddle. The captain hasn't said a word to me about my riding so I guess I'm coming along all right.

We had to jump over a hurdle. Everette, my chum, was the first one to go over and he was a little frightened; his horse didn't jump good and he had to try it over. I was fourth and by the time it came my turn one fellow had fallen off. I didn't have much time to think about it before it was over. We had to take our feet out of the stirrups, fold our arms, leaving the reins hang over the horses neck. The drill ground is hard as rock but where the hurdle is it is soft. One place where there is a mound it is quite a distance around it, and in the top is a ring. It is lot of fun to ride around and over it.

At the range they shoot 200, 300, 500 and 600 yards, slow and rapid fire. At slow fire, you have your ten shots, and at rapid fire, ten shots in 60 seconds, at 200 and 300 yards; 85 seconds at 500 yards, and about 105 seconds at 600 yards.

We, or rather "L Troop", marched from the barracks to the depot with the body of a fellow who died in the hospital here from appendicitis. We were lined up and listened to a Chaplin, then the firing squad of eight men fired three volleys over the casket. The infantry band led, then the firing squad, the hearse, with the pall bearers on each side, then his horse covered with black, and the troop. Every man carried a belt and holster, with his revolver in it.

There is a military library of a couple hundred books or more, monthly and weekly magazines and daily papers, so you see we have all kinds of reading, and Victrola for music. We also have free use of the gymnasium, bowling alley and pool tables.

We have all we want to eat and drink, not so much variety at one meal, but hardly have the same on two days, that is in meats and dessert.

Base Hospital, Laredo, Texas, June 13, 1917

I came here last Sunday. The water is bad and this weather very hot. It was 108 degrees in the shade yesterday. It seems to affect most all the Northern boys, but do not worry, we have plenty of army nurses and I am getting the best of care and gaining strength, though I am not on a regular diet yet. They give me milk-toast, soft boiled eggs, soup, cocoa, toast, milk and lemonade.

July 1, 1917

Have been out of the hospital since the 22nd of June and have been doing all right. The heat doesn't bother one bit now. The temperature was 112 this afternoon and one day went to 126. It was quite noticeable that day I go on drilling with the troop. You would never know that I had missed a couple of weeks. There isn't much to it if you pay attention to commands.

Monday, July 2nd, we start guard-drill to prepare us for duty. There won't be any chance for promotions for a long time. We haven't been trained for duty yet. After this has been done we are termed first-class privates, then are made Lance Corporals, then Corporals.

The reason we have been drilling so hard is to train the new horses and new men. Each troop has about 30 new men and as many new horses. The old men train the new horses and the old horses the new men.

A track meet will be held here on the Fourth between the 14th Cavalry and the 37th Infantry. A ball game will also be held. There is a rumor that this troop or a part of it may be ordered to France, but you never can tell. One can hear most anything.

Juell Hewitt
Co. F. 2nd Reg. of Eng., El Paso, Texas
June 28, 1917

To the Editor, Times-Indicator:

As I have so many people in Fremont to thank I feel that I can best reach them through the columns of your paper. I have been remembered with so many good letters from home that I want to say to the people of Fremont that I am well and happy and in the best of health, and am not sorry that I joined the army to fight for my country. We have plenty to eat and are used just fine. I hope every boy is fairing as well as I am.

As the majority of people know very little of what is going on in our training camps, I shall try to give a description, although it may be somewhat inaccurate in some cases.

The regiment of engineers is comprised of those who want to follow the positions and trades they had in civil life. This is a regiment of mechanics.

The duties of engineers are wide and varied. There is a pontoon section which constructs temporary bridges. There is also a section for reconnaissance. In fact the aim of the engineers is to keep things moving for the rest of the army. We are required to train the same as the infantry until we are able to handle the gun in military maneuvers. This drill and school of a soldier we will conclude in two weeks. Then we take over the engineer parts of the army.

Those of us from the North were affected by the climate and the altitude here. The temperature runs to 110 degrees and tonight we saw the first rain.

Camp Baker is located about five miles from El Paso and is at the foot of the Rocky Mts. Which reach an altitude of 4000 feet above our camp. We are 4200 feet above the sea level.

Two regiments of the engineers, the 2nd and 5th, are located here. The 5th will leave this week, part going to San Antonio and part of Fort Sam Houston. Our regiment will probably leave in about three weeks, although there is nothing certain about that.

The routine of the day is as follows. At 4:45 a.m. the reveille is sounded which starts the day; breakfast at 5 o'clock, cleaning up the camp streets at 6 o'clock. From 6:30 to 10:30 we have gun and foot drill and bayonet exercises. This consists of the manual of arms, squad, platoon, and company formations and movements. The period of 10:30 to 11:30 is given over to knots and lashings and their uses, and occasionally a lecture by a commissioned officer. From 1 p.m. to 3:30 o'clock we have target and aiming practice.

It is said 33 First Class Privates and Right Corporals will be chosen from this bunch and we are all working hard.

Hoping this will reach all my friends and they will correspond with me.

Austin Olney
Newport, R. I.
July 1, 1917

We left New York City last night about 6:30 on the "Commonwealth," best ship of the Fall River line, and arrived in Newport, R. I. about 3:30 this morning. We are now in detention camp. Probably will stay here only a day or two anyway, so I am unable to give any address yet.

First thing this morning we were taken to the shop and given a hair clipping. My hair now at the longest is from ¾ to ½ inches. Makes some pomp. He, the barber, took about one minute to chop my hair off. Some of the fellows surely looked funny with their lack of hair.

Then we were ordered to take a bath and then were vaccinated and given a physical examination and fitted out with part of our clothes. I have a complete white suit with black oxfords, three pairs of socks, two bath towels and some other things. I wear a pair of khaki leggings with my white suite.

We swung up our hammocks today and got things ready to spend a night in the camp. One company went on board ship today. There were over two hundred recruits who came in here last night and today from Maine to Indiana and West Virginia. Practically every state in that region is represented in today's recruits.

We passed under the big bridges connecting Brooklyn and New York while on our way out here on the boat. Saw several merchantmen in New York harbor. There were Holland, Danish, British, (French?) and Yankee ocean liners that I saw while in the harbor. The guns on the stern and sometimes bows of the ships of nations now at war looked very businesslike.

Saw one, maybe two, U.S. warships in New York harbor. Passed within a quarter of a mile of the statue of Liberty and close by one big fort and two or three smaller ones. There are around 1000 to 2000 fellows. Big lot of fine buildings here.

All the way from Albany we came on the train right beside the Hudson and the scenery is surely great. Place where Rip

VanWinkle was napping in the distance, a space of rolling country, then the river and the railroad after all. Passed through several tunnels and under the Detroit river. We sure get fed so far here. Guess I had better go mail this before I am sent to bed.

Well I am now in Barracks C, 2nd Regiment, 7th Co. and I am number 5. Any mail sent to that address for at least two weeks will reach me all right. It may be two weeks and it may be two months that we will be here. When we leave, it will be for some ship. The company here before us were allowed to leave after 22 days here. The officer in charge of our battalions said the 7th did very good work today.

Maybe you don't understand the terms. I am no. 5. My section contains 25 fellows, there are four sections in one company. One battalion contains three companies. We were held in sections at the detention camp or barracks. There are now either 200 or 300 fellows who will swing in their hammocks in the same room tonight. I said there were 1000 or 2000 men here. It would be more correct to say 8000 to 9000.

We drilled in the rain nearly two hours this morning and from 1:00 p.m. to 3:25 pm. Also in the rain. Then we came in and took a shot in the arm for typhoid. We have to take two more before we are through being vaccinated. My right arm was punctured for typhoid and my left for something else, either small pox or scarlet fever.

Dallas Darling
San Antonio, Texas
July 26, 1917

Dear folks at home:

Our new barracks are now completed. We have worked a long time to make this old cotton field look like home to us soldier boys. Have built barracks about a mile in length, made gravel roads and put it in sewer pipe so things look pretty good. Have a splendid artesian well 1400 feet deep that throws about 2000 gallons per minute. There is a small refinery here that puts out 40,000 barrels of oil a day. There are many cotton gins near by. I have been through the Alamo and around the city of San Antonio. Go to the church services usually every Sunday morning and spend Sunday afternoon at one of the beautiful parks.

The corn cutting is at hand now and cotton is from 1 to 1 ½ feet high. The greatest question now among the boys is "who will be drafted from the home town?"

Letters and Related Articles 1917

July 28 1917

When I wrote last I thought we—the 17th squadron—would get a chance to live in the new barracks, but our squadron is left out. The news comes to us that we are to move and I guess it is true for we have had our measures taken for new clothes, shoes, underwear, socks and overcoat. It must be we are going where it is cold, for our clothes are to be wool.

Our chances to go to France are good. We are called the Foreign Squadron. I like Texas and would just as soon stay, but if the squadron goes over the pond, of course I will want to go too. I am in to serve Uncle Sam wherever he wants me to be. I am going to do my duty as a soldier.

July 30, 1917

The mail man was good to me today. Had four letters, the Motor Age and Times-Indicator. The Times-Indicator always seems so homelike, even if the news is one week old when I get it. We are drilling forenoons and resting and sleeping afternoons. I eat good, sleep well, am happy, tanned and perfectly well. Weigh six lbs. more than I did May 1st, the day I left home, so don't worry about me.

August 1, 1917

I'm up and at work and it's only 4:30 a.m.

We are to move. Where? No one knows, not even the captain. But we are packing up and going to start tonight or to-morrow morning. You see, no one knows what is going to happen until it is over, and then you know it really was true. Such is army life. Well, no matter now where we go for it really seems good to start for somewhere.

August 2, 1917

We are now nearing Kansas City, headed north, but as yet our destination is not known for sure. Some say Canada and others think we are going to Illinois. Elgin Coburn and I are together yet. Our friend, Geo. Rosewarne, was sent a few weeks ago to Illinois. Texas is a big state. We have been a long time getting out of this state. We cannot leave the car at any place.

August 4, 1917

Just crossed into Michigan from South Bend. Will go through Battle Creek, Jackson and to Port Huron today.

I asked my sergeant if I could call up Fremont by phone when we got to Battle Creek, but he said I could not, as we were not allowed to leave the train while traveling.

We are on our way to Toronto, Ont. I tell you it seemed good to get into old Michigan again. I think we are to stay a short time in Toronto for further practice, but cannot say for sure until we reach there. I will write you as soon as I know. From there, we will be sent to the front.

August 5, 1917, Toronto, Canada

Arrived here all O.K. All are well but tired. Been riding since Thursday morning. It is cold, too. Some difference between this climate and southern Texas.

My address now is North Toronto, Ont., 17th U.S. Aero Squad., Canada, Camp Leaside, Recruit Depot.

Austin Olney
Barracks C., Newport, R. I.
August 2, 1917

We have been here three weeks this morning and now we are looking ahead to this coming week to be sent either to Boston or San Francisco, probably Boston. Most of us will not be sorry to leave this island. It contains only about 60 to 80 acres and it a big rock. New barracks are being put up all the time. Buildings that are nothing more or less than sheds about 150 feet long and between 18 and 20 feet wide. Cots are laid in just as thick as possible and still leave room to get to them. A company of 100 men is usually housed in one of those buildings, and a group of those buildings is consigned to some regiment. The hospital corps has a large administration building containing chemistry laboratories and lecture rooms. But the main part of the corps sleep in tents. All 3rd Regiment and all the yeomen are using tents, so there is plenty of use for more buildings. Each regiment has one or more hospital wards and its canteen or ship's store. There are two post offices on the island.

The recruits are building a house or rather it is a kind of club house, built of concrete and known as the "House that Jack Built." A new Y. M. C. A. building is being put up and then there is the rock pile which furnishes the stone for roads around the new barracks on the island. Every once in a while we get orders to work on the stone pile, building roads or in the House That Jack Built. Two companies have had to shovel coal from a barge all day. Expect we will get it before we leave. Here's hoping we don't. Our white suits are not what I would pick to shovel coal in.

Just a short time after noon today a small passenger steamer was going by the island when a man was either pushed, fell or jumped overboard. The lifeboat was lowered and the man picked up in a very short time. Of course we all ran over to the shore to watch the proceedings.

One of our favorite sports here is hunting starfish. Among the rocks in shallow water seems to be where they stay, and at low tide the boys pick up and dry a lot of them.

Each Regiment has its baseball team and a regular league schedule is played out. The 2nd regiment has had the pennant for some time now, but today the boys played a ragged game and lost to the yeomen 7 to 3. The team is still well toward the top. In fact, were leading until today.

Friday the 20th, was pay day. Since pay day there have been crap games in progress most of the time. It is strictly against orders to play any game for money on the island. A Pedro deck is sufficient for three days in the Brig. But the fellows got back of the butts behind the rifle targets an had some fellows on the lookout and went to it. One fellow in our company lost about $35.00 for the pleasure.

Went up to town last night on shore leave. There were just as many or more uniformed men on the streets as there were civilians. Of course, there were lots of soldiers over at Fort Adams. The Naval Reserve Station is here, and altogether, Newport would feel mighty homesick without the soldiers and sailors around.

Newport in itself is a genuine old fashioned town. Streets are very narrow. Barely room for three rigs to pass on most of the streets and some are so narrow that there are signs up which allow rigs to enter only from one end. Three people walking abreast are crowded on the sidewalks. Of course, that part of Newport which has been built up in the last few years is the same as any modern city, and millionaire row is elegance itself.

There is a dandy big Y.M.C.A. up town. We always get royal treatment there.

Lying at anchor here near the island are the two old U.S.S. Constellation, which fought and defeated three or four British ships in the War of 1812, and the U.S.S. Boxer. They are kept in good shape, although they are chained down and never moved.

Several people have sent cards and letters to me from around home. If they could see just once the eager crowd around the officer when mail is given out, they would know that their messages are appreciated

Chas. Wise
Great Lakes (Ill.) Naval Training Station, Co. J.
August 2, 1917

This station is surely crowded. They are bringing from five to six hundred fellows every day. The government bought 400 acres and is putting up new buildings and store houses to receive the new fellows. It is surely some hot here. It is so hot that lots of the fellows faint in line when they are drilling. Our company's commander has had us fellows making a flower bed in front of the camp and it is a pretty sight. All the other companies are trying to copy after ours. All last week there was a big show here and it was a different play every night, all free to the fellows in the station. I am writing this letter in our Y.M.C.A and there is some noise going on. They are building a bridge over the creek right back of our tents over toward Camp Ross and they are going to put a railroad track across it to get supplies over to the fellows there.

Don't know when I can come home for there are scarlet fever cases and other diseases have broken out. They have us in quarantine for 21 days.

Our company is the best drilled bunch of fellows on the field, so the Master at Arms said, and the commander trusts us so much they never search our company when we come in from shore leave.

I am picking up flesh and certainly feel lots better here, and am more than proud of the "blues" I wear. You ought to see me strut around. I have taken up boxing matches here every Wednesday afternoon and I am always on hand. I get along with the gloves pretty well, but there is plenty of chance for improvement.

Henry Felber
Troop G, 25th Cavalry, Fort D.A., Russell, Wyoming
August 2, 1917

I see that the boys are using the columns of your paper to tell their many friends how they are faring in the service of Uncle Sam. Perhaps you will print a few lines from me.

First of all, I must tell my friends that I am not in the cavalry anymore as the 25th Cavalry was converted into field artillery troops much to my disappointment. But Uncle Sam knows what is best and I am willing to abide by the decision. He surely does use the boys right and takes good care of us. We are like one large family. There are 105 boys in our troop and we know each other by name and pretty much nearly knew where each man's home is.

We have tennis court, basketball, and baseball and boxing gloves and have the best ball team in the regiment. Ours is the best drilled troop and we have the best horses. We are all proud of our troop. We are wearing hats a size larger than we used to.

I suppose I should say something about the country and climate. It is just great here. It is nice and hot in the day time and it takes three blankets to keep us warm at night. Trees are very scarce. The air is dry. We are all brown as Indians, but we are all feeling fine and are healthy. I never regret that I am in the device of Uncle Sam.

Len Gilbert
Aboard troop train to San Francisco, Cal.
August 22, 1917

I am aboard a troop train headed for San Francisco, Cal., where we will stay until September 5th when we board a transport to Honolulu. Hawaii Islands, out in the Pacific, halfway between the Orient and America—the land of coconuts, bananas and pineapples. I am real glad to go. We go to join the 8th U.S. Cavalry at some fort there.

We left Ft. Russell at 2 o'clock Tuesday, Aug. 21. There are fifteen coaches on this train, twelve Pullman coaches, a cook car and two baggage cars. There are 350 of us on the train besides a captain and some sergeants. We are traveling over the Union Pacific route.

We have just passed Ogden, Utah. And crossed the great Salt Lake; now we are spinning through Nevada. We just stopped and put on two big oil burning engines at a division point on the Nevada line and they are big, too, believe me.

I have seen some wonderful scenery here. Last night coming through western Wyoming I saw two large American eagles and also some coyotes and you ought to have seen the train loads of western sheep headed for Chicago or Denver. I saw two trains of them and one train had 22 cars double-decked and two engines, the other had 18 cars, all headed east.

We went through three large tunnels all about a mile long and very dark.

August 23, 1917

Well today is Thursday and we have just crossed the Rockies in California and are 107 miles from Frisco and the Pacific coast.

When I awoke this morning we were going up in the mountains and I never saw such beautiful scenery. We first would go around a mountain, then in under a long tunnel, among pines and rocks, over creeks and rivers, a mile or two down in the canyons. And the mountain air smells so sweet and pure.

We have gone through several different little towns where they would put a box of fruit on the car to pass around to us. We have a mountain engine on which looks like an engine going backward, with tender in front.

We can see lots of orchards, of peaches, apples and plums, and we see palm trees and rose bushes galore. This is some pretty country.

They tell me we will get into Frisco at 1 o'clock.

Ward Giddings
Co. F., 7th Infantry, Gettysburg, Pa.
August 30, 1917

J.A. Gerber is in receipt of a letter from Ward Giddings in which Mr. Giddings discusses camp life at Gettysburg. The letter in part follows:

I suppose everyone is wondering how I'm standing the army life. Well I never felt better in my life. The first couple weeks were pretty hard, for all the drills were strange and there was a lot of walking to do for a short-legged man who wasn't used to it, but finally all those flabby muscles which hadn't been used for years, began to get toughened, until now I'm in better condition than I have been in years.

The food is plain but substantial and there is plenty of it and it's clean too. I know, for I've had a couple days as kitchen-police and when I wasn't peeling potatoes or waiting on the table, I was scrubbing something. The kitchen is inspected every morning by the camp sanitary officer and if there is any dirt around somebody hears about it.

No doubt you've heard what we have to do every day, but it won't hurt to hear it again. The first thing after breakfast everybody has to police up. This means that every cigarette butt, match or piece of paper, in the company street, has to be picked up. If we don't get them all the first trip we go over it again. Then we cut wood enough to last for that day. It is hauled to the end of the company street in four foot lengths and we have to saw and split it. After that (if the wood isn't too tough) we have a few minutes to rest before we have to fall in for physical drill. That lasts until eight o'clock, when we have five minutes to rest to get a drink and also our rifles and belts. After that we have company drills for an hour or more, according to how good or bad we may be. Then we fall out for ten minutes to get our bayonets. From there we go out to the "battle field" to learn the proper way of sticking our friend the enemy. They have a regular trench, with stacks of hay for Germans. A civilian might think that is a simple matter to run a bayonet into a sack of hay, but it isn't. There is only one right way to do it for various styles of attack and we have to do it that way or come back and do it over again. Of course we all expect to forget everything we learned if we ever get into a real battle, but we can't say that we haven't been taught. After we have killed fifteen or twenty "Germans" apiece they let us put our bayonets away and teach us the proper way of walking post while we are on guard. We get through that at eleven and then we get another half hour at company drill. Then we don't have anything to do, except eat our dinner, until one o'clock. At that time we fall in again and are taught the proper way of aiming, also how to fix our slings for various positions which we assume while shooting.

That is about all we have to do until about three o'clock, except about a half hour of a delightful little exercise which is well named "push and pull" drill. You take the rifle to the shoulder just as though you were (going to shoot and push out) as far as you can reach and then jerk it back against the shoulder as hard as you can. If you do that from twenty to fifty times without stopping, you discover what a lot of fun it is. Try it.

From three until five-fifteen we have nothing to do except take a bath, wash our clothes and do any other small job that they might find for us. At five-fifteen we have retreat and then we are done except supper.

We have Wednesday afternoons off and all we have to do Saturday is stand inspection. That takes about an hour, unless your rifle happens to be dirty. If it is, you get an invitation to clean that first and then cut wood or sweep ditches for an hour or so. My rifle has been clean so far.

Friday is hike day. They give us all the way from ten to fifteen miles. If it is a nice day, that isn't bad, but if the thermometer is registering about 90 degrees, a man knows he has been some place. That's the way it has been most of the time. I beat the hike Friday though, for I go on guard duty tomorrow night at four-thirty and stay on for twenty-four hours. We have two hours on and four hours off. This is the first time I've been on guard. I hope I don't challenge a mule like one of our fellows did the last time F Company was on guard. Each company gets guard duty every twelve days.

They give us plenty of entertainment. Each regiment has a movie show and band concert every night. They also have a movie show here at the "Y". Also a piano and phonograph. Tuesday night is amateur night right here at the "Y". Any soldier who thinks he can dance, sing or do anything else in the amusement line is perfectly welcome to step up and perform. It may interest some for the boys to know that I haven't attempted to sing yet, although I think I have it on some who have tried. Thursday nights they get some regular entertainers.

They are also building a baseball diamond for the Seventh. F Company was out this afternoon. The third platoon played the first platoon and got trimmed, 10 to 7. I played with the third. Lieut. Greene, our company commander, has shown his confidence in our team by buying some balls and bats. He's a regular fellow anyway.

**Austin Olney
U.S.S. Transport Houston
September 20, 1917**

I know it has been a long time since you had news from me. But as you can guess, it was not my fault. It has been so long since I used a pen that it doesn't seem exactly natural.

I am ashore now on leave from the U.S.S. Houston. The Houston is a ship originally built by Germany for trans-Atlantic commerce. At the outbreak of war with the U.S. the Germans sank the ship in one of our southern harbors. Our government raised and repaired the ship and now has it manned and run by U.S. sailors. It is quite a large ship, being around 400 feet long. I don't expect to be kept on the Houston very long, but may be placed somewhere with the "destroyers" which are raising the hair on the U-Boats. Of course, I don't know for sure and couldn't tell if I did, just where I will be sent.

I am seeing sights in Europe at present. Doesn't hardly seem possible that such changes could take place in so short a time. Am seeing land and water fighters of almost all nationalities, and other sights which I am not likely to forget. We had good weather most of the way across but got into some places where the waves were rolling around 50 feet high. I had a slight attack of sea sickness but nothing like I had heard about. Maybe my turn is still coming. Our bunch is all in good shape with only one fellow slightly under the weather. Our feed is fairly good. Most of us are willing to get a meal ashore when we can.

Have seen several German prisoners at work under armed guards of the Nation we are in at present. Must be back to the ship by 9:30 so I cannot write very much; am not allowed to say very much, anyway, but am feeling fine.

I am one of the Signal Corp at present. Like it pretty well.

Mail for me can be sent to "U.S.S." Melville, care of Postmaster of New York.

September 3, 1917

Our first mail came today. I received 11 letters, two cards and three birthday presents. The Scottville Enterprise remembered me with a copy of their paper. I think I am lucky. Well everything is going O.K. so far.

I am a member of the signal squad and like it first rate. We surely do have big times ashore. Can't make ourselves understood unless we employ a lot of gestures, but we are getting used to that. I am getting souvenir spoons from different cities I visit. Expect I will have a collection. I expect to make a collection of the different pieces of money most in use in the different nations we may visit.

Maybe some of my friends and relatives will never see any but American coins if I don't. I guess I would not feel badly though to see a lot the good U.S. coin. We were given $15.00

just a couple of days ago so I'm financially at ease now. The sailors speak of a four-year enlistment as "one cruise" so we are on our first cruise and already have about four months in. It doesn't seem that long. Our bunch are second class seamen. When I talk about waves, swells and tides I will know what it means now. Last night the tide raised 20 feet.

September 10, 1917

Mail arrived again today. I got four letters from the folks. I am surely glad to get the letters. I am taking good care of myself and all in all, having the experiences of my life. Of course we are running risks as anyone must in times like these but I believe certain friends of "Old Bill" would be glad to be on our side of the fence. Everywhere we go we find the Yankee's Y.M.C.A. and we are always looking for them. Whenever a ship's crew receives liberty the "Y" is one of the first stopovers for all.

No, the boys are not such a homesick gang as one might expect. It is different now than in times of peace. In peace there is only one object, to serve your four years, but now the fellows are out to knock two or three "I's" out of "Bill and his family" and we are on the job. We have thoughts of home, get a little seasick, but seldom real homesick as many people think.

Sure, if you can chase up any loose papers, Indicator or any other don't worry but that they will be appreciated. After you get through with the dailies pack up a bunch and let them come. Anything which savors of the U.S.A is always welcome.

I asked for and received a new Testament from the American Y.M.C.A. up in the city. It is a little dandy.

Ward Giddings
Co. F., 7th Infantry, Gettysburg, Pa.
October 11, 1917

Nothing new ever happens here anymore. They have given us all the drills we need, I guess, and now we wear away the weary hours doing the same thing over again. I've had "squads east and west" so much that I can tell ten minutes ahead of time what the commands will be.

Aside from the bayonet exercise, the most thoroughly hated drill is the skirmish drill. The Company Commander gets out in front of us, blows a whistle and waves his arms about in an apparently aimless manner and we promptly (?) form a skirmish line, which means the whole company abreast. Then more arm swinging, we lie down, which is very nice on soft ground, but unfortunately they don't have that kind of ground out here. After we have fired imaginary shots at an imaginary enemy for five or ten minutes we jump up and beat it from fifty to a hundred yards to the front, flop down and do it all over again. It might be exciting if someone were out front shooting at us, but it certainly does get on a man's nerves to prop himself up on his elbow and make believe he is shooting somebody when he hasn't even got his rifle loaded. It also makes me sore because it gets my clothes dirty. The other day I had to lie down in the middle of the road and the dust was about two inches deep.

The second battalion of the Seventh assisted in the unveiling of a couple of monuments yesterday. We were supposed to fire three volleys at each monument. We did but it sounded more like a machine gun that it did like a volley. I hope it loses us our good reputation for it's no fun to get picked for all the parades and such things, especially when they keep us out until seven o'clock as they did last night.

In their excitement over the fellows who were drafted, have the good people of this fair land forgotten about the fellows who enlisted? It looks like it. Every paper we get hold of contains notices of the ovations tendered those brave boys who are leaving the paternal fireside after they discovered they weren't exempt, of the big feeds, fine speeches, wrist watches, etc. tendered them by an admiring populace. Why they have got it on us in very way. They live in good barracks, with floors, they have warm water to bathe in if the weather is chilly, and they are kept in their own state as much as possible, where they have a chance to get home once in a while, while we live in tents with dust for a floor and if it gets much colder we will have to break ice in the pail before we can wash ourselves in the morning, and most of us are so far from home that we couldn't get home and back on a five day pass, even if we could get one, which we can't.

I'm only expressing in my poor way, the feelings of nine-tenths of the regular army and the other tenth don't know enough to have a whole thought at one time, so they don't count. Of course, I know that there are a great many who had regular reasons for not enlisting, but they are in the minority. But please don't imagine that we are pining for wrist watches and house-wives*, for I wouldn't wear a wrist watch anyway and we are well supplied with house-wives, which only about one man out of a hundred ever uses, anyway.

(*A sewing pouch containing items a soldier would require to make repairs to his clothing.)

Private Lynn Crawford
Battery C., 25th Calvary, Fort D.A., Russell, Wyo.
October 11, 1917

I feel it my duty to let folks know what the Y. M. C. A. is doing for the soldier boys. I suppose you notice that many of the letters sent home are written on paper furnished by them. They also furnish all the reading material that one could wish for, such as books and magazines.

One of the great helps is the educational opportunities they offer. There are classes in English, French, mathematics, typewriting and spelling.

We also have the old Sunday night meeting which I enjoy very much, and last but not least, are the Movies, which are more or less educational and help to pass the time away.

With thanks for the many helps of the Y.M.C A.

**Austin Olney
U.S.S. Jenkins
November 22, 1917**

Since my last letter I have been in one port that is certainly rich in natural scenery. High hills or young mountains in height having a white cloud cap most of the time and down the sides are little fields surrounded by stone walls and fences, queer little farm buildings and altogether it makes some picture. Ships lying at anchor or sailing around. The town in the harbor is only a patch of dwellings on the hillside with lots of mud for streets. Expect to take a four day furlough in about a week or so from now. Am planning to see some of the places we read about back home. Will tell about them later.

If it isn't too much trouble have my church letter transferred from Mt. Pleasant to Fremont. You can count on me for $15 for the church. So far as clothes are concerned I am pretty well fixed now. You remember those all leather boots Uncle Adam used to wear, well I have a pair like those large enough to hold all the heavy socks I care to carry around. But if you want to send postage stamps I sure can use them. We run short over here and of course have only what is brought to us. I am standing my sea watches in the Radio Shack and act as Decoder. Hope someday to wear a little crow on my arm and stand watch with the wireless phones on my ears.* Have you kept track of "old Cappy Ricks" in the Saturday Evening Post? Some of his stories tell more truth than fiction.

(*When U.S. Navy Sailors achieve 3rd class they achieve what is called their Crows.)

November 25, 1917

We are in port just now and will write. The officers have given me full time for work in the Wireless shack now so I probably will make better headway. Old Michigan with all its snow, ice and wintry weather would be very acceptable to me. Not that I am sick of my job, not at all. Things here never looked better. But all the same I am interested in Michigan. We can't send any more mail without stamps but I have a good supply right now. It is tough all right that we have to get in this war. But I guess the Old Kaiser is some sad too since our fellows got started. Haven't seen any snow around here yet. Don't care if I don't. Say, do you folks eat over there; 21 meatless and wheatless meals a week. Well don't try to fast until the end of the war. I don't believe you would have much waist left.

Those Liberty Loans are surely going great. It's a great country filled with great people that is back of Our Old Glory.

Should you care to have the spike of Kaiser's helmet just send word to that effect. Your letters surely do make me feel lots better. Keep them coming. I think I can be more prompt in answering them now.

December 4, 1917

The Popular Mechanics and Science magazine sent surely made a hit. The Radio gang are interested in anything of that nature. I have not opened the package marked for Christmas yet, but the cover of it was broken and I fished out the candy. Tasted real (good), that did. You know I am beginning to think the folks back home are the ones who have the real hardships of war to contend with. Me, why I am getting fat and sassy on this navy life. I'll be glad enough to be again where letters won't be needed. But I haven't had any serious fit of craziness due to homesickness or anything else. I am here to see the thing through and guess I will, too.

Sure did have some feed on Thanksgiving day. For dinner, turkey with rest of fixings. For supper went ashore and had more turkey, plum pudding, mince pie, celery, mashed potatoes, coffee and—well it took two days to recover. Expect to go on furlough in about five days. I will take about $35 and think that will do. Some of the fellows are taking $100 to $200.

December 8, 1917

Have been ashore a few times the last few days or evenings and have seen some good plays. Saw one that went all over the U.S. either on screen or vaudeville; the name is "Damaged Goods". Have been to one Pipe Organ concert. The organ was the largest I ever saw and the fellow who did the playing was an artist. Guess start on furlough soon now, from reports we may have an interesting time.

**J. Hewitt
Somewhere in France
December 6, 1917**

I have seen three European cities so far and hope to see more although we have not seen the first line of trenches yet, but we have heard them as we often hear the heavy guns although not like we did when we first came here because the French are gaining very rapidly on the front. We have not had any training on this side except with a pick and shovel.

We expect to see the front before Spring but I never did lose anything in that first line of trenches that I want to get. But when they say go, I'm there, and will be ready to go with the rest and try and do my part.

It seems so strange to us to see the French people and the way they do things. They don't live on the farms like we do, but they have a small town every couple miles. They have one large building in which they live, and a barn. Well the whole works are in the building. Of course we are among the peasant people but they are very good to us in every way they know as they can't talk to us.

If they call this Sunny France give me cold United States for mine. But I suppose we will get used to the climate in time. At least I hope so.

We haven't got paid since Sept. 5 but we expect to get our pay soon. The worst of it is we can't buy any American tobacco over here and that's what hurts us. Of course we will just have to put up with it. We got a little a couple weeks ago. Our captain got it for us. I have one package of Bull Durham left.

Your card of Sept 27 reached me Oct 31 so you can see how long it takes mail to get to us. When they get things straightened out I don't think it will take so long. We have only received mail twice while here and it is surely appreciated when we do get it. If there is anything that makes us feel good it's the mail and to know that the folks at home think of us. Tell all my friends "hello" for me. I am a long way from home but often do think of the people back there.

I have been in the army over six months and have traveled over 11,000 miles, and hope to travel several more.

Selah M. Reber Wins First Lieutenancy
Son of A. P. Reber Given Commission at Second Officers' Reserve Training Camp
December 6, 1917
Fremont Times-Indicator

The friends of Selah M. Reber, son of A. P. Reber of this city, are rejoicing over his success at the recent officers reserve training camp at Fort Sheridan, Ill., where Mr. Reber was awarded a first lieutenancy in infantry when the commissions were handed out at the close of the training period last week.

While now a resident of Milwaukee Mr. Reber spent several years of his boyhood here and is a graduate of the Fremont high school. About eight years ago he went to Chicago to work in the Marshall Field establishment and his advancement has been rapid. For some time past he has had charge of a wholesale branch of the Marshall Field Co. in Milwaukee.

Mr. Reber has been notified that his field of service will be in France and expects to leave for foreign soil about the first of the year. As first lieutenant he will draw a salary of $2000 a year with 20 per cent increase for European service.

Mr. Reber left yesterday for Chicago and will spend a week there and in Milwaukee on business. He will then return here for a short visit before he receives his call.

Renard Looyengoed
Columbus Barracks, Ohio
December 6, 1917

I can assure you my heart is in the work and work for promotion I will, as everything I ever go into I do my best, and that is what I will do now. All intoxicating liquors, tobacco and anything that will hinder my promotion I will leave alone.

People do not realize what they are doing for us in the Y.M.C.A. But if they were in our position one week there would be plenty of funds for their work. Men in charge of the Y.M.C. A. work incessantly to help us in every way possible. On Sundays they try to get as many boys as possible to go to church. Not only that but they encourage them by getting the members of the church to take the boys home with them for dinner. And the dinner that one of the members gave me reminded me of the good Sundays at home. They make you feel at home. They try to do everything possible for your welfare. It is a very good thing to help keep the boys straight which is an important thing in a soldier's life so that he may be fit to serve his county. A man who is not in condition is worthless and more of a burden than a benefit. Boost for Y.M.C.A. Tell the people to boost for the Y.

Letters and Related Articles 1917

Bugler Carl Felber
Co. A., 18th Infantry, Am. Exp. Force, France
December 6, 1917

Love sickness is very catching here in France. If some of our ugly looking girls from the U.S. were here they would be the belles of France and would be able to catch a soldier boy with money. Now you can imagine how many girls are left here in the smaller towns. The prettiest have gone to Paris, Nancy and Bar Leduc and some of the larger towns of France to work on street cars and in big munition plants. So you can imagine how hard France has been hit by this war.

Well I hardly know what else to write with the exception that our regiment wins the $500 silk American flag offered by some American woman for the capture, dead or alive, of the first German prisoner.

Dallas Darling
139 Areo Sgdn., Camp Hocks, Texas
December 6, 1917

Saturday night I went to Waco to see the home town boys who left in the National Guards from Muskegon and Grand Rapids, Milon Jackson, Dan Gerber, Mason Brace, Frank Raymond and there were a number of others from Fremont. They are in the 126 Infantry, Co's. L and M. They are real soldiers doing 8-1/2 hours drilling per day with the rifle. That is real life.

Elgin Coburn came back and told me some about where he went while he was home for 24 hours. Tonight I am going to corner him and hear it all.

Well a car full of mail just drove up, about 20 bags. Here is where I quit and sort for an hour or two.

**Austin Olney
U.S.S. Jenkins
December 13, 1917**

Started a letter last week (November 13) while we were in port but did not have time to finish, so will try again.

Your letters keep coming and each time we get in I have a few letters waiting. You can know I look forward to those letters. I received several fine letters from people around Fremont and I certainly appreciate them. Have received two bundles of newspapers. From what I can find in the Grand Rapids papers I don't believe you hear much about what we are doing. Of course I can't tell you, but The New York Times on Oct 21-24 had a few articles which were right from our neighborhood.

Was on patrol duty ashore last night. Got back to ship at 12 p.m. We are not allowed to smoke or drink while on patrol, so I didn't. Went ashore last Sunday and found an old cemetery. In one corner was an old chapel and in it a vault. The fellow I was with and myself found monuments dated 1830, 1750, 1730, and 1705 and 1701and lots of dates in that same period in 1804. Have more about the castle in my diary. The estate surely bears ear-marks of old age and still people live in the castle. It is pretty too.

I have not been in the signal corps since coming on the Jenkins. I work on deck most of the time, but some way found favor with the officers and am now studying to become a wireless operator. Can pick up once in a while a word on the set. Got some from a French, some British and some Berlin stations the other night.

We are very well fixed for winter so you don't need to worry about our being cold.

I know what "canned Billy" and hard tack are now.*

Well goodbye for now. Don't worry if letters seem far apart for we are kept very busy.

(*Cans containing beef along with biscuits were main field rations during World War I.)

Frank Raymond
Camp McArthur, Texas
December 13, 1917

We are getting along as well as can be expected considering the disappointments and trouble in securing equipment, but in spite of all that, we are doing fairly well and I think I am safe in saying that we could give old "Bill" a run for his money without any further training.

The meals at first were nothing to brag on but are fine now. Today we were issued what are commonly called hob nailed shoes. They are real heavy and are guaranteed to last a life time. We get the rest of our equipment just before we leave for France, which I think will be about the 15th of January.

In the morning we are called at 6 and at 6:45 we have mess. Then at 7:30 we assemble and march out to drill until 12 o'clock. At 12:15 we have mess and are free until 1:30. Then we again go out to drill until 4:30. At 5:15 the mess call again sounds and at 6 o'clock the bugle calls retreat. After this we are free until 10:30 when we all have to be in bed and the lights out.

At sundown the flag is taken in while the band plays "The Star Spangled Banner" and everyone, no matter where he is, faces and salutes "The Stars and Stripes." This is very impressive and seems rather sacred.

Our work so far has been very hard, but we are all in the best of health and enjoy it all immensely.

The Y.M.C.A. is in camp and has large buildings in which are many writing tables, a reading table and library. They also have programs and old fashioned song services there. Always be a booster for the Y.M.C.A. for it deserves much credit for the wonderful work being carried on in army camps.

I have just completed a fifteen days course in "Grenade and Bomb construction" at the divisional school of arms, and I am going to act as company instructor until transferred to some other place where this line of work is being carried on.

"America" is the synonym for "liberty" and it's up to everybody to do their bit for the continued protection of future generations.

I am writing this in my tent and most of my squad which consists of eight men, are here and they too are writing. Can you imagine eight men crowded around a small cast iron stove all trying to write and talk at the same time?

Lieut. S. C. Hilton
44th Infantry, Camp Lewis, American Lake, Washington
December, 15, 1917

The Regiment moved up here four weeks ago, where we are supposed to be recruited to full strength and prepare to go across. I hope this happens soon as I am getting pretty well bored with this spot. It is located about twenty miles from Tacoma and in one of the wettest valleys in the world. Since coming here it has failed to rain only three days. We have drilled but one day a week, spending all the time digging ditches and holes to take care of the water which covers the parades.

I enjoy getting the paper each week and thereby keeping in touch with things in Fremont, especially the news concerning the young fellows who are in the Service. Wish some of them were out this way.

I had a letter from George Caldwell last week. You may be interested to know that he also has a commission in the Regular Army, being a Second Lieutenant in the Veterinary Corps, stationed at Fort Sill, Okla., with the 14th Field Artillery. Thank you for your kindness in sending the paper.

Ray E. Bassett
61st Aero Construction Squadron, Morrison, Va.
December 26, 1917

I doubt if any of the men folks at home are dead tired from digging stumps, or anything like it. I've done about everything one could think of today. Started out this morning by digging out stumps, then wheeled dirt until nearly noon, when a bunch of us were sent to police up around some new barracks. After dinner we were sent down the line to build sidewalks. It snowed nearly all night last night so we have wet feet about all the time now, for there is not staying in the barracks unless one is sick or on duty in there. It is pretty crisp this evening. I wonder how the boys at the Michigan camps get along. Yesterday about half of us were down on the river eating oysters. The tide is out in the afternoon and one can walk out on the river bottom about a quarter of a mile. Some places the oysters are thick as hair on a dog's back. Those places are oyster beds though. That is, they are staked off, they are private property. We have had one bunch of oysters to eat, all they cost was the time it took to get them. I was out all the afternoon and dressed but little heavier than I had to in August. The storm was coming though, and drove us back before the tide had risen but a very little. I want to see the tide come in some of these days. From where we were we could see Norfolk, and the ships in the port. Some of them looked like battle ships. We were at least five miles from them. I have heard some boats whistle while I have been writing.

This place is cut right out of the woods and it is awfully hard to get reading material, especially as there is no "Y" here yet and I have not seen but two kids in here selling papers. I bought both of them. The woods around here are mostly pine, but there are also beech and other hard wood trees. Holly and mistletoe also grow here.

I don't know when we will go across but probably in a month or so. I wish to goodness they would hurry and put us where we might do some good.

Morrison, Va., January 3, 1918

No wonder you couldn't find Morrison on map. You couldn't find it in the dark if you were here. I never imagined Reeman was so large until I saw Morrison. They don't even know there is such a thing as a three cent stamp here. There is a depot, two stores and two negro churches; I guess they are negro, anyway

I am going over there and see some of these days. The camp is chopped right out of the woods. I don't know when it was started but it couldn't have been started much earlier than August. There are 24 barracks with a warehouse to each barracks being divided in two parts. We don't have to go outside for anything but our meals and to work. Each end of the barracks has a hot air furnace and the bathroom is heated by steam and there is also a water heater. There is a large range in the kitchen.

We get mail twice a day and once on Sunday. We are right down on historic territory. There are some civil war trenches within walking distance from here just as they were, they say.

We get up at 5:40, reveille at 6, breakfast at 6:30, fatigue call at 7:25, recall at 11:30, dinner at 12, fatigue call at 1:25, recall at 4:30, supper at 5:00, lights out at 9:15.

Henry Felber
D. Batt., 83rd F.A., Fort D.A., Russell, Wyoming
December 27, 1917

Perhaps it would be of interest to Fremont people to hear of a club that is being organized in Cheyenne. It is called the Hundred Percent American club. Its object is to promote patriotism, investigate cases of disloyalty where such exist, to aid and assist the government in locating traitors and prosecuting same.

Accounts of the treatment given Kunnen seem to have traveled across the whole country as many of the boys showed me accounts of it in their home papers.

I might say that I am enjoying my stay here at Russell since the coming of the 'Y". We expect to remain here for the winter. Our regiment is the only one out of three to remain here. The other two are on the border. We are well supplied with wool clothes now except a few things such as socks and gloves, but as the weather is fair at present it is not causing any hardships.

In Time of War

PART TWO

In Time of War

War Continues
1918

In 1918, the prolonged war intensified as American troops flooded France. By summer, 10,000 soldiers a day were setting foot on French soil. In early July President Wilson announced one million troops were stationed on the Western front. Ultimately by the end of the war that number rose to 2.8 million. The arrival of U.S. troops greatly altered the war, but in the first few months after the U.S. declared war the process of moving American troops across the ocean was agonizingly slow, mostly due to the shortage of ships to carry them. The U.S. began pressing every available ship into service including cruise ships and seized German ships. They also borrowed ships from Allies to transfer men and supplies. Once troops arrived they were used to support the fatigued British and French troops who had been fighting since 1914. It was only on August 10, 1918, the that U.S. had enough properly trained manpower under General Pershing to announce the creation of the U.S. First Army. Pershing was put in command of 500,000 men at the Battle of St. Mihiel on September 12. At another successful battle at the Argonne from September 27 to October 6 he commanded a combined total of one million U. S. and British soldiers. Their success included taking back 200 square miles of territory from the German army for the French.

The number of troops was staggering, yet sheer numbers alone did not win the war. Armies on both sides faced an entirely different war from any fought in the past. Much of this was due to the onset of new technology which increased rapidly during the war. From the use of submarines and aircraft, to long range artillery and machine guns, chemical warfare, and trenches reinforced with concrete and barbed wire, the war looked nothing like anyone had seen before. Though horses were still used to pull cannon and move wagons filled with supplies, they were no match for machine guns or gas warfare.

The introduction of tanks in 1917 was very effective in ending stalemates, especially if they preceded artillery. They were big bulky machines that generally moved slowly in large groups. They traversed right through barbed wire and across trenches knocking down anything in their path. Inside, soldiers had little visibility and no radios. Overall, they were the beginning of the downward spiral of morale for the German army.

Like tanks, airplanes could also be used to end stalemates. Weather permitting, airplanes would scout enemy lines, report troop movements to the ground, drop supplies, and even take photographs. They were relatively new in the early 1900s, but by war's end their use was widespread. By the end of 1918 Germany was out-numbered in the air five to one by the Allies. Sources vary widely, but Great Britain was able to produce approximately 55,000 aircraft during the war; France contributed approximately 68,000. Production by the U.S got off to a slow start, but by war's end they had produced 15,000

War Continues 1918

aircraft. The difficulty lay it seems in not getting automobile factories repurposed as aircraft manufacturers quickly enough. Due to the lack of manpower and materials Germany was limited to 14,000 aircraft. By June the British and French had joined forces creating fleets of forty or more aircraft which they flew deep into Germany loaded with bombs.

Though there were some famous World War I Ace pilots, being a pilot wasn't as glamorous as it might sound. It was a dangerous job with a generally short life span. In aerial combat opposing planes fired at each other as they tried to knock each other out of the sky. This was done with the pilot completely exposed. Guns were mounted on the front of the plane forcing the pilot to shoot between the propellers. By war's end, from all nations 15,000 airmen gave their lives.

Another aircraft, found mostly in the nighttime skies, were German dirigibles known as Zeppelins. They were described as flying weapons, "lighter than air, filled with hydrogen, and held together with steel." They were used both for reconnaissance and bombing missions. Zeppelins could reach heights of 10,000 feet taking them out of the range for artillery fire. Stocked with two tons of bombs and reaching speeds of 85 mph they created terror on the ground. Under cover of darkness a loud hum would alert those below of their presence. The sole purpose was to induce enough fear and panic to destroy the morale of those below. The British were used to watching the sea for possible attacks, but now had to look upwards to the sky. Zeppelins attacked Britain 51 times during the war causing considerable damage and loss of life, but never succeeded in causing the British to retreat from the war.

Though not new to warfare, trenches were extensively used in WWI. When the two enemies reached a stalemate, they dug in. By the end of 1914 the first set of trenches extended 415 miles from the North Sea to the Swiss borderland. A trench was dug deep enough for a man to stand upright. A ledge or step allowed the soldier to "step up" and peer over the top, usually through sand bags piled two to three deep. This was the front or fire line trench. Behind and parallel to it, another trench was excavated to be used as a support trench. Men and supplies were kept there ready to be moved forward quickly. Finally, a third trench served as a reserve trench. Smaller connecting communication trenches allowed the movement of men, supplies, and messages to pass to the front. These trenches lined with barbed wire zig-zagged with numerous twists and turns to prevent the enemy from firing straight down a line. Inside the walls were supported by the addition of sand bags, concrete, logs, or anything else available to keep the trench walls from collapsing during heavy rainfall. Underground rooms similar to cellars were sometimes dug twenty to thirty feet below the trench floor where beds and sometimes even a stove could be found.

When not engaged in battle soldiers were engaged in working the trenches. Sentry duty was rotated and lasted two to three hours. Wall repairs were continuous, new latrines needed to be dug or pails of waste emptied. The removal of standing water

War Continues 1918

when possible was critical. After heavy rain men often stood in deep water, their feet bogged in mud, unable to leave their post or change out of wet boots, socks, and clothing for days at a time. This could lead to a painful infection called trench foot. Dead tissue would spread across the feet which sometimes led to amputation. In these filthy conditions soldiers also had to contend with body lice which caused trench fever, rats, swarms of flies, overflowing latrines and the spread of diseases such as cholera, dysentery, and typhoid fever. The stench that filled the trench was ever present, from putrid standing water, unbathed men wearing the same clothes for weeks at a time, bloated dead rats floating in the water, and corpses of dead soldiers that could not be readily removed.

Trenches could be occupied for weeks. Men would spend four to six days in the front line, and then be moved back, spending equal amounts of time in support and reserve trenches before being rotated back to the front. There they again faced "No Man's Land", the space between Allied and enemy lines, waiting for the call to go "over the top', bayonets fixed to attack. It wasn't until tanks became more present that trenches began to be seen for what they were, useless attempts at resolving deadlocks between enemies.

The filthy, disease ridden trenches, feelings of being trapped, the incessant sounds of war, and the fear of being called to go "over the top", often with no end in sight, led some soldiers to develop what was then called "shell shock." We now know this as Post Traumatic Stress Disorder or PTSD. It was not understood then, and often soldiers suffering from it were accused of being cowards and received little sympathy. Some were even shot.

Germany released a weapon in 1915 that exposed soldiers to a peril before unknown. The ugliness of war reached new heights with horrific results on April 22 at the Second Battle of Ypres in western Flanders. A greenish-yellow cloud smelling like bleach rose from German trenches in a south-westerly breeze and descended on Allied troops, completely enveloping them. The German army had released 6000 cylinders buried in the ground containing 200 pounds of chlorine gas. This gas causes immediate irritation to eyes, nose, lungs and throat. In high doses it brings about a slow terrifying death by asphyxiation. The Allied troops were taken completely by surprise. Immediately after its release soldiers could be seen staggering and falling to the ground. In the end 1000 French and Algerian troops were left dead and 4000 injured.

The Allied response was two-fold. By 1916 they had developed British-made Small Box Respirators and French-made M2 gas masks. The M2 masks could give protection up to five hours. By 1917 they were standard issue. However, troops from the United States were often not well trained in mask use. Many would begin with the Box Respirator and then switch to the M2 masks for longer protection, inhaling deadly gas in-between. The masks covered the whole face and became filled with condensation, making it difficult to see and causing many soldiers to remove them too soon.

In the second response, as devastating as gas warfare was, the Allies began manufacturing their own chemical weapons and used them on the enemy.

One chemical weapon used was six times more deadly than chlorine gas. It was phosgene. It was colorless, hiding its presence until it was too late. Sometimes victims didn't realize they had been gassed with a fatal dose until two days later when lungs filled with fluid and they died of painful suffocation. Phosgene killed not only people, but plants, insects, and horses. It was the number one gas used by the Allies. In all, 85% of fatalities from chemical warfare came from phosgene.

Lastly, the third most used chemical was mustard gas, a known blistering agent. The effects were not immediate, but within hours some victims began suffering blindness, followed by extensive blistering. The affected areas often developed infection. In this case, gas masks were of no use. The use of mustard gas could also leave behind contamination of the soil where ever used. It caused the most casualties of any of the gases used in WWI. At the end of the war the American Chemical Society estimated that these gases and others caused the deaths of 90,000 to 100,000 people with 1.3 million injured.

Another unseen enemy began its global journey in late August 1918. Transported by unsuspecting soldiers, three cases of flu were confirmed in Boston. In a matter of days the number of infected skyrocketed as thousands of trainees at Camp Devon overwhelmed all medical facilities.

Prior to the war many Americans still led very rural lives with little social contact involving large numbers of people. Then the war began massing soldiers together in railroad cars, training camps, and trenches. Many soldiers never left American soil before being quarantined. They had been vaccinated for typhoid fever and small pox, but scarlet fever, mumps, measles, and other contagious diseases flourished. Without antibiotics or a vaccine this new virus soon became a devastating illness of pandemic proportions as it left the nation and put the world in peril of the Spanish Flu.

Spain remained a neutral country during the war and was not responsible for the flu despite its name. Spain had censor-free newspapers and became the first country to report the flu epidemic, and by doing so the virus became known as the Spanish flu of 1918-1919. The very contagious and deadly disease was downplayed by other countries, thus keeping the public uniformed and vulnerable.

The flu not only infected and killed soldiers, it also overwhelmed civilian populations. Often times there were not enough healthy workers to do basic jobs such as garbage pick-up or driving buses. Businesses closed as bodies stacked up in morgues. The war left many at home without the aid of doctors or family members to care for them. Those medical people not already in the military were often too sick themselves to

War Continues 1918

minister to the needs of the infected. Antibiotics had not yet been developed, so aspirin was given in doses of up to 30 grams a day. This is now known to be a toxic dose. Today only 4 grams is recommended. The result was the death of many people by aspirin poisoning. Many patients developed pneumonia causing it to be listed as the cause of death rather than the flu. All that could be done was to keep the ill as comfortable as possible with some victims dying within hours.

From September until the Armistice in November the flu had the world, and the war, in its grip rendering much of the army and navy ineffective on both sides. Quarantine conditions in military life, such as trenches, was not possible making those already in weakened conditions easy prey for what had become a killing machine. As those who died or became too ill to perform their duties were removed, new healthy replacements were sent in and exposed. During battles, such as the Meuse-Argonne, combat support had to be rerouted to care for the sick and dead, weakening the effectiveness of the military.

The flu caused more U. S. soldiers to die than those from combat. As many as 2.8 million American soldiers were sent to France. Of those, 116,000 died. Half of these deaths were attributed to the flu. Some sources suggest world-wide 50 million deaths occurred, more than all combat deaths from the entire war, though the total number was most likely higher due to lack of good records.

In spite of the many hardships caused by disease and manmade forces of destruction, the war ground on to its brutal end. In the spring of 1918 the Communist Party seized power in Russia bringing about the Bolshevik Revolution. On March 3, 1918, they signed the Brest Litusk Treaty with Germany terminating Russia's involvement in WWI. Germany was then able to withdraw its troops from their eastern border and place them on the western front in anticipation of a spring offensive. From March through June, Germany achieved many breakthroughs on the western front. Then with the aid of American troops and the coordinated French and British Troops commanded by Ferdinand Fock, the Allied Supreme Commander, Germany gave up ground and finally had to withdraw from positions once held in May. It was then it became apparent that with the addition of U. S. forces Germany was not going to have its military victory. The Allied Hundred Days Offensive from August to the Armistice was a time of hard fighting on both sides with many lives lost. By then mutiny had broken out in the German navy and uprisings in German cities took place as the people saw continued fighting as useless.

In November it was again a house of cards, much as the beginning of the war, only now country after country withdrew from the war. By November Bulgaria, Turkey, and Austria-Hungary had signed armistices; Kaiser Wilhelm abdicated and fled to the Netherlands. Germany was then declared a republic.

War Continues 1918

By the time Germany signed the Armistice on November 11, 1918, the American Expedition forces had become known as one of the best armies in the world. But that notoriety came with over 320,000 American casualties. The world and its people would be forever changed.

In Flanders Fields

In Flanders fields the poppies blow
Between the crosses, row on row,
That mark our place; and in the sky
The larks, still bravely singing, fly
Scarce heard amid the guns below.

We are the Dead. Short days ago
We lived, felt dawn, saw sunset glow,
Loved and were loved, and now we lie,
In Flanders fields.

Take up our quarrel with the foe:
To you from failing hands we throw
The torch; be yours to hold it high.
If ye break faith with us who die
We shall not sleep though poppies grow
In Flanders fields.

John McCrae

Home Front
Newaygo County, 1918

Patriotic fever still ran high in 1918. Every loyal American in the community was urged to attend a "monster Win the War" mass meeting in March. Special effort had been given to the attendance of area farmers, even going as far as making sure the hours of the meeting would not interfere with evening chores. The local farmers, as with those across the nation, had been hard hit in their efforts to meet the demands of the war.

Preceding the meeting, the Home Guard dressed in full uniform performed a twenty-minute drill in the streets led by Captain Erwin C. Tinney. Once gathered in the Fremont auditorium Attorney W.H. Eastman addressed the crowd on the topic, "The Menace of Prussianism." He put forth his study of the great conflict in a way described as "alive with Patriotism."

Another Mass meeting, again dubbed a "Win the War" demonstration of loyalty, took place in April at The First Christian Reformed Church. A call went out to every person in the county to gather and join hands in solidarity. "High caliber" men from Grand Rapids were solicited to speak beginning with Rev. Johannes Groem, the man behind the 100% Patriot campaign. Next on the docket was Sam Young, president of the Grand Rapids Furniture Manufacturers' Association. The *Fremont Times-Indicator* stated Young was "expected to furnish oratorical fire-works" for those who were willing "to make sacrifice at the altar of liberty." As before, the Home Guard drilled on Division St., followed by a march of businessmen to the church.

To further inform the public a series of patriotic meetings were organized in rural areas. Halls across the county were procured for the purpose of accommodating those unable to make more urban area meetings. Though the farmers were gravely concerned about supply and labor issues it was made clear these meetings were to be used only for the purpose of presenting the hard facts of the war given by speakers with first-hand accounts of the trenches, and not for the airing of grievances.

The fourth Liberty Loan campaign was given a boost by the arrival of the Trophy Train. Escorted by a company of soldiers and sailors, three flat cars were loaded with German airplanes, cannon, and other larger spoils of war, while a box car contained thousands of smaller confiscated items. A lecturer traveled with the train. Of special interest was a German airplane, a high speed Fokker, riddled with bullet holes testifying to the marksmanship of Allied aviators. An anti-aircraft gun still mounted on an automobile displayed distinct damage from American shells. The spectators were captivated by guns used in Verdun, the French 75's that helped stop the advance of Germany on Paris. The mud covered guns were proclaimed to have come straight from the trenches.

The train would stop in its travels for only two hours on an October Friday afternoon in Fremont. Everyone was urged to make the effort to see the largest exhibit of war trophies ever collected. And while there, they were encouraged to buy liberty bonds so the Allies could continue on to victory.

Another source of government income was something everyone could afford. At twenty-five cents apiece even children could buy Thrift Stamps. Once a thrift card was filled with sixteen stamps it could be exchanged for a War Savings Certificate. To make purchasing stamps convenient, every fifteenth day of the month teachers around the county sold stamps to children eager to belong to the Thrift Stamp Club.

Patriotic activities by area churches continued to support the men who had left for war. A service flag of the Fremont Methodist Episcopal Church was dedicated to seventeen servicemen. As their names were called a star was placed upon a flag of white. Prosecuting Attorney W. J. Branstrom gave an address using quotes from the Kaiser's speeches to demonstrate how the German peoples' thoughts had been infused by the Kaiser's policy of "blood and iron".

Similarly, Sitka M. E. Church had a service with eighty people in attendance to dedicate their service flag. The nine young men honored were each represented by a family member. In his oration Rev. A. R. Elliot discussed the war practices of the Prussian military and listed ways in which those at home could help win the war. A solemn march then led the congregation past the platform where each person stopped to salute both Old Glory and the service flag. One of those present was Civil War veteran J. B. Ruggles, whose son and three grandsons were in the war. Across the church community servicemen were acknowledged with flags, speeches, songs, poetry, and food prepared by ladies of the church.

A new campaign was launched called the Four Minutemen. Forty thousand men were trained and sent forth in the U.S. to actively warn people about pro-German propaganda and explain their methods. It was hoped informed people could defeat such propaganda by denying its truth. At the same time, a tight hold was still held on those of German descent. A German man or woman moving within his or her registration district must immediately inform authorities. If moving to a different district the alien must first obtain a permit.

As the war progressed the Red Cross stepped in to provide aid to American soldiers in German and Austrian prisoner of war camps. Regulations for sending money or parcels to prisoners were posted in the newspaper. Checks or money orders were to be made payable to the Bureau of Prisoners' Relief, American Red Cross. Privates could receive five dollars a month. Officers were allowed fifty dollars. Letters could not exceed two pages and must not mention the war. Parcels of eleven pounds or less could be sent. They contained a sundry of items: combs, tooth brushes and tooth powder, shoe laces and boot brushes, buttons, hard candy, cigarettes, gloves and belts not made of leather, sewing articles, soap, towels, socks, underwear, photographs, and periodicals published before the war began. These packages forwarded to loved ones were addressed the same as a letter, but must also be labeled clearly with the relationship to the prisoner, that is, mother, sister, wife, etc.

To continue their work the Red Cross needed money. Readers of the Indicator were told numerous times in numerous ways to support the Red Cross by becoming a member and help *"a boy in France fighting for you"*. Several methods for raising money were used. One of the strongest Red Cross auxiliaries in the county was that of South Sheridan. At an auction on the Eberly farm in Bridgeton they sold lunches to the crowd raising $57.19. They also prepared and shipped boxes of clothing for Belgium relief for thousands of people who still lived under German rule after three and a half years. This auxiliary led in Red Cross membership, partly by strongly suggesting anyone attending community gatherings should be a member of the Red Cross.

Uncle Sam's Free Auction Sale was held to benefit the Red Cross and as an opportunity to buy Liberty Bonds or Thrift Stamps. On the corner of Main and Division Streets in Fremont, on a Saturday afternoon in April, people began bringing items to be sold free of charge. All sales under five dollars benefited the Red Cross, while sales of up to ten dollars required the seller to buy five dollars' worth of Thrift Stamps from money received. Sales over ten dollars required buying a

Liberty Bond out of their profit. This auction continued each Saturday alternating between Fremont and Hesperia.

In May the Newaygo County War Board was challenged to raise funds for the Red Cross by a national campaign hoping to secure one hundred million dollars. The state of Michigan was assessed three million dollars with Newaygo County's apportionment coming in at $9000.

Michigan had still another quota to fill. As nurses left to join the service in the army and navy, they left behind understaffed hospitals. With the purpose of closing the gap both at home and abroad, the Red Cross engaged in enrolling 25,000 women between the ages of 19 to 35 for nurses training. Mrs. H. R. Barnum opened her home to be used as a recruiting station for women who wanted to do their patriotic duty. Application could be made through the local Council of National Defense or local Red Cross chapter. Once enrolled the women became part of the United States Student Nurse Reserves. Michigan was tasked with providing 1,500 applicants.

As people took part in other Red Cross opportunities, or quit jobs for better paying positions left behind by those gone to war, a shortage of teachers arose. As a result some schools faced closing and had to send their students to other schools with hopes of reopening when the war ended.

Adding to the list of troubles for farmers was the shortage of machine parts. They were encouraged to order extra parts to keep on hand that tended to wear out quickly, such as screws, bolts, rivets, snaps, harnesses, and machine oil. In a way this seems rather like a type of hoarding, but it was necessary to keep farmers producing food. On the other hand, people did get in hot water for all sorts of hoarding practices. For instance, as wheat supplies dwindled some farmers began holding back wheat. They were considered pro-German farmers for their refusal to put their wheat on the market. Such acts were said to be disloyal and to give aid and comfort to the enemy. Notice was sent to the unpatriotic farmers from the Food Administration informing them immediate possession of their wheat would take place if they continued to refuse to sell it.

But in reality, it was the shortage of ships causing the wheat rationing that was taking place. There was enough wheat in the U. S., but lack of Allied ships and ship space due to other goods that must be transported, forced the United States to send more U.S. wheat abroad.

Whatever the cause, the shortages were real. In May Americans were told to cut wheat consumption in half. In June the Indicator headline stated, "If you are a patriot" you are observing the schedule of flour rations in your home. Households were not to exceed one and one half pounds of wheat per person a week. This was to include not only bread, but macaroni, crackers, pastries, and cereals.

June also brought new rules for beef and sugar. From the Food Administration in Lansing people were told to observe meatless days by not serving beef more than four times a week. The rules were very restrictive. Families were to serve roast beef only on Mondays; stewed or boiled beef or hash could be served on Wednesdays and Saturdays. Steaks and hamburgers were on the menu for Thursdays and Saturdays. To everyone's excitement oxtail, liver, tongue, hearts, kidneys, brains, and tripe could be served anytime. One wonders how closely people adhered to these rules and if neighbors turned in those who did not comply.

Sugar was not to exceed two pounds at any one time to be sold to a family living in town; five pounds was available for those in the country. Three quarters of a pound a week per person was considered sufficient. For those canning and preserving twenty-five pounds of sugar could be acquired at one time, but the customer must sign a statement before the retailer could sell it. As in the wheat shortage, sugar was diverted to the Allies because of the shipping problems. In August the County Food Administration authorized all Newaygo County residents to use sugar cards. Merchants were not allowed to sell sugar to anyone without a card and then must adhere to the regulation of half a pound to each family member per week. Care was to be taken that cards were not duplicated and presented to multiple merchants.

Of the many restrictions one of the most unusual was the restrictions on the color of children's shoes. It was prohibited to manufacture shoes in anything but brown, black, or white. They must have low heels and cost twelve dollars or less.

There was no limit on buying shoes above government grade as long as they were purchased from surplus retail stock previous to the ban. However, a twenty percent luxury tax would be applied to surplus shoes costing more than ten dollars.

Home life became very stressful and chaotic as people worked around shortages, constantly changing rules, and meeting the demands of being a patriot. Their much needed social lives were often interrupted when gatherings of family or church were canceled due to lack of food to prepare for the occasion.

Finally, it must not be forgotten that mumps, pneumonia, flu and other contagious diseases persisted on into 1919. There was even a rise in the number of cases of tuberculosis. It was not unusual for churches and schools to be closed for weeks while people recovered from these debilitating illnesses.

The biggest concern of all, though, was that of family and friends gone to war. One could withstand a shortage here and there, a noisy patriotic rally, or the hampering of social life, but the constant worry for those overseas, not knowing sometimes for weeks of their well-being, was a source of anxiety that clung to them without ceasing.

When the Armistice was signed there was great joy after so much fear and chaos. The men were coming home! But it would still be months before many of the soldiers touched American soil again. Some would never return having been buried in foreign soil. For others their whereabouts and what happened to them would never be known. They became part of the great number of missing in action. For those Americans who spent the war years on either side of the ocean, nothing would ever be quite the same again.

Home Front Newaygo County, 1918

Celebration Follows Peace Announcement
Thousands Participate in Monday's Program When Holiday Was Declared
November 14, 1918
Fremont Times-Indicator

Nothing could restrain the pent-up enthusiasm for peace when early Monday morning the whistles of the tannery and canning factory heralded the news that the armistice had been signed by representatives of the German government. The signing of this document meant peace to the world, the peace that hundreds of thousands of American mothers and fathers and wives have been hoping and praying for during many months past. It meant the kind of surrender that the American people have been demanding, an unconditional surrender.

The employees of the tannery began the day's celebration by marching from the West End to the municipal flagpole dragging an effigy of the Kaiser which was burned on the public square.

The city was not slow in catching the spirit of the occasion, and the business places were closed for the day. The public school was also dismissed so the young Americans could also enjoy the occasion of the re-establishment of world peace.

At a meeting of the board of trade held at 9:30 Monday morning it was decided to start a formal celebration at 1 o'clock, and Mayor Tinney was chosen president of the day.

In Time of War

Other committees were also appointed and plans for the afternoon and evening were soon consummated.

At one o'clock one of the best parades ever witnessed in Fremont was formed near the school building and the line of march extended to the west end of the city and returned.

The procession was headed by Clark's Band, which was followed by the children and teachers of the public schools and all the employees of the Fremont Canning Co. A number of floats and attractively decorated automobiles also added to the gaiety of the occasion. The Beast of Berlin was represented by several effigies not all complimentary to His Imperial Highness. The big bell of the old Congregational church was mounted on a truck and tolled the death-knell of Kaiserism. A Cleveland tractor drew the hearse containing the effigy of the deadest live man in the world (The Kaiser). And Postmaster McCarthy impersonated Uncle Sam, the victor.

Later in the afternoon more than fifty cars including a number of the floats drove through the county to Newaygo where the band played several selections and Prosecuting Attorney W. J. Branstrom gave a short patriotic address. A big crowd assembled.

Monday evening several thousand people saw the fine display of fireworks on the City Park square. Later in the evening the crowd resumed on the Main-Division corners where short talks were given by Mayor Tinney, J. A. Gerber and H. McCarty.

W. J. Branstsrom ended the speech making with a short but impassioned patriotic address.

November 11 is a day that will long be remembered by the people of this community.

In Time of War

Home Front Newaygo County, 1918

Letters and Related Articles
1918

In Time of War

**Bugler Carl Felber
Co. A, 18th Inf., A. E. F. France
January 2, 1918**

To Mr. and Mrs. H.C. Buck:

Kind Friends—The kindness and thoughtfulness of Mr. and Mrs. H.C. Buck, also Mrs. Chas. Buck and Clarence will never be forgotten by me. It came to me entirely unexpected and was a pleasant surprise. Perhaps I will have a chance to return the kindness if the war devil (the bullet) spares me to come home safe and well, but we must hope for the best.

Well just a little about conditions here in France. It is real cold here with not much snow. Our sleeping quarters are of French model and are very cold at night, otherwise there is no complaint.

**Richard Ashford
Hdqts. 2, Cav. Brigade, Fort Bliss, Texas
January 6, 1918**

I have received the papers you have been sending. Thanks for the "Times-Indicators". Since I heard from you last, we have moved to Presidio, Tex. This little town situated on the Rio Grande is merely a group of clay huts and the inhabitants are Mexicans. Regardless of its lack of beauty, it is full of excitable happenings. Villa makes it hot for us. Two weeks ago we chased a number of Bandits to the border. One of our soldiers was killed and another wounded. Nearly sixty of the Mexicans were killed. In all we have made four expeditions into Mexico. While at Presidio we seldom took off our clothes so as to be ready for immediate action. This kind of duty ought to give us a good training for France.

On New Year's day I transferred from the Eight Cavalry to Headquarters Second Cav. Division. Here I do a little office work and act as motorcycle messenger. This is a better paying job and avoids the monotonous drills. The brigade is a new organization or regiment for service in France. Possibly before long we will cross the pond.

I spent Christmas at Presidio which is 75 miles from a railroad. I was unable to get even Christmas cards there, so pardon me for not remembering you this Christmas.

February 4, 1918

This transferring upsets all correspondence. I suppose the next move will be off this hemisphere. Any place to get out of the God-forsaken Texas. Did you ever live in Texas? Keep away from it. It reminds me of the Sahara desert.

Yesterday, I took out my first naturalization paper renouncing George V for the first time. Don't you think I make a better "Sammie" than a "Tommie"? I have three of Uncle Sam's Liberty Bonds, also ten thousand dollars insurance from the government, so you can see that the soldiers are not only giving their lives but also their money. There is some talk about taking the soldiers from the southern camps and bringing them up north for the summer. The weather is tropically hot during the summer here. When soldiers are taken from the hot camps and sent over to France they easily take cold. Too good to be true. How would you like to be enjoying nice sunny days like we are having now? Of course I am not mentioning the sand storms.

Howard Schoolmaster
Great Lakes Training Station
Co. F., 2nd Reg., Camp Dewey, Ill.
January 10, 1918*

I am getting down to a fair physical shape and am going into boxing, basketball and athletics of all kinds. We had fields of sport Christmas day and our company won two events. Our boxers from this barrack won both of their contests; they are not much, either one. I am sure I can stop them both when I get in trim.

We have sporting events again tomorrow. They want me to go into sprints and I am going to run the 220 yard sprint for this company. The training station does everything in its power for the fellows to encourage them to take up athletics for they know it's the best of training, and if a fellow mixes in all athletics he is bound to shine above the rest. You get acquainted with more commanders.

I must tell you about our Christmas eve. Our company marched to the Christmas tree. They had a mammoth tree and all decorated in red, white and lights and a large U.S. silk flag floated on high. Search lights and other lights played on us all over the Administration building. It was a sight of a life time to see all of us Jackies out attired in the same uniforms. Many people from Chicago attend the tree. We all received boxes of candy and smiles and cheers from some pretty Chicago girls. They always have a cheer for us.

I received a dandy black sweater, a pair of wristlets and a dandy pair of socks, also some other presents from relatives and friends near home.

For our Christmas dinner we had turkey, mashed potatoes and gravy, pie, cranberry sauce, bread and butter, soup and coffee, also bananas and apples.

*This letter appeared in the newspaper the same day as the following notice:

MENINGITIS FATAL TO FREMONT "JACKIE"

Howard Schoolmaster Died
at Great Lakes Training Station
January 10, 1918
Fremont Times-Indicator

Howard Schoolmaster, son of Mr. and Mrs. Louis Schoolmaster, died at the Great Lakes Naval Training station at Great Lakes, Ill., Tuesday evening at seven o'clock after a few days' illness from spinal meningitis. Word of the young man's death reached here Tuesday night shortly after his father had left for his bedside. Mrs. Schoolmaster left for Great Lakes Monday.

As Mr. and Mrs. Schoolmaster were out of the city yesterday no detailed information regarding the illness and death of their son was available.

Howard enlisted in the naval service about the middle of November and was sent to Camp Dewey Great lakes Training Station, where he was being schooled for the service of his country. He was a member of Company J., Second Regiment. That he possessed a fine spirit of loyal Americanism is predicated in a letter written to his mother and father December 30 in which he wrote:

Please don't feel bad about the war for it's you we are fighting for. If we did not subdue the militarists of the Central Powers this world would not be a safe place for us to live in. It would be worse a thousand times than death to have them rule this country, to make us slaves, taking away our homes, etc.

I took out a ten thousand dollar policy to protect myself and you people.

Funeral of Local "Jackie" Held Tuesday
Large Number of Sorrowing Friends Attended Services for Late Howard Schoolmaster

The funeral services for the late Howard Schoolmaster, local "Jackie" who died at the Great Lakes Training station at Great Lakes, Ill., Tuesday, Jan. 8, were held Tuesday afternoon at the Congregational church. Rev. F. W. Magdanz, pastor of the church, officiated. The church edifice was filled with the sorrowing friends of the young naval recruit who came to pay their last tribute of respect to Fremont's first real sacrifice in the world war. The casket was enshrouded in an American flag.

The Fremont company of the Home Guards in uniform acted as escort from the church to Maple Grove cemetery where the body was interred. As a further mark of respect the business places of the city were closed from 1: 30 to 3:30 o'clock and the flags were lowered to half mast.

Howard Schoolmaster was born in this community September 28, 1894, and spent his entire life here. He has always lived at the home of his parents, Mr. and Mrs. Louis Schoolmaster, and in later years has been associated with his father on the farm. He was 23 years, three months and 11 days old at the time of his death. He is survived by his parents. His sister, Marion Schoolmaster, passed away last summer.

Those from away who attended the funeral were Mr. and Mrs. Henry Schoolmaster of Lansing and Mr. and Mrs. Lyle

Letters and Related Articles 1918

Edwards, Mr. and Mrs. Glen Rice and Mr. and Mrs. Dawson, all of Newaygo.

Chas. Coburn
V.S.S.S.C. 128, care Postmaster, Norfolk, Va.
January 15, 1918

Well I am aboard the little packet called the V.S.S. Submarine chaser 128. I don't know as I ever dreamed of living or trying to live on such a wagon as this. It would be O.K. if there was more room and a wash room. I have a dandy spring and mattress bunk, lots of extra heavy clothes and rubber boots and etc., furnished by the government. I think I will be a machinist before long. I have made quite a hit with the captain and leading petty officer. I am the oldest timer on the ship excepting the leading petty officer who had five or six months more in the service than I. The captain is an ex-sailor but not a naval sailor, so they look to me for lots of things. We are mixed up closely with our officers as the ship is small. I should say boat instead of ship. Gee, I get so goaty at times I don't know what I am saying, but I will get used to it before long; it comes better now than it did.

I told you in my last letter to address me in care of P.M. at N.Y. after Jan. but don't do it, for we will not leave here for a couple of months unless orders change. We may go out for a trial trip but aside from that we will be right here. I am insured for a thousand dollars with the government.

We had lots of cold weather here, the most this country has known for over 40 years. Had some snow. It was nice today. We have no snow here now.

It is hard to get settled on a brand new (ship) boat. Takes most of our time getting tools and so on board. Lots of things to think of.

Harold Zerlaut
Camp Grant (Winnebago County, Illinois)
January 15, 1918 (from family archives)

Dear Lavinna:

How are you coming? Going to school every day I suppose and studying hard. How is the school mom, gitting pretty cranky? (Note: Older sister Neva was her teacher at the time.)

Well I am still at camp grant. We have ten days more under quarantine, that is if nobody brakes out in that time. We get out quite a lot on hikes and so on but nobody is allowed out alone without a pass. We were vaccinated again Saturday I have been vaccinated five times since I joined the army but none of them took.

We are getting about an hour a day infantry drill and about an hour physical drill each day. We have a French class here and are learning French. Some noise believe me. We see quite a lot of Allied officers such as French and English in their uniforms. They have their cars decorated with their own flags. There was a French flier in here the other day.

There has not been any mail in for a couple of days and so I have not got any mail. The last letter I got came from Columbus. A letter John Thill wrote a long time ago. I can not write very much as we can not get paper and envelopes at present. Everything is free but they are all out at present. Write and tell me how all the folks are. How is mother? We may leave any time as soon as the quarantine is lifted. They are sending mechanics to school right along. There is going to be a great call for fliers. Anyone that can pass the physical examination stands a good show. Will be glad when we can try out. Well I will close.

Ray E. Bassett
473rd Aero Const. Sqdn., A.E.F. France, Morrison, Va.
January 18, 1918

Well, it is goodby Broadway for us. All we have with us is our equipment which we have to carry. It only consists of three blankets, half a tent, mess kit, toilet articles, suit of underwear, three pairs of socks, towel and a bed tick, all hooked on to as a convenient a harness as some poor nut could devise. O yes, we carry a rain coat too; you would be surprised at the amount of junk we can get in so small a space, and the small amount of space it takes. We harnessed up yesterday morning and went for a hike. We only went about a mile but double timed or ran a good share of that distance and the roads are muddy and we were glad to get back. I started this before breakfast, all the clothes I have off since yesterday morning is my legging, hat and coat. It was rather cold in the barracks and our bed ticks emptied and blankets rolled up, so to pass the night away I went up to the Movie show and when I got back the fireman and I played Rummie 'till midnight and then I got my bed tick and overcoat and went down to the furnace room and slept behind the furnace until near morning when the fire got it too hot for me, and then I came up and laid down on the bare iron cot. We are in the army now. Several of the fellows slept in one end of the mess hall and our lieutenants in the other end on the tables and on the floor, we could be away from here inside of ten minutes. If I don't get a chance to mail this before we embark I don't know whether that would pass the censor or not. If I was to mail this at the gangplank it would be censored and held until we arrived on the other side and then mailed. I shall try to get it in the mail before then though. None of us know when or where we are going and couldn't tell if we did.

Last Monday a Penn.-State Pedagogue about 35 years of age and I got off for the day and hiked up the road about 14 miles, got our dinner and came back. Most of the way afoot. Going out we were looking at the tomb of some old Englishman who lived some time during the 18th century. A old Confederate soldier came along and we got to talking and asking about the Civil War actions in this neighborhood. He walked on down the road, took us up in the woods and showed us some of the old trenches and told us war yarns. He is 72 years of age but very active. He seems to think that if the Confederate Army was over in Europe at the present time, the war would last about half an hour.

I began to worry a little for fear I wouldn't get a chance to write and let you know I had gone. They kept me so busy yesterday, but for a wonder they can see some one else besides me for details this morning.

Juell J. Hewitt
Co. F., 2nd Engineers, Am. Forces, France
January 21, 1918

Dear Editor:--I have finished the story which has been running in your paper, "My Fourteen Months at the Front" and needless to say I have read it all since I have been in France. I think it surely gives the ways and important occurrences of this war.

I was surely always glad when the mail came and brought me a paper from home so that I could read some more of that story.

Well it runs in my mind if you folks at home are having anything near the same weather we are having it should be appreciated. It is only the latter part of January and all our snow has left us, although it is some wet from the rains but is drying up very rapidly and the French people say we won't have any more snow.

I also saw in the paper last night a letter from Ward Giddings. I was very much interested in reading it as I think he has the right thing in mind about the boys who left at the declaration of war. They are long forgotten. No doubt you have all read the poem, "Only a Volunteer" by Corp. Thos. Baker. I think it fits the case exactly.

Now as to the statement that Ward made that it wasn't a wrist watch or housewife he was looking for. He stated that the housewives were never used. I think if they were over in France they would be mighty glad they had a housewife. They are a mighty handy article over here, and it a case of use them or go without. You can guess the rest. I don't mean by that that I am asking for a housewife as I had one and the Red Cross from home sent me another, so I am not suffering any.

As to the wrist watch, well in my business I find that they are mighty handy things, although I never wore one until I came to France and at the present time I have two watches. I do not know how long I will have two as those who know me know that I never had anything I would not trade or sell. During my time with the colors I have had about twenty watches, all kinds and colors

Ward speaks about lying in dust. I think if he were over here dashing around in mud knee deep he would be glad to see a little dust. I felt the same way about Texas but learned that dust was easier to clean off than mud.

Well, I don't want "Babe" to get sore at anything I may say so I think I had better change the subject before I say something I had better not.

We are beginning to think that Christmas comes sometime in the year wherever we are as we are just getting our Christmas packages and they surely look good to us and it seems good to feel that someone is thinking of us although we are many miles away. I can honestly say that we appreciate what we get if it isn't anything more than a safety pin. They certainly come in handy some times.

I received five Christmas packages this week and have some on the road yet so the letters I receive state. Well, I will quit, hoping to hear from my friends if I have any left.

James Coburn
20th Eng. Co. D., 4 Bn., American Forestry, A.E.F. France
January 1918

I got on the other side at last. I am just able to walk and sit up and write. I was taken sick with mumps when I was two days out at sea, I must have taken cold for I was awfully sick and thought I would die for sure. I am poor as a crow and reel when I walk. I suppose you wondered where I went when I did not write for so long. Maybe this won't reach you, I hope it does. I like the looks of things here in the hospital. I have a good bed, so I can't kick if I just get well so I can go back to my company.

How are all the folks at home? Tell them I send my best regards and I am not sick of being where I am. As for the war, I don't know much about it as I have not seen a paper in a month.

The children and the sailors here wear wooden shoes. I am in a French hospital and they are good to us. They are glad to see American soldiers come. The streets are narrow and dirty. The street cars are little things about 20 feet long and funny looking. The people are down hearted.

The German prisoners seem happy. The French think the war will soon be over. Don't worry about me. I will be along all right.

January 31, 1918

I am well and feel fine, a little weak yet and poor.

This is a queer-looking place, lots of wooden shoes and two wheel carts. I like it here petty well. I will go to my company in a few days. I don't know where but will find out. I wrote a letter one week ago and wonder if you got it.

We have a plenty to eat and wear and a place to sleep if it is on the ground some times in a dog tent. But that doesn't worry me.

The weather is good and no snow, but some rain. The French are good to us and all the men here have on uniforms. We can't talk much to them but can do lots of hand talk like the dumb. The girls are pretty, as good looking as I ever saw but if the guards catch us talking to them they put us in the brig.

We went to France in a hurry when we got started. Have you had much of a winter? I have not seen over two inches of snow this winter.

I am all over the mumps and don't worry.

**Frank Raymond
Camp Merritt, N. J.
February 14, 1918**

To Mr. and Mrs. Art Edwards:

We left our tent city at Waco about sundown Sunday, Jan. 20th, and arrived here Saturday 10:30 a.m., Jan. 26th. We located in nice warm barracks quite different from our tents, and have nothing to do but take hikes, in order to keep us in trim while we await the arrival of transports at the Port of Embarkation.

This is February 6th now, and I don't want to leave here without writing you a few lines and telling you of our trip from Texas.

It was early Sunday morning Jan. 20th when the captain gave the command to pack up and be ready to leave camp on a minute notice, and from then until we marched from our Co. street everybody was kept busy scrubbing tent floors and putting everything in first class order for the troops that are to be sent there from some northern camp.

The journey through Texas and Arkansas was the most tedious part of the whole trip, cotton fields and negro villages were all one could see and I was mighty glad when we crossed the line into Tennessee. We passed through the timber district and stopped in Nashville, capital of Tennessee, for exercise, also passed through Memphis, Bristol and other large cities on our way to Alabama and Georgia. It was dark when we entered Alabama and when we awoke we were back into Tennessee, just about to cross the line into Virginia. Our journey took us through the Blue Ridge mountains of Virginia. It was about 3:30 p.m. when the porter came through the train and told us that we were about to enter the foothills of the Sony mountains and that we soon would be passing through tunnels that lead to the Blue Ridge mountains. About sundown the train came to a halt and another large engine was coupled on behind, oil tanks filled, and everything made safe for the trip through the mountains, which took all night on account of the heavy load and the many steep grades. Most of us stayed up that night as we had never seen a mountain before, and those who retired early got up later, complaining of the noise and what poorly managed road, etc. It was a beautiful moonlight night and we could see for miles, nothing but snow covered mountains and an occasional farm house in the valley.

We crossed the Potomac just at dark Friday and entered Washington, D.C. It was too dark to see much, but the Government buildings were all lit up and were easily distinguished. The Capitol and the congressional Library were brilliantly lighted and they are certainly beautiful structures. We had a good view of Washington's monument from the train. We took a short hike there but couldn't see as much as we could from the train. From Washington we traveled across Maryland to Baltimore and caught a glimpse of the Chesapeake Bay. We went almost directly north from there, crossing the Susquehanna River, passed through Wilmington, Delaware, and arrived in Philadelphia about midnight. We crossed the Delaware river and came into New Jersey at Trenton. Came through Jersey City and Hoboken within sight of New York harbor and arrived here 10:30 eastern time.

We are quite sure that we are going across very soon, but the present indications are that peace is coming in the near future, so our stay in France will probably be short. I hope so for I am looking forward with great hopes for the future. It is almost time for retreat so I must close, hoping that you will cheer me up with a nice long letter soon.

It is hard to get settled on a brand new (ship) boat. Takes most of our time getting tools and so on board. Lots of things to think of.

Pt. Fred Hoad
Co. 3., Pla., 16th Sussex Yeomanry, Royal Sussex Regt., E. E. F., Egypt

Mr. and Mrs. Chas. Hoad of this city are in receipt of an interesting letter from their son, Fred Hoad, who is with the British forces in Palestine. Mr. and Mrs. Hoad have three sons and one son-in-law in the British army.

February 18, 1918, Palestine

Dear Father, Mother, Brother, and sister:

In answer to your most welcome letter which I received Feb. 13th, and many thanks. You wrote to cheer me up and I can assure you all that it did cheer me up, as you seemed quite close to me when reading it. As you say, it must have been hard to leave a wife and six children. I felt it very much at first but am now getting hardened to it. I know it is for me or my boys to fight this war so I am doing it with a good heart, as it is a sin to throw a young life away. I often wonder if it will be finished before Fred is old enough. Now I can assure you that if only I return this war has made a better man of me, God has opened my eyes and showed me my folly and I mean to lead an upright, straight forward life.

I have fought in three battles, one at BeerSheba where a shell came and killed one, seriously wounded another and slightly wounded me in the right arm. I was also in the battle for Jerusalem but have not had the pleasure of entering in yet.

When holding a service in the hills that surround it I heard the bells chime. I shall get a chance to go as they are giving leave to soldiers to go, but we learn from our officers that the place is like all other places, diseased by loose women. What a character for the Holy city.

I am sending a photo to Pollie of a few of us taken after driving the Turks away, taken at the bottom of Neve Samuel, one of the keys that held Jerusalem, and suppose to be Samuel's tomb. Whether so or not I cannot say. I know you all picture Palestine as being a land of beauty but it is not worth seeing. It is only a wild country, with very few trees, no hedges and very few birds because of the absent of trees. There are orange and olive trees and oranges are very cheap here. You have heard of Jaffa oranges, one can buy them six for 2-1/2. I was in a village from which we drove the Turks and there were figs there. The name of the place was Ramallah. The Christians had crosses on their doors but they are all very dirty people and the street buildings only fit for a horse to live in; one never sees a chimney. Life for a woman here is a dog's life as they do all the carrying. I see daily men walking behind a donkey loaded with oranges, carrying a stick, and the woman following behind like a dog, carrying on her head nearly as much as the donkey does. One sees a man with boots on riding a donkey, and running at his side a woman with no boots on. It makes one's heart bleed to see the way a woman is used. If the men only knew English they would hear something. Women carry water on their heads in pitchers the same as in Bible times. If there is any moving the woman does it on her head. I have seen a little child nine years old carrying on her head a cradle with a baby in it. Anything that a girl has to carry is carried on their head; one can see them at three years old.

Now putting Palestine in a nut shell—if it were not for it being the Holy Land it would not be worth two pence to see. I shall never forget how I spent my Christmas but should not care for you to know. Even camels were dying from the cold weather. A wet snow fell at Bethlehem but I was in the hills of Judea, some of which are from five to three thousand feet above sea level. To show you what a wild place it is, I have seen wild deer running about not more than six miles from Jerusalem. The most interesting place I have been to is the village which Christ visited after He rose from the dead, which you will read about in the 24th chapter and the 13th verse of St. Luke.

Now I must close as I am snatching the time and I am to fill water bottles now. I am sending you a leaf picked from the hills of Judea which are the same that run around Jerusalem. It is Sunday and the weather is like weather in England.

Ralph Beisel
Cambridge, Mass.
February 19, 1918

Just a few lines to let you know that I leave Cambridge today for New York. From there I take a boat sometime for somewhere. The nearest I can tell you now is that it will be in foreign service in foreign waters. There are twenty of us going, the twenty out of our class with the best marks, and I was chosen as one. I leave with a third class radio electrician's rating and expect to make first class of chief at the end of my cruise. I may not do it but I hope to.

Stockbridge Hilton
44th Infantry, Camp Lewis, Washington.
February 1918

From 5:45 a.m. until 7:00 or 8:00 at night is all work, and often there are things to do after that. Although we have not immediate hopes of going across very soon, we carry on intensive training just the same. We should be in very good shape when we are called to get into things. I am rather tired of this camp life and the Washington rain and hope we can get a change pretty soon.

I spent last week-end with the Meyers of Seattle and had a very delightful time. It was the first time I had been in Seattle since last August. It is a very nice city, more like the Eastern towns than any others out here.

You will be glad to know that I am promoted to First Lieutenant in the Regular Army, with rank from October 26th.

There is not much doing out here, just work and drill. Am doing quite a lot of riding lately, which I enjoy much more than walking. Have the choice of two horses, both of them good ones. One of them was used by General Morse at Camp Custer when he was Colonel of this regiment, and I must say he was a good judge of horse flesh.

I hope everything is going well with all of you and that Fremont is pirking up with the coming Spring.

France, February 1918

Well I am safe and sound and rearing to go. And it seems good not to have to chase my meals all over the table. We had pretty good weather. After the first two days the water was quite rough and the ship did a bird to roll, and believe me, Charlie Chaplin had nothing on us at meal times. One day I slid to the side of the ship and was followed by about a dozen others and they proceeded to give me a very unpleasant shower of hot soup, I am quite sure I have enough launch ride to last me at least a month. Lake Michigan is big enough for me. I was a little sick one day. I was a berth deck orderly and digging around under the bunks was too much for me. It was extra rough that day any way. I will be glad when we get where there is a Y.M.C.A. building.

So far France looks good to me. The hills are green, the buildings are mostly stone and quite large. There were some girls out here today, pretty good looking.

Austin Olney
U.S.S. Jenkins
February, 1918

I found your letters and package of papers when I came back from shore leave last night. Sometimes when I read of the hardships of the people of U.S.A. I think that we fellows in the service are the lucky fellows after all. I am glad I enlisted when I did. Only had I known a little more about the navy, I would likely have specialized on some branch of work instead of coming in as apprentice seaman. The experience is worthwhile though and it certainly beats teaching. We know we have a big U.S. backing us all the time and we never worry, so that you could notice it. We take everything as it comes and treat it according to its merits in so far as we are able (Huns included.) The people here weep about their cold winters. Honest, I never spent such a mild winter in my life. It beats the weather we had in Texas. Last time out at sea it was often nearly as warm as our early summer.

Saw a man plowing two days ago. The milk wagons are two wheeled carts with a donkey about as large as a big dog and shaggy with long hair, for the motive power. Their teamsters here would hardly be allowed to drive the sheep to water on an ordinary farm there.

Once in a while we see a Ford. But we have "Jaunty Carts" instead of taxies, high two wheeled carts with passenger seats over each wheel and a driver's seat in front, drawn by one horse, and when you go for a ride in one of those things you don't need any further exercise. The nearest thing to it is a lumber wagon on a corduroy road. You surely do hang on.

I am seeing lots of different places and lots of salt water too. We have seen flying machines and dirigibles until we don't hardly bother to go on deck when they come along.

February 20

Just returned from shore liberty. Had a dandy show and concert on at the Navy Men's club tonight. It beats all how prices swell when it is a U.S. Sailor holding the pocketbook. The fellow I was with bought some chocolates the other night. The clerk said, "We have some cheaper ones for 75 cents (U.S. money) but you wouldn't want them."

No, I didn't get lost, that is, very badly. Had lunch in a restaurant and then we started to walk back to the Y.M.C.A. hut and after walking for about half an hour, were right back in front of the restaurant again. As we wanted to take in a play that afternoon we hailed a Jaunty Cart and went back to the hut. It only took about 45 minutes for the cart to make the trip. Some speed.

We had lots of fun. Saw a regular soccer football game between branches of the British Naval and Aviation forces. It was a 1-1 tie game.

Do you ever get any reports of what the destroyers are doing?

David Thomas Hopkins
Columbus, O.
March 11, 1918

We got here all fine and dandy. This is some place, believe me, all you can see is soldier boys and large buildings. It is raining here today, but we are all inside where it is dry.

When we got to Kalamazoo the Red Cross ladies came out with baskets of oranges, tobacco and most everything you could think of. They certainly used us just fine.

Walter Robbins and three other Fremont boys are with me, so we won't get lonesome. We certainly had a fine time coming down here. I believe we made noise enough to almost wake the dead.

They marched us around in Grand Rapids a half hour and then we took the train for Columbus. We got here at eight o'clock this morning and didn't have any breakfast until eleven o'clock but we had a fine dinner.

Well, you had better wait until you hear from me again before you write.

We are all through with our examinations and have our suits. We leave here for Texas in the morning. I will send you my address when we reach there.

Letters and Related Articles 1918

Russell Crawford
A.E.F. France
March 14, 1918

I am pretty nearly lost over here where everybody speaks French except the rest of the boys. I am getting so I understand it pretty well now though, and talk it some to, enough so I can ask for bread or coffee or go to the store and buy toilet soap or to the laundry and get my clothes.

Dallas Darling
139th Aero Squad, Somewhere in France
Extracts taken from letters and printed together.

We, the 139th Aero Squad, left Fort Worth, Texas, the last week of February for New York. Had a fine long ride and arrived in camp not far from the city of New York in good shape. I was on guard duty the first night after arriving. We made a visit or two into the city and saw so much that it's hard to say just what did please us most. Perhaps the ice cream parlors were visited with the most interest. After one week there we were transferred to a ship which was to take us "across the pond". I was getting anxious after 10 months of drill and work to get where there was something doing. It took only seven days to cross over to England.

After two or three weeks of more drilling with the English such as we had last summer in Toronto, we were called to

France. We are now (April 20) too far away from the front to even hear a noise of battle. I am still on the mail job as I was in Texas. Am promised a truck when we move on. My arm is well and strong. I am growing and feel fine. Weigh now 168 pounds.

April 2, 1918

Well, this is my birthday. 19 years old and have been away one year—the shortest year I can remember. Have received my truck and made a trip with several others of 180 miles across the country to get wood. It was a great drive through the country and through small villages every five or six miles. The farmers were working in the fields with horses with only a bridle, collar and chain tugs. No harness. All the houses we passed were of stone.

A year ago when I was sent to Texas the first person I saw that I knew was Geo. Rosewarne and he looked good to me, and now over here in France, not knowing where any of the Fremont boys are to be found, who should walk into my barrack but our old friend Rosie. Talk about talking! We certainly did not forget anything from the time we were working for Mr. Graff in the garage up to the time we landed France. We are about four miles apart at present.

We are all happy and wanting to move on near action. The flicker show will begin in 15 minutes and the boys are making themselves heard. One is at the piano, a bunch are singing, another bunch playing basketball, some playing volley ball and others are having a game of baseball, while some of us are trying to write letters home.

In the Saturday Evening Post of April 6 on page six you will see a picture of our barracks, a guard and a Red Cross nurse in front. But I cannot tell you where we are. That long board side walk you see in the picture we walk over many times a day.

Always glad to hear from Fremont friends.

Walter Hindes
Co.____, En route, Aboard S.S._____
April 1918

Isn't that an enlightening heading for a letter? I'll bet you know exactly where I am from that.

Am not allowed to tell any details of our moving date or ship on which we sailed, at present. In fact there isn't much we can say, only that we are going to be in England for awhile, haven't any idea how long.

Since I haven't dated this letter, can also tell you that we expect to dock tomorrow. Have had a wonderful trip. Couldn't have been better. Have had a state room to sleep in and have wonderful "chow" in first class dining room. Am getting fat. Didn't get seasick as I expected to and have had a very interesting trip. There are lots of things I would like to tell you about but am not allowed to now. May be able to tell more details later.

For some reason or other have not received much mail lately. Ha! Ha! We all kid each other about getting the mail, going down town, etc., these days. This is one jolly crowd. They certainly are very cheery when you consider that they didn't put themselves into this Co.

We have boat drills every day to get the men used to getting to their life boats in order. We wear life belts constantly and it is so apparent that we won't need them that one hates to wear one.

You probably will have received the card I mailed before leaving quite a while before you get this. This will probably be a month or possibly longer, since my last letter. Don't worry about me, if I felt better I'd be ashamed of myself. Expect to be pretty busy as soon as we land but will try and write regularly.

Am studying French quite a bit now and like it

John B. Brookhuis
Co. A., 39th Infantry, Camp Green, Charlotte, N.C.
April 4, 1918

Will try and write you a few lines today and let you know that I am feeling fine and hope that everybody at Fremont is the same. It rained here last night and is pretty muddy around here. This ground is great when it rains, for it's all that red clay. It's nice and warm here. The Camp Custer boys are not used to this kind of weather. It seems to make them all a little lazy at first. We had a nice ride when we came here. When we came into Toledo the Red Cross ladies were at the depot and gave the boys apples, oranges, and other things. We came through Pittsburg, Pa., Cumberland, Md., Roanoke, Va., and Salisbury, N.C. When we left Pittsburg we followed a river for about ten hours. They say it was the Alleghany. We also crossed the Potomac river. From Camp Custer down here is about twelve hundred miles. That's quite a long way from home for me.

This camp is very different from Custer. We don't have any barracks around here. It's all tents, eight men to every tent.

We went for a march out in the county last Friday and the apple and peach trees were all in blossom. I guess it don't look much like that at Fremont.

It's a great place out here for darkies. A big crowd comes in Camp every day.

Bugler Carl Felber
Co. A., 18th Inf., Somewhere in France
April 4, 1918

I wish to express my most sincere thanks to the people of Fremont, who so thoughtfully and generously sent gifts, bearing the best wishes of the Fremont citizens to one who is serving in France for a righteous cause, so I am taking this opportunity of sending this small message of humble thanks to the Fremont citizens, and may it bear with it my best wishes and thanks.

Austin Olney
U.S.S. Jenkins
May 14, 1918

It has been some time since I last wrote home but it was only because we have been so busy and not around the mail buoy very much, Your letters of April 15, 19 and 22 all came today (May 14) so I had mail again. Yes I would miss those weekly letters and they are always the first ones I read. It is certainly good the way Uncle Sam is coming across. The people were long in getting started, but they will be much slower in stopping, and we are only started in some ways.

Personally I don't envy the Pro-German in America or any where else. Not even in a submarine.

I realize you would find accounts of our trip very interesting. I wish that I could feel free to tell more than I do, but you will have to wait until later on before I can say very much. I haven't got the navy on my back or anything of that kind, I am simply doing my part as I see it in keeping any information from the mails which might possibly prove useful to the Germans. I don't think Germany has a chance on the sea, but accidents will happen you know, so it is safety first. The letters surely had a lot of news this time. Must be some lively city these days. The "Harps" over here are dreading the time when the Yankee sailors with their flow of cash will be called away. Lots of them have just about made their fortune since we came.

Say, do you realize I have been away from Michigan for nearly a year, and the U.S.A. over nine months? Well I ran across a party of four American girls in a café in France. Girls in the U.S.A. Reserve Corps. It very nearly made me homesick to hear the good U.S.A. language as those girls handed it out. Didn't realize before what I had been missing. Talk about travel, say I intend to have dinner in Berlin someday, then I have seen most of the principal European countries. That is, I will have by the time we get to Berlin. I have trouble in making myself understood in France, but in England, Ireland and Wales it is a cinch (when they go slow). The money in any of the countries I have been in has been fairly easy to master. Well as we say here, it is a great life if you don't weaken. I expected to have a furlough soon but it has been postponed. Hope it comes after I have had a pay day or two more.

I happened to be in port last Sunday and saw that it was Mothers' day. Seems that just now all I can do is think of you at home. Someday I hope to do more. Glad you are all well, I am too. But I am some sleepy tonight from having night watches the last two nights.

We have been kept very busy for the past weeks and months. We are getting lots of trips and not all joy rides either, but everything is going good here. Our baseball team is a regular winner, which we enjoy when in port. Must get ready for sea now.

Lee A. Somers
Signal Corps, Buzzer School, Barrack 231, Fort Leavenworth, Kan.
May 16, 1918

My dear friends at Fremont:

As a writer I am a good cat chaser. But I'll try.

Fort Leavenworth is located on the eastern edge of Kansas, in fact, only the river separates us from Missouri. The Missouri river is full of dirt and mud, but also full of history and romance. It flows to the north and to the east of us, bending near the Fort. The Fort is an old stone wall fortress of Civil war times and for years it proudly commanded the river, but now it is used as the Disciplinary Barracks for Military prison.

The way those prisoners can go through a drill is wonderful. Not a command is given—only music.

After the civil war this became an officers' school and the War college is a beautiful structure overlooking the river and the Missouri shore. A large number of officers' homes are here.

This is strictly an Engineers' and Signal Corps' camp. I of course belong to the later. In sight of my barracks is the Government cemetery, the high power radio station, and over the hills the roof of the Federal prison. The barracks are very strong substantial brick buildings built for War College students.

The entire camp and surrounding country are beautiful. The climate is much warmer than Michigan but pleasant. The sun rising across the river in the Missouri hills is beautiful.

The work consists of two hours drilling per day and the rest of the time at buzzer, which is the same as radio or wig wag or semaphore signaling or electrical class. The latter is very hard for me.

I enjoy my life here now that they have stopped inoculating me. They inoculate against everything. I expected to be inoculated for dandruff.

Of course the discipline is rather strict but one expects that in the army. When will I go to France? Honestly I haven't the least idea but we hope to go before fall. There are now 21 of us here from the Grand Rapids school.

Joe Jewell
Camp Lee, Va.
May 18, 1918

Two letters came today, one of them written May 2 and forwarded from Custer.

Every right thinking young fellow is dreading that trip and is at heart wishing it would not be necessary. But, and here is the part that we must play without flinching, every right thinking young fellow dreads more to have someone ask why he is not doing his share. Or to have someone say he was afraid and showed it. It is failure to play up that we dread. Sometime you understand and be glad if you can say I played up. Sometime someone is going to ask about things or say something that would hurt if it were true. No one could want to have the chance to go home more than I and I know that it worries you all at home to have me where I am. I left something pretty soft while it lasted and even if I thought it would last, would have still left. I know you dreaded to have me move, but dreaded more having some one point out that I side-stepped anything. When I come out of this as I surely will a better man than when I entered, I am going to be able to look every man in the eye and say that I played the game. Otherwise I do not want to come out at all. And so far it has worked as I knew it would. I think you take a little more pride in me here. When it's over there will be two kinds of men: those who were in it and those who were out of it. Those who by various ways side-stepped the main issues will have a rocky road to travel and those nearest them will have a still rockier one.

You have one thing to always take satisfaction in and that is that the education you have given me affords me a chance to get into one of the highest branches of the service. Engineers are classed as non-combatant troops, so we have a little better chance. Then too, I am more than a little proud to be able to even compete for a commission. It means more than you think to me, just for my own satisfaction, to be able to wear an officers' bars. I came back the first time with a sergeants' chevrons and the second time I want the shoulder bars if for no other reason than to show that it is in me.

(name of serviceman not given)
Battery D., 83 F.A., Camp Fremont, Palo Alto, Cal.
May 23, 1918

We have been on the range with the big guns for the last week and have made some good hits. I hope we will do as well over there. If we do it will be "Goodby Bill". Up to the time of our arrival we have been held back with our training on account of not being fully equipped, so we are getting our training in double measure now seven days in a week and twenty-four hours in a day, and we like it too. You would be surprised to see how wild the boys are to get across and at Bill.

The government has decided that we must learn to sing now and has sent a professor to lead and train us, or rather wished him on us. There isn't a dog, cat or bird that can live around here nowdays. I guess Uncle Sam figures to scare the H—out of the Kaiser and then get his goat. There is going to be a contest in a few weeks and the Regiment that sings the best gets a prize of $50. I think after the judge hears the first Regiment he will be willing to give us all a prize of $50 to keep still unless we do better than we have.

David Hopkin
23rd Prov. Col, 7th Div. Recruit Camp, Camp Arthur, Waco, Texas
May 26, 1918

To the Times-Indicator and folks at home:--Your kind letter came today and believe me, it makes me feel good to hear from home. I am well and having a fairly good time. Just think I am 1800 miles from home and no bell on. This is the first job I ever had that I could not quit when I wanted to. Well we have all we want to eat, potatoes, bread, once in a while butter, beef, hash, tomatoes, beets, carrots, coffee, lemonade and orangeade.

We have to get up at 6:30, have reveille at 7 o'clock, breakfast at 7:30 and at 8 o'clock we go out and drill until 11 o'clock. Then we come in and wash up and have dinner at 12 out and drill until 4 o'clock, come in and wash up and have supper at 5 o'clock. At 6 o'clock we have roll call and are free until 11 o'clock at night. We have a tent to sleep in and cots to sleep on. Have one woolen blanket over us and one under us, but we don't have any pillow and there are eight of us in one tent.

It is awful hot here but the wind blows all the time. If it did not we boys from the north could not stand it. But they don't drill us very hard at first. We drill a while, then go in the shade for a while. We have certainly got a dandy corporal, he is good natured and if there is anything we don't understand he is willing to show us, but our lieutenant is crankier than the devil.

We started from White Cloud May 10 and May 11 at 8 o'clock in the morning we landed in Columbus, O. We stayed there until May 14, then started for Texas. We arrived in Texas Thursday night, May 16. We surely saw some beautiful country. Went through Indiana, Ohio, Illinois, Missouri, Kansas, Oklahoma and Texas. The Red Cross came out at Grand Rapids and Kalamazoo and other places and give us tobacco, candy, cake, oranges and other things. They certainly used us fine. Hurrah for the Red Cross.

Well I can say I like everything we have had so far, only I get a little lonesome sometimes when I don't have anything to do. Well, I could not get lonesome yesterday, I got three letters and two cards, also the Fremont paper. It seems good to get it to read what is going on in and around Fremont. Well we are going to be all split up next week, then I don't know who I will be with.

We are going to have a ball game tomorrow afternoon and I am in it. I have to pitch. I guess we are going to move some time next week but we don't know where. They don't tell us but it is either to El Paso or the Mexican border. If we go to the border we stand a good show of never going to France.

Emer Doud
1st Reg., 2nd Co., Barracks B.N.T.S., Newport, R.I.
May 31, 1918

Am taking advantage of a short rest period to write you a little note. Glad indeed to tell you that I am feeling extra well today. I have gained just what I lost while I was sick and weigh 154 pounds now.

Yesterday was Decoration Day. Of course we had a little extra work as we served a very fine meal. You will note below our noon chow.

Giblet soup, radishes, pickles, olives, fricassee of chicken, sweet potatoes, green peas, roast spiced ham, Spanish sauce, lettuce and tomatoes, crackers, cheese, bananas, oranges, peach pie, raisin cake, ice cream. This meal was served to all the many boys on the Islands.

I have a friend, a Mr. Gaylor, and he and I have attended church several times. We go to church parties in the afternoon and the good mothers of Newport feed about 200 sailor boys every Sunday afternoon. The boys are asked to go to church after being served with the good home baked cakes, pies, etc.

Mr. Gaylord is a Christian boy and a Southern, from Alabama. He is a good-hearted fellow, like most of the boys from Dixie. They are different from the Northern fellows. You remember I told you recently about joining the Pocket Testament League, and am glad to say I read my chapter every day and carry my Testament in my pocket at all times.

I note you are having wheatless and meatless days. We boys in the navy don't know what a wheatless or meatless meal is here. I think the navy is a good place for a young man, it helps a fellow in many ways. It encourages good morals, the training gives a fellow good energy, and I said before, the experience of military life will be very beneficial to us when we return to civilian life. I have been in the navy nine weeks, I enlisted as apprentice seaman, I rate Second Class seaman at present. The chance for promotion is good and any young man can do a patriotic deed for his country by joining the navy. He not only encouraged our navy by enlisting but helps himself. If they would offer me an honorable discharge and I could go home before the war ends, I wouldn't take it now. Don't think because the papers talk peace, the war will end soon. But Uncle Sam has sure got the material to swat the Germans.

C. C. Upton
American Marine confined to unknown hospital
June 24, 1918

C.C. Upton, son of Mr. and Mrs. C. H. Upton, who is with the American Marines at the front, has been confined to a hospital. He writes:

You have no doubt learned by this time about my being on the wounded list. Am in the hospital now but am getting along first rate.

Got a light dose of gas and if affected my eyes mostly. Was blind for over a week and can see only a little now, but expect to be "up and at it" again in a few days.

I suppose you have read about our stopping the "Huns" on their drive for Paris? We surely did some awfully hard fighting and I guess the Germans are well aware of the fact that we mean business.

They call us Marines the "American hellhounds"

My eyes won't allow me to write any more.

**Walter Robbins
Co. E. 55th Inf., Camp MacArthur, Waco, Texas
June 26, 1918**

I left White Cloud May 10 for Columbus, Ohio. There I took my examination and on May 14 left for Texas. Thursday I arrived at Camp MacArthur. We were taken to our quarantine camp. I was vaccinated three times and none of them worked on me so I am free from diseases. My health is good since I have been in the army. I have plenty to eat and plenty of clothes. It is hot enough to go without anything on. It was cool in Columbus but it is different here.

I was in seven different states coming down here but there is none as good as old Michigan. I hope we will all be back soon. I have seen some pretty countries and have had some rough riding on the train. I have looked out of the car windows and all you could see was stones and trees. Texas is some place. All we can see here are tents for about 10 miles across. We have a nice bunch of officers. We have lots of drilling and some hikes with our full packs. They weigh 85 pounds; a nice load over the hills, but we stand it alright and will be a good deal better men when we come home.

When we got to Columbus the Red Cross women gave us oranges, apples, cigarettes and cigars. We can buy everything we want here if we have the money. Everything cost so in the army. They furnish everything at first, but I believe all that they give us our clothes and food and our gun and a hat. The

Y.M.C.A. gives us our writing paper and envelopes. We have good times just the same and we never will be sorry for being in the army either but will be glad when we get the Old Kaiser Bill, and we will get him before long.

Well, everything is awful dry in Texas. I suppose everything up in Michigan looks good. Nothing to see here but soldier boys. That is some sight to one who never saw many.

Well, they took us boys out at noon and we had to pitch our tents. It is no fun until you get used to it, but we have lots to learn.

Lieut. Darrel Alton
Aviation Concentration Camp
Camp Dick, Dallas, Texas
June 27, 1918

It is so dreadfully hot here that I can readily conceive how the Southern people get the slow lazy attitude that is so characteristic with them. The highest official temperature by the weather bureau was 99.8 but our thermometers around the Camp have gone as high as 120, due to the reflected heat.

Orders from Washington were received to assign 35 men to take a special course in Aerial navigation to be given by an English captain and I was one of two from the school department that was allowed to take it. We finished the course from a practical standpoint a couple of days ago, but officially the course is not yet over as we are going over the ground again and more in detail now that the Captain has left and will finish up in a couples days.

This work consists of the study of the navigation of the air and all the useful instruments connected therewith exactly as the sea is sailed with mathematical exactness. Just as the mariner can sail thousands of miles across the ocean and arrive exactly at a predetermined point so is it possible for the aviator by paying proper attention to conditions in the medium in which he travels the air, to so regulate his flight that he also will arrive at a predetermined point in the predetermined time.

This mathematical application to flying is a comparatively new thing and offers a large field and I believe that I was lucky to get in on it and if I am not mistaken, I believe that I will get considerable benefit in addition to the knowledge as I understand that it is the policy of the war department to put in a modification of our course at all the flying fields in the country and naturally the rumor follows that those of us that took the course are to be made instructors. How much truth there is in it only time will tell of course.

As near as I can tell now from the way things are going it looks, disregarding the navigation possibilities, that I would go to Fort Sill from here, stay four or five weeks and then return here for another three or four weeks and then go to Mt. Clemens after that. I am almost sure to get to Mt. Clemens sooner or later because all army corps men are going there at some period of their training. That would make it sometime in August.

It is almost useless to attempt to try and do any figuring though as so many unexplainable things are constantly occurring. Some of the men are sent out of here within four or five days of the time they report, most of them stay ten days to two weeks, a very few stay three weeks and hardly anybody a month, but I am soon to enter that classification.

We are right in a good town now though and get quite a lot of time off although it is an awful expensive town to live in. When it costs from thirty to fifty cents to go to an ordinary movie you can imagine that most other things are in proportion.

Watermelons and okra seem to be about the two most common edibles around this section judging from our mess at least. We get pretty fair chow though as our chow and the cadets comes out of the same kitchen and this is how they work it. For example, take the watermelons, we get the large round slices with lots of heart and the cadets and enlisted men get the ends, so you see there is a little advantage in having the bars on one's shoulders besides the personal satisfaction.

Letters and Related Articles 1918

Sgt. D. F. Gerber
Co. M., 126th Inf., American E.F.
June 28, 1918

Mrs. Frank Gerber, Fremont, Mich.

Lieut. Johnson has been killed and it is needless to tell you how much a man of his type is missed but it has given every man a new incentive to fight for.

Dad asked where we are issued pork and beans. Well, the only place we had canned pork and beans is in traveling as a travel ration. The only canned goods we have had issued over here are corned beef, salmon, tomatoes, milk and a little jam. Canned fruits and jams of all kinds can usually be bought at the Y.M.C.A. and commissaries. Most of the canned foods to be found in the French stores are in individuals with the exception of peas, which are usually in a 3-lb can. A great deal of canned jam is sold in the stores over here and the price is very high. I have paid five francs or about 60 cents in our money for a No. 1 can of cherry jam.

I forgot to tell you the last time I wrote that I have been decorated with Croix de Guerre by the French.* I don't think I spelled it right but you probably know what I mean.

Tell Oosdyke that I appreciate very much the way he is looking out for my interests.

(*The Croix de Guerre is a French military decoration created in 1915 to reward feats of bravery.)

July 17, 1918

I have received all of your letters up to the one with Bob's picture in it. I have destroyed all of your letters so I don't remember the date or number of the last one.

I just returned from a nice swim and am writing in a pup tent by candle light, so you will have to pardon my penmanship.

Last Sunday was a big day all over France. I had a pass to a neighboring town where they had quite a celebration, partially American, but mostly French. Most of the girls were dressed in the picturesque peasant costume but a great many were dressed just as our American girls would dress on such an occasion. Several boxing bouts, a soccer game, and a few speeches that I didn't understand, were the leading events of the day. I had two splendid feeds in a small French café and was lucky enough to catch a ride home in a baggage wagon.

I haven't been with the company for about two months but I still draw my pay there and I see someone from there nearly every day. I have a job that I like very much, in fact I don't think I would like to trade with any one. My work is extremely interesting and somewhat exciting but never have to work long at a time.

Well, good night, and I will write again soon if I have an opportunity, but don't be surprised if there is quite a time before you get my next letter.

Pvt. Otto W. Smith
Field Hospital, Co. 331, 308 Sanitary Train, A.P.O. 762
Am. E.F., France
June 28, 1918

Dear Mother:

Will write a few lines tonight to let you know I am o.k. We are in a fine place and are well satisfied with France.

We found the French people here about 150 years behind the times but are big hearted and their hospitality couldn't be beat. They treat us fine. The old ladies will do anything for us. The French are hard workers and deserving of our help. They are doing their share.

The people live in villages and go out every morning to till their lots from daylight till dark, the gray haired grandmothers and small children alike.

We are learning some French. The children are our teachers. They learn English very quick. Its lots of fun anyhow.

They have fine large cows here and nice large horses. You hardly ever see a four-wheeled wagon in France. Occasionally you see a dog pulling a cart as in Holland.

Expect it will be some time before you get this and it may be some time before you get one again, as it's a proposition now about our mail. But don't worry about me because I am going to be O.K.

Some of the boys who just couldn't see the use of coming over here are well pleased to be here now. Have seen many German prisoners. They do work all over France. They are happy too. There will be more happy Germans when we are finished with them.

Hope you get this letter all right anyhow. It's a month's job to get one started.

July 9, 1918

Dear Mother:

Will write a few lines to let you know I am all right as usual. Have been getting along fine and the time is passing very fast for us now. It doesn't seem two months since I saw you at Camp Sherman. Everything has gone fine so far, much better than I expected. We will certainly remember our stay in France. I can't conceive of the great ocean now between us, which is not so far when we think of the time it took Columbus to cross it. The reception which the French have given us makes us feel at home, so our little journey has not changed our environment so much. The climate is about the same as that at home. The air is better I think, and it doesn't get as sultry on hot days.

I haven't received any mail so far and am not expecting any for a month. So if you don't hear from me twice a week you needn't worry because we are sort of up against it in this letter business. But we hope to get it organized a little better soon and then it won't take so long.

I suppose you folks are making hay now. I have helped make some here. We help the people unload it at times when we aren't busy, for fun. They repay us for all we do in many acts of kindness. It seems like we were among real people again, but of course when they get to talking too fast to us we are up against it and once more we realize we aren't home.

Clarence L. Misner
M.G. Troop, First Cavalry, Douglas, Ariz.
July 4, 1918

I have been in the service for three months and like it better all the time. It is the easiest life I ever had. We drill about six hours a day, have three drills in the forenoon with a fifteen minutes rest between each one, and in the afternoon we have mounted drills which is just fun. It is a great sport when a horse bucks to see the fellows hang on them. Some are from town and don't know much about horses and are so afraid of them that they hardly dare to get close to them. We surely made some showing the first day we were out. They gave us slow trot for about half an hour. Believe me, we were shook up good and proper. But we have got on to it now so it is not as bad.

They give us cross country rides through the sage brush and cactus. The horses are jumping in all directions so it makes it exciting. We all feel as if we were cheated when we don't go on one. We ride over hurdles three feet high which seemed like 30 feet the first few times we crossed them. A fellow will sure be able to ride when he gets across the pond.

My regiment was ordered across but they canceled the order so we had to stay in this "beautiful" state of Arizona. Arizona is about as poor a place as I ever saw except the part next to New Mexico. When we came through New Mexico we had all the windows closed in the train and then we could hardly get our breath for dust. There isn't but a little grass growing here. There is nothing except cactus and sage brush. We were out about 20 miles Friday and saw three or four houses and one herd of cattle. The houses are made of the surface soil mixed with straw and water. When it dries it is almost like cement.

We have all kinds of people in Douglas but mostly negroes and Mexicans, and some white. Douglas is the second largest city on the border, the south side reaching the border. I was about a rod over the line in Mexico. Did not see any difference in the looks of things except that the sign boards were printed in Spanish and Mexican, which I did not read. I would be glad to hear from all my friends around Fremont.

Chas. Baker
Presidio, San Francisco
July 5, 1918

Editor, Times-Indicator, Fremont, Mich.,

Dear Sir: Just a word from an old Fremont boy who is in the service of his country and trying to do his bit.

I am stationed at the Post Hospital at the Presidio of San Francisco. I belong to the Medical Dept. of the U.S.A. We have no patients at our hospital but merely look after the health and sanitation of certain branches of the army. We have however, the Letterman General Hospital across the road from us and in that they have eleven hundred patients, many of them home from the front, and about three hundred Med. Corps men.

We are working very hard to get prepared for overseas. We drill three hours a day and have classes the rest of the time. I am the only one here from anywhere near Fremont. It would seem good to hear or see any one from one's home town where I spent about 20 years of my life.

Being above draft age, I am a volunteer. I could not stay out of the service when my country needed me. I went through the Mexican crisis and am therefore once a solider, always a soldier. My brother, Glen has been in France since last September. I am in hopes of getting over seas before long, every man in the U.S. Army to my knowledge wants to fight the Boche. "My only regret is I have only one life to give for my country."

We expect to be sent to Siberia, as we understand that U.S. is going to send troops into Russia and have us doped out for the base hospital. This is mostly a volunteer post. We have here in all about 15,000 soldiers, I should judge.

People in San Francisco are very good to the men in uniform but some of the merchants rob you when you try to buy anything.

We are treated very good at this post and no one has a complaint to make. We live well and have good quarters to sleep in and the Y.M.C.A. has entertainments nearly every evening. At that the volunteer is not treated as good as the drafted man, but they (the volunteers) are the boys they call on when they want things done up in a hurry. Several of the boys that I knew in the West have gone to France since I came to this post.

I would like to hear from some of my old school mates in Fremont. I don't know if you or any of my friends will ever see or hear from me again, as before this letter reaches you I may be on my way across the water to fight the Hun, but wherever I go I will do my best for the U. S.

Merritt Beisel
C.I., 339th Inf., Camp Custer
July 11, 1918

Well, we are here because we are here. We arrived Monday evening about 4:30 o'clock. But they didn't let us get to bed until about 12:30. We sure had a fine trip coming. When we got to Grand Rapids there was the Red Cross with a nice big lunch, hot coffee, cigarettes and newspapers; when we got to Kalamazoo there they were again with ice cream cones and post cards for us. Now you can see what your Red Cross is doing for us. It sure made the boys all feel good to be treated in that way and not only that, but the Y.M.C.A had men on the train all the way entertaining us with music and talking to us. That kind of treatment makes us feel as though the people were back of us; although we know they are back of us. That just impressed the fact a little stronger and makes us feel like doing all we can. Why, I had no idea that they were doing what they are. It's sure a great work, back it up all you can, and tell your little bunch of Red Cross out there what I had to say about it.

It is sure fun to hear some of these little "Willie" boys that never had their feet from under mother's table kicking about the eats. But I say they are feeding fine, for I know from past experience. Why they are doing better than I expected. We get all we want to eat and a good place to sleep, what more do we want.

We have had gas drills already. This afternoon they had us in a house filled with gas to see how we could make out without masks. They are training us to put masks on in six seconds. You can go into the most deadly gas with these and it will not hurt you, and then if you are able to put masks on in six seconds you can see that we are well protected from gas. Oh, I'm telling you those Huns have a very small chance in front of us, we're going after them to the last one.

Corp. Dewey S. O'Neal
Troop No. 1, 8th Cavalry, Presidio, Texas
July 11, 1918

Well, I have been waiting for a letter from home because I thought that I wrote last and was just preparing to write home when I received the letter. Now don't think if I do not write you every week that there is something wrong, because I am in the best of health and haven't been sick since I joined the army, and although we are 75 miles from a railroad and civilization, we have a good doctor and also pretty good hospital.

Things are pretty quiet here just now; we haven't had any trouble for two or three months and all the soldiers are wishing that Villa would attack Ojinago again so we would have some excitement. Just think, I haven't seen a railroad engine for nine months. It doesn't seem possible that in the United States one could travel the country for that length of time and never see a train.

Well, I am still holding my job down as Troop Clerk and like it quite well. Of course there is a great deal of paper work, but it is the best thing to learn in the army because it helps fit you for a position on the outside, and you learn to do your work right, because you have to have everything right or you will be court martialed, but I am not afraid of that as I don't do my work any other way but right. Our Liberty Loan bonds run out next month and I think mine will be sent to you.

Well now I am a corporal and am sending my warrant home and you can frame it or do anything you like with it, but be sure and keep it. I would like to come home on a furlough but it's almost impossible to get one in this regiment, at present. Now if I am a little slow in writing sometimes don't think that I am on my way to France, because I will let you know right away if we leave here.

Give my friends a good word for me. I would like to see them all. I receive the paper right along. Well I guess I will have to quit for this time, hoping to hear from you soon.

Roy Parker
Camp Mills, New York
July 14, 1918

Well, I am a long, long way from home now but it seems as though I was just down to Fremont. We sure had a fine trip, I would not have missed if for a good deal. You haven't the least idea what it is like to go so far, but it was sure great.

We left Camp Custer at 10 a.m., July 12. There were fourteen coaches on our train. We got to Detroit at 2 p.m. and the Red Cross ladies were there and gave us coffee and candy, etc. Believe me the Red Cross is sure doing good work. They should be supported by all. We left Detroit and went through the tunnel and stopped at Windsor where the Red Cross met us and gave us cards all stamped ready to mail. We went from there to St. Thomas. There were guards to keep people from the train. We got there at 4:30 Central time, that would be 5:30 Eastern time.

The crops aren't very good through Canada, they are mostly hay and grain. The country is very level all the way through there. Well we got to Niagara Falls at 8 p.m. where we stopped and all got off the train for 15 minutes to take in the sights. They were very interesting. We got to Rochester, New York at 11:30 p.m. It was dark so we could not see much there. I went to sleep then and woke up at about 1:30 a.m., July 13. We were then in Syracuse. We got there at 1:45 and were there about 15 minutes. Later we went to the Hudson river where all who wanted to went in bathing. It was about a mile from the train.

As soon as the train left there, I was guard on the train as we were not allowed to go from one car to another. I rode on the platform so I could see all and believe me, it was sure interesting. We only went through seven tunnels and three were as long or longer than the one at Detroit. But all were cut through rock. Some places along the Hudson river there is fine scenery. Some of the Catskill mountains were so high they pierced the clouds and some places there were rocks about three hundred feet straight up from the sides of the car.

Well, we got to New York at 3:15 p.m. We marched about two blocks and got on a boat and were there about one hour and then we went about eight miles along the shore of New York. The boats were thicker in the river than the Fords on Fremont Main St. There were also lots of battle ships. It is nothing to see 35 story buildings in New York. I also went under the Brooklyn bridge. It is only wide enough for five trains to go over at one time.

We got to the port where we unloaded and we were in the street from 5:30 until 10:30 p.m. We had supper with the Red Cross people there. We got on the train at 10:30 and had about one hour's ride out to Camp where I am now.

We are just 20 miles from New York. Who would have thought I would have ever seen New York, the largest city in the U.S. We got to our tent at 12:30 a.m., July 14. We are all in tents here now. The weather is just the same as in Michigan. The ground is sandy and a little gravelly. Each tent holds eight men, just one squad, so our company covers a large space now. There are lots of aeroplanes here, I just saw six in the air at one time. It is lots of fun to watch them.

I was on the train about 29½ hours and only in a day coach, so I didn't get much sleep on the way. Today I am a little tired and as it is now 2:30 p.m. I guess I will have to close for this time.

Griffin H. Smith
Field Hospital Co., No. 15, 2nd Division, A, E.F., France
July 21, 1918

Dear Mother: I will try to write you a few lines.

We are now stationed where the boys are making the big haul. We have been very busy the first three days while here, but today has been a little easier. The first three days we took 20,000 prisoners and over 400 guns, several of them were 16 inch guns and some were 6 and 8 inch guns. The rest were 75's, trench motors, and machine guns, also a lot of ammunition, supplies and gasoline and I think the Boches* are getting their fill of this war. Some of the wounded prisoners we had here at our hospital say the Kaiser and Crown Prince are crazy. We have had nearly 100 wounded Germans in the last three days.

The morning the Americans started "over –the-top" the Boche said they were all asleep and did not expect anything.

When the drive started our hospital was about four miles back from the front, and now we are out of hearing of the artillery, so you can see that the boys have been going some.

The day we came up here the road was just lined with all kinds of tanks, armoured motor trucks and troops, and the morning of the drive saw nothing but cavalry for four hours.

The morning we left our rest camp we were shelled. We were called at 12 o'clock and told to be ready to leave by daylight, so everyone was out of their tents and dressed and were packing up. It was so dark we could hardly see our hands before us, and at 12:30 Bang! went a shell right over our heads, and shrapnel falling around us, but we did not go to the dugouts till they got a little closer, and we never got out of there till daylight. They shelled that town for 36 hours, destroying parts of it, and another one a mile from here.

Well, I must close and try and get a little sleep, for as soon as it gets dark the Boche bomb us. They have been doing this for four nights straight. Am well and happy.

(*Boche is a derogatory French slang, meaning "Cabbage Head", used by the Allies in WWI to refer to German soldiers.)

LIEUT. VICKSTSROM IS PRAISED FOR BRAVERY

Following Communication Gives Official Recognition to Conspicuous Conduct in Service
July 18, 1918
Fremont Times-Indicator

Lieut. Oscar Vickstrom, brother of Chas. Vickstrom and formerly a resident of this city (Fremont), has received official recognition for conspicuous conduct during action June 13-14. The communication follows:

Headquarters 32nd Division, A. E. F.
June 21, 1918

1. The Division Commander takes pleasure in announcing the conspicuous conduct of Second Lieutenant Oscar Vickstsrom, National Guard, in repulsing an enemy raid on the night of June 13-14, 1918. The official reports show that Lieutenant Vickstrom was in command of a platoon of his company, that he took part of this barrage that was approximately 200 yards wide in order to strengthen an outpost cut off by the barrage and prevent its capture. After passing the barrage with a part of his platoon, he took command of the advance post and successfully repulsed the enemy's raid.

2. The conduct of Lieutenant Vickstrom in this case is well worthy of mention as illustrating quick decision

and prompt execution; both qualities of the highest importance in successful offensive or defensive operations.

By command of Major General Haan; W. D. Conner, Colonel, General Staff, Chief of Staff.

A barrage is a heavy artillery preparation covering any amount of ground. This artillery throws gas shells, high explosives and shrapnel so that they fall like rain.

Wm. A. Woodlief
Captain, National Guard
Assistant Division
Adjutant.

John R. Stone

337 Inf. Supply Co., Camp Mills, Long Island, N.Y.

July 25, 1918

Well we are on our way at last, left Camp Custer Friday at 10 o'clock and reached here last night, Saturday night. The trip is great, it's worth five years of one's life. The Red Cross sure was good to us. In all the large cities we came through we could not mail a card or letter only by giving them to the Red Cross ladies. We went through Battle Creek and Detroit where the Red Cross gave us a lunch and tobacco. From Detroit we went under the water through a tunnel to Ontario and from there to Niagara Falls. Canada is very level, I did not see a hill. I can't remember the names of the towns we went through, there were so many of them. We stopped in St. Marks but did not leave the car until we reached Niagara Falls where we had half an hour to see the Falls. They sure are wonderful, the sun was shining through the mist and sent up a lovely rainbow about 200 feet, it was some sight. Later we came to Albany, N.Y. and all at once we jumped out of the hills over the city 300 feet below. You can't imagine what sights there were and I can't begin to tell you the fine cities and grand sights there were from Albany to Jersey City (or Hoboken as they like to call it.) Mountains so high we couldn't see the tops from the car windows, the roads in most places being cut through solid rocks.

We followed the Hudson river for 200 miles, on the other side were mountains reaching above the clouds. Pretty cities nestling among the hills and a great suspension bridge reaching from one town to another. My eyes were tired from looking but I still had to gaze at the wonderful sights. There were crowds at every city waving flags and shouting. We yelled until there wasn't a single yell left. At last we pulled into Jersey City where we left the train and marched over and got on a great float; there were six companies. I never heard such shouting in my life. Across from us was New York city. We didn't land there but steamed up the river, went under the Brooklyn bridge. The Red Cross served sandwiches and coffee or milk on the boat. Left for Long Island about 10 o'clock. The city reaches out to the island and the camp is made up of tents. Aeroplanes are flying over camp all the time. We don't expect to be here but a few days—but who knows.

David Hopkins
Co. A. 55th Inf., 7 Div., Camp Merritt, New Jersey
July, 1918

I have received mail of some kind every day since I left home. That is not so bad. I don't have much time to write only when we have days off.

We have Saturday and Sunday all day and Wednesday afternoons off. All we have to do is wash our clothes. We wash them after supper about every other night.

We have to change our clothes every night. We sweat so that they soon get dirty. No, I don't have any tub or wash board. We just have a scrub brush and we have to scrub them some, believe me. We don't have much time to play. They are shoving us through fast.

I have learned a lot since I have been down here, and will have a lot to tell you when I come back, and I presume I have got lots to learn yet, but I am willing to learn and do all I can for my country to help win this war. That we must do and shall do. Well, we had a large fire here in camp. The damage was $2000. It was a mule stable and hay shed. They got the fellows that set it and they both got twenty years in jail.

I think we are going to move somewhere next week but we don't know where. Some say we are going to New Jersey and if we do I will be near home. Maybe I can get a furlough to come home before I go to France.

We were all out in the field to-day. It was some sight to see. There was 50,000 of us boys.

Well, this is Wednesday afternoon and I am off and I am glad, because it is awfully warm here. The Michigan heat will never bother me when I get back.

July 16, 1918

Well, we are all packed up ready to move but don't know where. We have got our woolen clothes. We got two woolen suits and one woolen overcoat and a raincoat. We had to turn our khaki suits in when we got our woolen ones. They are nice clothes.

Well, our captain just came by my tent and said we were going to start to-morrow, July 17. That sounds good to me to get out of this warm climate. But I guess it must agree with me, as I now weigh 135 pounds and only weighed 110 pounds when I went into the army. I have got to get ready for the rifle range. We are shooting now. My captain said I did good shooting. I shot the other day and got 20 per cent out of 25.

The firsts shot at 100 yards I got 68 shots out of 100; at 200 yards I got 72 out of 100; at 300 yards I got 40 shots out of 50. We have to go out again today and shoot rapid fire which is 10 shots a minute.

Well this is **July 23.** I arrived safely in New Jersey. We were four days and nights on the train. Some ride. Believe me, I certainly enjoyed it. We had Pullman cars, so you see we had a good bed. There was 14 coaches, 1 cook car and 1 baggage car. Some train. We came through Texas, Kansas, Oklahoma, Missouri, Indiana, just 40 miles south of Fort Wayne, Illinois, Ohio, New York, Pennsylvania and New Jersey. I have seen most every state in the union. The Red Cross and other people treated us just fine. We got off the train in St. Louis, Mo., and the Red Cross gave us ice cream, cigarettes and matches.

The next day we got off in Indiana we were treated there to ice cream, cigarettes, cards and oranges.

The next day we got off at Cleveland, O., and went up to the Y.M.C.A. and took a bath. We looked just like negroes. After we got our bath we were treated to ice cream, candy and cigarettes.

The next day we got off at Buffalo, N.Y. We were treated there to ice cream, cigarettes, cards, and candy. The next place was here, New Jersey.

I never saw so many people in all my life. They came to the train waving flags and I could see people one half mile away waving flags and cheering to us. Well, this is a nice place and is cooler than Texas, but we aren't going to be here long. We are just waiting here for the boat to take us across the big ocean. It takes 18 days to cross. Some trip.

Well, this is **Sunday July 28**, and you will surely be surprised when you get this, as I am not started across but am still moving. I am now Cleveland, O. Am well and enjoying the trip. Will write you soon.

**James J. Kuypers
U.S.S. Pensacola, On the Coast of France
August 4, 1918**

Dear Mother and Sister Bess:

We began again in France as you will see by the heading of this letter, but had an uneventful trip. This is our third trip across the briny Atlantic.

I am still well and getting along fine with the work as there is always plenty of that to do.

During one of my trips several of the jackies were given a forty-eight hour leave of absence, and we went up into the city of Bordeaux. It is a very pretty city, about the size of Detroit. It was a relief to get off the ship for a short time.

At other times we have made stops at Charleston, S.C., Baltimore, Md., and Philadelphia, Pa., for as you know that a great many of our important supplies must be loaded at said places. While at Philadelphia I went up town one evening and saw the movie which is taken from the book written by our late Ambassador Gerard to Germany, "My Four Years in Germany". It surely was well worth seeing and one can gain very much value from the pictures.

I do not know when the ship will be ready for her return trip, but at this writing we are being unloaded. The docks over here are all crowded with ships and the trains and trucks are running day and night carrying the junk inland.

In Time of War

According to the Grand Rapids Press reports the soldiers have the Square Heads* running pretty fast, so I think the war will not last very much longer, for if they keep on at this rate they will soon be home. Some of the prisoners say they are glad to be captured.

I cannot tell you much news as you know there are so many rules about the mail.

I will carry you and Bess some French cologne on my return trip and send it from the first port I hit in the states. And as Bess is still an old schoolmarm I have some foreign coins and a couple of pieces of the Rock of Gibraltar for her, too.

I hope this letter finds you both in good health and please give my best wishes to all the other friends who may inquire about me.

Newspaper Note: The above letter writer is now carpenter's first mate on board the freighter Pensacola, which plies between the States and Frances. This is his second cruise in the service of his country, having reenlisted in July of 1917 after spending several months at his home in Fremont at the close of his first four years of service, which was on the Pacific coast.

(*An ethnic slur referring to cranial features of people from Germany.)

**Gerrit Deters
England
August 5, 1918**

Dear Parents:

Just a few lines to you. I know you will be anxious to hear from me often. I arrived safely overseas in England. We are still here but expect to go farther very soon. I am not with my other friends just now. I am helping with the baggage and freight, loading and unloading. As soon as we have that done I will go to my old work again. I came across with the Hq. Div., 169 Inf. Brig., and two of the boys from that division are with me.

Fred Eppink and Geo. VanOss are on the same detail. The rest of the bunch left as soon as we landed and we are to follow slowly. I am as happy as a bird. How are all you folks? This is some country. No wooden houses or barns, everything is built of stone and brick. We traveled over some beautiful country yesterday. The crops look just fine. Two crops I haven't seen as yet and they are corn and beans. This country is just full of potatoes. That seems to be their main crop. All look great. No weeds to be seen anywhere, but a thistle now and then. Wheat and oats are pretty fair crop. Hay is very poor. The barns are not as large as the houses and are very few.

The country is rather thickly populated, children by the thousands. Every city we came through was just like a bee hive. Very few men to be seen, whether they are all gone to war or that they are scarce, I can't say. I can't understand how thy have such good crops and no men to do the work. Must be the women and children that do the work.

The horses and cattle are dandies. Big heavy horses. What the animals live on I don't know. The cattle are nice and fat. They have plenty of pasture but what in winter?

The railroad traffic is way behind the U.S. Freight cars (box) are about 14 ft. long, 6 or 7 wide and 5 ½ high. Capacity from 5 to 10 tons. We could hold on our farm wagons what the cars hold. Coal cars are not over two feet high on the sides and the same in length as the others. They don't look and aren't any larger than some of the big auto trucks of ours. The wheels look like our small wagon wheels. Four under each box car and six under the passenger coaches.

The passenger cars are divided into sections. Eight and six sections to the car. Each section holds eight passengers. No toilets or wash rooms at all. The fastest train runs about 30 miles I guess, and the largest engines are like our smallest ones. The little freight cars make me laugh. If saw such in the U.S. I would call it a Gypsy wagon.

I am in the American Y. Hut writing this letter. The climate is about the same as the U.S. here; rather cold today. The farmers just commenced harvesting. Some aren't through haying yet. You folks no doubt have started threshing by this time.

It's 1:30 our time here now and you folks are just having breakfast, 6:30. Seven hours difference between here and there.

Guess I have written enough now, will write again later. With love and best wishes to all.

Pvt. Bryon Dragoo
D.Q. M. American P.O. 102, American
Exped. Forces, Paris, France
August 5, 1918

Dear Friends:

I have found out during the last five months that this world covers more space than our little town of Fremont.

I have been in many states and have seen their beauty and enjoyed a few good times and especially Florida. I cannot see anything great about the state but nevertheless I had many good times there and some pretty hot ones.

I have stepped from good old U.S. soil on one Friday in June and journeyed to a land across the deep.

The trip was not one of those pleasant ones at first on account of rainy weather and high seas. The result was that I fed the fish for five days and then I felt pretty good. We celebrated the Fourth on the waves but it didn't seem natural. On landing in

France everything was curious to us. And we did lots of eye strain looking at peculiar sights. We saw many German prisoners and talked with them.

We rode in the famous French coaches and also in box cars at first and were very tired when we arrived at a rest camp where we did not stay long until our company was sent in all directions, and I being lucky came here to _____. But by being separated as we were I only have a very few of my pals and buddies with me.

Although I did not get what I enlisted for I am very well satisfied, being as I am a clerk in a warehouse and think I'm doing a lot to help win the war, and probably more than if I were a chauffeur. I don't have hard work to do but it's seven days a week.

There certainly are many great sights here and I'd like to describe them to you but it would take some space to do so.

I have been doing my bit nights by acting as stretcher bearer at the hospitals, where I saw many of the results of war but saw no one from home there as yet.

Nothing troubles the people here and they all seem to be getting on very well. They don't pay much attention to "Bertha"* any more, neither do I.

Well, I must close for this time but will try and write again. Will be glad to hear from any one that cares to write and would very much like a Fremont paper so I could have the names of the boys over here.

(* A nickname for the 420-millimeter howitzer used by the German army.)

Austin Olney
Edinburg, Scotland
August 8, 1918

Dear ones at Home:

Well, you see I am on leave once more. As Scotland was the only division of the British Isles I had not visited, I decided to come here and so avoid offending these people. You see they might think I was neglecting them. (If they ever guess I existed).

This is surely some place. Today I went thru the Castle, Royal Palace, Royal Museum, and climbed to the top of Lord Nelson's monument. Certainly can get some view from either the Castle or monument. Both are on high hills and give a view out over the Firth of Forth and, until the hills shut off the view, way inland. Have certainly been going some today. Started in at 8:30 this a.m. and just now am laying off for a few moments breathing spell at supper time. So here is a brief account of doings lately so far as I am concerned.

We were out on a trip when we got a wireless order to return to base, which we did the next day. We were then ordered to Liverpool for refit, and with refit goes "leave". I got the first part. So leaving the ship at noon three of us caught the 1:15 train for Edinburgh, or Edinboro as it is sometimes called here. Arrived here at 10 p.m. it was distinctly wet and so were we before we reached our bunks for that evening. Well, this morning we three split up for different places. I remained to see what I could of this place.

First I went to a rather imposing looking bunch of buildings and towers surrounded by a stone wall. (Nearly everything here has a stone wall around it). Found it to be a cemetery but it certainly contains a lot more vaults than those I had seen before. Among others I found the one erected for Robt. Burns, by the widow and 12 surviving children.

Right opposite was Nelson's monument. So I crossed over in order to inspect that. Found it to be quite some monument. Built on the order of a lighthouse, and containing accounts of most of Nelson's work. Part of it is in his own handwriting. While there I ran into a couple U.S. fellows in the Signal Corp of the Army. They also are on leave. We have continued together on our tour of inspection.

Next we went to the Royal Palace and saw in one wing the furniture used in different rooms by different members of royal families of several generations ago. In the chapel are tombs and slabs marking burial places from the nobility. The main part of the Palace is used by the present Royal Family of Great Britain on their trips to this city so of course we concluded there was no contraband and didn't inspect it. You understand that of course.

The Castle is on a hill whose sides for the most part are almost perpendicular rock. It would seem to be almost impossible to capture it without good artillery. Yet it has been done at least a few times. Partly by strategy and then hard fighting. In it the Nobility and Royalty used to have their dwelling places. The old banquet hall is now filled with armor of the early centuries and is an interesting collection. Somewhat similar to that of the tower of London. Only not nearly so large.

Guess I forgot to say we also went through the picture gallery. It has several masterpieces of different centuries of each of the Italian, French, Dutch, Spanish and British schools of art.

The museum is similar to most other large institutions of its kind. It has one peculiarity in that nearly all of the different machines shown are connected up with motors so that by pressing a button one can observe the actual working of the various internal and external parts of the machines. Also there are lots of African curious (curiosities?) to be found.

That is our record so far. Am surely enjoying my leave.

Ford Brooks
13 Service Co., Trans. Dept.,
Camp Alfred Vail, Little Silver, N. J.
August 9, 1918

Dear Father and All:

I have not written for several days because I have been too much on the go. Have been to Camp Dix and Camp Merritt since last writing. So you see I have done some driving as it is about 100 miles each way. There surely is some beautiful country in New Jersey. The southern part of the state, where we are located, is very flat and level, while the northern part is hilly. In going to Camp Merritt I left camp about 7 a.m. and made beyond Jersey City before dinner. The place where we ate dinner overlooks the Hudson river and the bank of the river at this place is 200 feet high and very steep, in fact in some places the bank is perpendicular and of solid rock. Just across the river are many New York apartment houses. Boats were constantly passing up and down and they looked very small to us because of the height of the banks. We stopped at a country inn for our dinner and as we ate from the veranda could watch the traffic, and it sure made an interesting sight. Shortly after dinner we reached Camp Merrit. I should judge this to be about the largest camp in the United States. It ordinarily contains about 75,000 men, and as it is an embarkation point the men are coming and going all the time.

When we returned from the trip I found mother's letter awaiting me telling that Harry Dursema is at Camp Merritt. Had I know he was there I surely would have kept my eyes open for him.

We were there until about 4:20 p.m. then started back by the way of New York City and Staten Island. At these places the traffic was so great we could not make good time. The roads were posted and much of the way we were on Lincoln Highway. We arrived at Camp Alfred Vail at 12 midnight. Needless to say I was tired all through. I am getting used to this continued driving, as I average sixty miles a day and change tires anywhere from two to three times each day, for this hot weather is playing hob with our tires. Here we do not stop speed for tires but just change and on we go. Sometimes the tires are so hot that, in taking them off, we have to protect our hands with a bunch of waste or anything we can get hold of. I have gone when I had two other calls awaiting me. When we are sent to a train it means speed. I made a train at the station one mile away in just two minutes from the time ordered. Chester (Miller) has taken some trips of equal length to any made by me. Where we make these fast runs of course we have good roads to drive over. (Words missing from microfilm.)...yes, he is, and I still think there is not a better fellow living.

We sure do get some eats here. I suppose we get better than most camps, but even at that I have been through what is called the worst station in the United States and lived through it, so think I can stand over sea grub. But it does not look as though we would get a chance at that. I sure would like to get a chance at one or two of those Huns. And that word should not be spelled with a capital letter.

I just was called to the telephone and invited out to dinner tomorrow evening, so probably will not write again until Sunday. These people who invited me are the same ones who invited me for last Sunday and I was in New York instead.

Well father, I guess I must close. Love to all.

Pvt. Austin Olney
U.S.S. Jenkins
August 10, 1918

Dearest Mother:

Have been tardy about writing this time, but we have had extra work also liberties, (Ha) which accounts for it. We ran into a regular old storm the other night. It only lasted for a little over a day and night but it reminded more than a few of us that our little ship can roll and go some. Maybe you won't believe it but we rolled at least 55 degrees from the vertical. Last winter such storms were common. A trip was not complete unless we did a few days rolling. But this was the worst for several months.

You must have had quite a frost from all accounts. Hope it runs out better than it at first appeared.

While on leave I met a couple of fellows who are in the aircraft squad. Both from New England states. We spent most of our leave together and surely had a fine time.

Say I haven't seen any popcorn since I left the states and the peanuts over here are not worth much.

As for clothes, I am all fixed up in good shape. The only drawback is that when we want a tailor made job we are up against it, because the tailors here don't seem to know how to make a suit to fit.

So Pa received a "Hun killer" did he? Ha. How many notches has he on the handle?

Not meaning any reflections on the girls in the good U.S.A., but they will have to go some if they equal the mark these patriotic girls over here have set, and are pushing still higher. Of course I haven't seen the States for several days and of course things are different now.

Just tell Pa that he said a mouthful when he mentioned my looking back now to what I thought and expected when I first got on the "Houston." As I see it now most things that I thought and did or expected of the Navy then are rather humorous, to say the least.

Say sometimes I think the Navy is the greatest experience yet for a young fellow. I am far from sorry I joined up, I only wish I had known more about it. It seems to agree with me to, as I have had to get entirely new outfits of clothes. My old ones simply wouldn't go on and so---you know how it is.

Tell Florence not to forget me with her snapshots.

Sgt. Dan Gerber
Co. M., 126th Inf., Am. E. F.
August 10, 1918

Mrs. Frank Gerber, Fremont, Mich.

Dear Mother and Dad: I have received your letter just after we had moved a short distance back from the front. I have seen so much and lived so long in the last few weeks that nothing could surprise me.

Have been in the midst of the big fight; it was pretty tough but a wonderful experience. We drove them so hard that it took four days for our grub to catch up, but we kept right after them. If you run across anyone who does not feel able to buy many Liberty Bonds, just tell them that they should be willing to go without a few meals as cheerfully as we did.

There are no trenches up here but I am never without a shelter, because a very effective one-man dugout can be made in short order that will protect one from high explosive fragments and machine gun bullets. I wish you might have seen Captain Gansser with a rifle over one shoulder and a big shovel on the other. Col. Westnedg left his headquarters and came right up on the line with the rest of us with the seat of his pants all ripped out, and the General was there too.

Did I tell you that I received a Croix de Guerre (Cross of War) a couple of months ago? (P.S. will write more when I get more paper.)

1st Lieut. Henry A. Geerds
Co. M, 126 Inf., France
August 11, 1918

To Mr. and Mrs. Gerrit Bode:

I am so pleased over the success which has attended the efforts of our army, and so relieved to know our troops can face without flinching, all the "frightfulness" the Boche is capable of, that I must take time today to let you know a little of our deeds.

I trust you are all well and enjoying the blessings of life in America, that you one and all appreciate the greatness of our country and thank God for allowing us to call such a country our own. From the privileges we enjoy at home, we cannot do too much. We, over here, are doing all in our power to uphold the standards of our land and shall continue with good spirit to make possible the continuance of the liberties we have enjoyed. When France, Belgium and Russia are freed of every Hun, when peace has again clothed the world in love, then we are going home to live the lives of freemen, knowing posterity will be safe from further holocaust.

I think I have voiced the sentiments of every trooper over here, for every man who was in the recent drive conducted himself in a manner worthy of every praise. Through artillery and machine gun fire our lads ate up the miles and kept Fritz dog-trotting toward his kennel.

Our unit picked up the fight on the Ourcq and kept them going day and night until across the Vesle. One town exchanged hands three times, so you can see, it wasn't all pie.

Machine guns have always stopped infantry advances, but for some reason it didn't stop our lines. We went against them and through them, leaving no Huns behind, but capturing many, and many machine guns. They are dirty fighters. As soon as they see they are done for, they put on Red Cross Brassards, and expect to get away with it. And the litter bearers, who are safe from infantry fire, carry away machine guns on the stretchers, so we can't get at them. We have learned, so he will have to pull something different. The amount of ammunition and material captured is unbelievable. And one more argument against Germany is the dates on the shells. Germany is still using ammunition manufactured in 1900, although she used a lot made just a month ago.

Personal experiences are naturally numerous and exciting, but do not cover the scope of ground a general report does. Hence, the men of a unit often tell two different stories, both being true. I mention this, because I could not verify it with my own eyes. It is claimed there were German women manning some of the M. guns. Men were chained to the guns, of that I can be sure, but whether or not the woman story is true I dare not say.

I was with my platoon during the earlier stages of the drive but was later taken away to command the battalion combat and supply train. Not a pleasant duty, I assure you, for it required 24 hours of hard work each day. We had rainy weather to contend with, and as the roads were shelled to nothing, the bridges blown down and the fields soft and hilly, the transportation of eats and "crackers" was some proposition. And we delivered cooked rations up the lines.

Quite a few times I thought the whole train was a goner from shell fire, but we were lucky and still able to operate. One morning I was caught by a battery which sure jarred me up, gassed me, and sure did scare me for the minutes I was in it. Men have been killed two hundred miles from a burst and we are living when the shell burst ten feet away.

I am as well as can be expected. Rather tired and depressed, but lots of reserve power to go farther. Wishing you all the best of luck and health, and hoping God will make possible the culmination of our desires.

Don M. Dickinson, Son of Mr. and Mrs. C.A. Dickinson Believed to Be German Prisoner
August 15, 1918
Fremont Times-Indicator

The sympathy of the entire community goes out to Mr. and Mrs. C. A. Dickinson of Brookside, who received a telegram last week from Adjutant-General McCain of the War Department, notifying them that their son, Don M. Dickinson, "was officially reported missing in action July 15." This is the first instance of the report of a local boy in the casualty list since this country entered the war. The young man is the only son of Mr. and Mrs. Dickinson and is 20 years of age.

Mr. Dickinson was fighting in the Conde Woods near Jaulgonne, France on July 15. It was on this date that the Germans reported the capture of a large number of Americans in the neighborhood of Jaulgonne, and it is probable that he, with a captain, first and second lieutenants, other officers and more than 100 privates, fell into the hands of the enemy. Mr. Dickinson was a member of the second unit of the 28th division, known as the Keystone Division, under General Muir.

That Mr. Dickinson was possessed of the true American spirit is evident from the fact that he made three unsuccessful attempts to enter the military service of his country before being accepted. He tried for three branches of service in Chicago and was rejected. Determined, however, to get into active military service he went to Pittsburg and was accepted by the National Guard on the 13th day of July, 1917. His division left for foreign service the latter part of last April. He refused to try for the Officers' Training Camp, fearing that he might not be sent to France for active service.

Mr. Dickinson comes from thoroughly American stock. Members of the Dickinson family have fought in every war since the founding of this nation. His father is a Spanish-American war veteran. He is a descendant of John Dickinson, one of the signers of the Declaration of Independence from Delaware, and a kin of the late Don M. Dickinson, postmaster general under President Cleveland, and Ezra Dickinson who was an ambassador to England.

The young man was born in Cheboygan, Mich., and finished his education at Valparaiso, Ind., University. He trained for automatic rifleman at Camp Hancock, Georgia.

F. H. Raymond
Co. M., 126th Inf., American E. F.
August 15, 1918

To Mr. A. O. Edwards, Fremont, Michigan:

Just received your letter so shall answer right away, as it takes so long you know. It has been about a month since you wrote yours.

I have received letters from Loraine, Miss Cherneski, a note from Miss Dragoo, Mr. Gerber, Bill Mee, Earle and Charles Vicstrom. I wish I could express to each one of them personally my grateful appreciation but as this is impossible will you kindly tell them that I am pleased and should like to hear from them again.

I am proud of the great work that the Canning Company employees have done in supporting the third Liberty Loan drive. I know that the one great question on the lips of every man and woman is, "What can I do to help?" Sometimes this question is answered with an opportunity to buy a Liberty Bond. Never the less to play a small part in the winning of this great conflict is a rare and splendid privilege. Some of the members of Co. wish to congratulate you on the magnificent success.

We have put in another hitch at the front. I will tell you a little about the time we had while up there. The first time we experienced shell fire was in a small town a short distance back of the line when "Hans and Fritz" got busy and dropped about fifteen shrapnel over the town. But that didn't amount to much. The next time was when we were up near the front line. I happened to be in reserve at the time and was in a dugout. This lasted about fifteen minutes. They all landed about fifty feet to one side of us and left a few holes in the ground. After that we got it quite often, sometimes high explosives, very little gas.

You can think of me most anytime standing in a shell torn trench, always on the alert and ready to give Fritz just what he is looking for. He is a sly little devil and does most of his dirty work at night.

I must tell you of a joke we played on one of the boys who at times gets a little nervous especially while standing upon the firing step on a dark night. You know we are pestered to death with trench rats, some I dare say are big as a full grown cat, and, like the Boche, are very active at night. Well, we saved up several crusts of bread and one dark rainy night planted them directly in front of the parapet. About ten o'clock, the usual hour, they ventured forth; he commenced seeing things and the following morning he had a terrible tale to tell. Of course, all were wise so it didn't cause much excitement and unnecessary rifle shots.

One particular thing about this country is the roofs of the houses and barns. All the buildings are of stone, for wood and lumber are very scare articles. The roofs are all of red stone slabs about two inches thick and can be seen for some distance. France is the home of some very fine horses, very large, and would be worth a great deal in the States. They have very nice Holstein cattle, although goats are used to great extent, mostly for cheese.

Just a word about the hill-towns of France and then I'll call it off for now. They are of four distinct types: First the large town, second the castle which is sometimes built on the side of a steep hill surrounded by tall trees, third the farm town, fourth the real hill-town which is usually built on the highest hill they can find, overlooking beautifully cultivated fields, which from the distance look like a checker board.

Saw Dan (Gerber) yesterday looking good and feeling fine. He was rewarded a few weeks ago, but presume he has written his father about it.

Mail again to-day, had two letters from home. I surely did expect one from you. Kindly remember me to Mr. and Mrs. Gerber, the family, and all the employees.

Juell J. Hewitt
Co. F., 2nd U.S. Engrs., American E. S.
August 15, 1918

I will try and drop you a few lines as I very seldom have this privilege. I know I owe letters to many around Fremont and take this opportunity to answer them through the Times-

Indicator. While I would like to write many things and tell of the places I have been to, it would be useless for me to try such a thing. I am hoping that someday I may be able to tell my many friends of Fremont my experiences in France, although they are not as great as many, and as far as I am concerned I am just as well pleased as trench and front life is not what you would call enjoyable. I haven't lost any flesh nor have I gained any pounds. I am in good health and hope to continue so for some time. We are having fine weather and hope it continues.

I suppose you have heard and seen much of the boys who went back to boost for the Liberty Loan. One of the boys from our company was in Chicago. He is Corp. George Edgar Barnes. One of the boys got a Chicago Tribune with his picture in it. I never did begrudge George his trip but when he left little did I realize what it meant to really go back to the good old United States. When I saw his picture in the Tribune I did actually realize what it meant to see the home folks once more.

Now I can't say that I have been in front line trenches but I have been close enough so I could hear the revolver shots here, and once an aircraft shell fell through the roof of our barn. I was just outside. The fellow who was on the wagon with me and I could hear the shell coming, and he jumped. I couldn't say just what my thoughts were for the second, as that would be mighty hard thing to explain. Again, I had to drive through a town when Hun shells were plentiful, at least for me, and my main trouble was to keep the horses in control. They did get the best of me at that and we sure did travel from there.

At that a skirmer's life is rather dull, except at times when things get rather warm.

If some of my friends have not received answers to their letters they should not blame me, as we had to destroy all mail as soon as received, and I have lost all track of the letters.

Corp. Frank H. Raymond
Co. M., 126th Inf., Base Hospital No. 3, Ward B, Am. E. F.
August 16, 1918

Mr. A. O. Edwards, Fremont Mich.:

Dear Art and All:--Am writing this sitting up in bed and as I am feeling tip top and in the right mood for writing this no doubt will be a lengthy affair.

It has been about two weeks since I left the line and I think two more will find me back with the company or in a casual camp. I am in hopes they will send me back to the company for I was next up for Sergeant. If I am put in a casual outfit it may be sometime before I am made a Sergeant.

You have already heard quite all you want to know about the present drive. You no doubt have chosen that part of your time to study and by means of complete descriptions published in the daily papers you are sure to form some ideas about the present battles. But until you have served a hitch on the firing line, face to face with a real Hun, and experienced the sights, sounds and smells of war, you'll never know nor will you find a picture that could really describe it.

I'm going to tell you a little personal experience and take a chance on it passing the censor. It all happened in the morning of August 1. We advanced the night before, gained our objective, and remained there until morning when we were supposed to make an attack on a certain patch of woods just at the top of a steep hill.

Daybreak found us all on the job, willing and eager to make the rush, and a few minutes before the signal came to go over the top, _____ a friend and pal of mine, came to me and said "Frank, what do you say we stick together going through the woods?" He had charge of the group on the right and I had charge of the left group so this could be arranged very nicely. So we started out with the understanding that if I took a trip west he would write _____ a nice long letter, and in case he went I was to write his girl. About half way through the woods we got separated and I didn't see _____ again until we had reached the other side. In the meantime the Germans had flanked us and almost before we had time to think there was a steady flow of hot lead coming our way. We waited a few minutes to collect our wits, and the officer in charge of command finally came to the conclusion that this was no place for a minister's son and gave the command to retreat.

We made a rush for an opening that led to the hill, and in spite of the heavy machine gun barrage a few of us managed to reach it safely. I was nearly the last one to leave the woods, and I can't understand how I ever escaped with just a bullet wound in the shoulder. It seems that nothing could ever live through a hell like that.

Just before I left the hospital I inquired about _____, and I learned that he had not returned. One of the boys said he was wounded and others said he had gone "west".

He was a good looking man, Art, and I admired him for many things. His greatest ambition in life was to return after the war wearing a silver bar on either shoulder. He was witty and had always talked about doing something big and worthwhile.

It will only be a matter of a few days until I'll be able to return to the line and if it is true that _____ is dead, I hope that I am spared long enough to get revenge and if I ever find a Boche that looks anything like the one that shot me, "God pity him".

I can't tell you any news about the Company as I have not had any mail since I came here. Have written to the Captain but have not received any reply. Am expecting a letter soon though.

Well, Art, I've reached my limit for today, so will close. Please answer soon and tell me all about the factory, etc. How are Ernie Chapman and Randolph Zimmerman getting along? Tell the bunch "Hello", and that I am anxious to get back on the job again. Best regards to all.

Pvt. Kay W. Towne
Co. H, 115th Infantry, Am. E. F., France
August 20, 1918

Dear Mother and brothers:

As I have plenty of time today I will tell you as much as I can of my first experience in the front line trenches. One night not over two weeks ago we rolled our packs, put them on and started for the trenches. It only took us a short time to get there for we were stationed in a small old _____ about a mile back of our front line, and believe me, it shows it. It is a shame the way cities are all shelled to pieces. Well as soon as we got there, which was about midnight, we were placed on our posts, which were about 10 yards apart and two to four men at a post. There were three men at my post. A post is nothing more than a place dug in the side of the trench high enough to look and listen out over "No man's land," for the trenches are about two feet higher than a man's head. Some of the posts have steel sentry boxes and I happened to get one of them.

It was a still quiet night and we had not been there long when we heard a noise a little way from us. One of the fellows threw a grenade at it but it was nothing more than a rat, as we soon found out, for they were running all around us and once in a while one would bite another and it would squeal so loud (or so we thought at least) that it could be heard a mile. Of course it did not take much of a noise to sound loud to us. So just imagine when about four o'clock in the morning the German artillery opened on us. The shells were bursting all around us and all three of us crowded in the steel sentry box which was about large enough for two. That was good enough to protect us from the flying shrapnel but if a shell should hit it, we would be going yet. It lasted about 30 minutes, then our artillery opened on them and sent so many shells into them they had to quit. This is supposed to be a quiet front, but the boys say if this is a quiet front they had just as soon stay away from a noisy one.

We were on posts nights and slept days. One morning right after we had breakfast instead of going to bed I took my rifle, got up in one of the posts and watched for a German to show himself. After about 30 minutes of waiting I saw one get up on their parapet which is about 600 yards away, and start to walk along their trench. He had taken four or five steps when I took my first shot at a German. I don't know whether I got him or not, but he dropped d_____ quick and I didn't see any more of him. I waited about 30 minutes, then went to bed.

Letters and Related Articles 1918

We were expecting General Pershing to visit today. I hope he comes, for I certainly would like to see him.

September 5, 1918

We have been in rest camp for about three weeks and tonight we go back to the trenches again. Now if I could be lucky enough to be the first one to capture a German prisoner I could come home, for our Battalion commander has just made an offer of 500 francs, which is about $100, and 30 days in the U.S. to the first man that captures a German. Since we have been in this camp I have seen two German aeroplanes brought down by the French.

St. Ralph R. Lewis
Moutchie-Lacanan (Gironde), France
Northern Bombing Squad, U.S. Naval Aviation Forces,
Foreign Service, France
August 21, 1918

My dear Mother and Father:

At last we are again settled among the aeroplanes on the west coast south of Bordeaux. This is a beautiful place among the pines with a lake to fly over. We have been sent down here for some advance training in bombing and gunning. Looks as though we would be here for a month or more. Very healthy here and we are getting good healthy food but without any frills whatever.

I had a wonderful trip over. Surely looked (?) and was inspiring to see the ships coming over and realizing that there were thousands of troops for the Allies. There were 20 naval aviation ensigns on board and most of them came through to London with us. We had a very interesting time in London. All lights out at night and food very expensive, but with it all people seemed happy and convinced that America would win the war for them. Both the French and English seem fed up on it, but determined to whip the Boche with our help. I tell you it was a close call for them through at that.

We came over the channel and landed in France, then went to Paris. Was there for three days then came down here. Had everything arranged to go to Italy to fly large caprone's over the Alps to Northern France. Would have been wonderful but an accident caused them to stop it so I came here. May go down there later.

You will note I had to cut out much detailed information.

Please send me all the candy, cigars, sugar, etc., that you can.

Do not worry. Hope you are all well.

Pvt. Otto Smith
Field Hospital 331, Am. E. F., Italy, A. P. O. 901
August 21, 1918

Dear Sister:

Tuesday noon and I have just finished a husky dinner. Don't know as I will be able to write very well. We are having much warmer weather here now than we had in July. Hope it gets cooler soon. But I guess it never gets very cold here. Have had a couple rains here in the last month.

When it comes to fresh air and beauty we have to tip our hats to "Old England", the island of holly and rosy cheeks. I will never forget how green and handsome were her shores when first she loomed up before us. It was a sight to behold. Everything had a neat appearance, on the landscape. The houses were beautiful. She must be a jolly old place in peace times.

Now England's cities are crowded with soldiers and army traffic. Women and girls are taking the places of men, and we saw them as they rode to work on bicycles or went on foot, basket in arm.

The "Stars and Stripes" hung from many windows. We cheered them all as we passed them. It was a great day and from then on we were satisfied that England was doing her bit.

But our stay in England was limited. Soon we stole away from her shores to see the land of Lafayette. Here we were given the glad hand of the hard pressed French. Here we were treated as are the sons of France themselves. We shall never forget the people of France.

We learned enough of their language to understand tales from the front during the big allied offensive of July. They spoke of the Americans as good comrades and marvelous soldiers. Altho some companies were badly shattered the survivors were in high spirits, and took delight in showing us their Allemagne (a French name for Germany) souvenirs, which all went to show that Germany received a worse beating.

But as luck would have it Uncle Sam wished to pay tribute to another country. We were some of the lucky ones chosen to journey on to the native land of Columbus, who was first to discover our own great country. We found the name of Columbus, (Christophorus) upon the tongues of the Italians as the name of Lafayette upon the tongues of the French.

We found the people of Italy much the same as those of France. Their homes are of rude stone with open fire places, their kitchen ware mostly of copper. The people live mostly in villages and cities, silk and fruit being their main products. Here, as in France, the two wheeled cart is in prominence. The horses (cavelli) are much smaller than those of France. The large horses of France could not endure the hill climbing necessary here.

The people are pleased over the entry of American soldiers. "Vive La America" (Hurrah! America) was upon their lips.

You people back home don't realize how the nations of the Old World look up to the U.S.A. It takes Yanks to give them "pep". There is quite a bit of merriment in the Italian people and we have some jolly old times with them.

We have seen many cities and towns of Italy, every village having its church and priest. Our priest here is a checker player and comes to play with the boys. Checkers and chess seem to be popular here. The smaller churches have fewer number of bells than the larger ones. The chimes of the larger churches are very pretty, the bells are made of fine metal and have all resounding qualities of a good bell. Much of the money of the country goes to the churches, they are very elaborate inside. Some of the best are rich in paintings, sculpture and gold edged tapestries. The altars are of fine marble.

Nearly every village has some monument or another to some hero. Italy has been a battle field for hundreds of years. The larger cities have their arenas where the gladiators fought years ago, when Columbus was sailing the dark blue brine. Today they are used for public gatherings and auctions. These are marvelous products of masonry. Now and then we see monuments to such as Victor Emanuel II, Napoleon and Garibaldi, the Lincoln of Italy.

The troops which we have been assigned were recently reviewed by King Victor Emanuel III. They certainly did credit to the U.S.A. He said they were the best troops he ever reviewed. They are much larger than the Italian soldiers, and they made a fine appearance. They were cheered to the limit. They didn't come from a warring nation, but from a nation that can war to the limit, if the standard of liberty which she has set for the whole world is endangered. This standard has made more of an impression upon us since we have visited these foreign countries, and these are growing more and more democratic now. America has made her impression.

I am on night duty now and nearly every night we hear the large guns roaring away at the foe. We can always tell when a battle is on. Well, I guess I have better stop or the censor won't get all this read. You can pass this letter around to the rest of the folks whom I haven't had time to write to.

Letters and Related Articles 1918

Frank H. Raymond's Name in Casualty List Last Week
August 22, 1918
Fremont Times-Indicator

The many friends of Corporal Frank H. Raymond were shocked last week to learn that he had been severely wounded in action. The news was wired to A. E. Edwards of the Fremont Canning Co. from a friend of Mr. Raymond in Kent City, his home. Corporal Raymond enlisted in the 126th Infantry in June, 1917, leaving Grand Rapids for Grayling a year ago, He is 28 years of age. At the time of his enlistment he was in the employ of the Fremont Canning Co.* and had worked for this company for several years. He was a fine young fellow and had a wide circle of friends here. Corporal Raymond was in the same company with several other local boys.

A letter from Mr. Raymond to Mr. Edwards written August 6 and received yesterday, states that the corporal was wounded in the shoulder by a machine gun and that the patient is doing nicely following an operation.

(*In 1928 this company evolved into the Gerber Products Company which produced Gerber Baby Food.)

Pvt. Walter U. Robbins
Co. C, 104th Inf., American E. F., Somewhere in France
August 25, 1918

My dear Mother, Father, and Brothers:

I am feeling fine and dandy and hope this finds you all the same. Well there are a lot of us boys transferred to the 104th Infantry. Dave Hopkins is in the same company that I am in so I will see him oftener. This is a fine place here.

I haven't had any mail since I got across but I think we will get mail better now. Tell all the rest I will write to them when I get time and some paper.

How is everything in Fremont coming? It is hard to make the French people understand what we want but we get what we want just the same. They do everything they can for us.

This is a great farming country, they raise mostly all grains, and everything looks fine. We went to church this forenoon. It was the first time I had been there since I have been in the army. I have a testament with me but I haven't read it yet. Well this is a beautiful morning. The sun shines so nice and bright. We sure have great times camping.

I just went down to the Y. M.C.A. and got one can of tobacco. Tobacco is the only thing we can't get very handy.

It probably will take four or five weeks before you get this. It seems a long time since I read a letter. I don't suppose we will get mail very often but write as often as you can. We are having good times in France. It is a pretty country. It's the nicest place that I have ever seen. We have great times counting French money. They think that our money isn't any good.

I am with a nice bunch of boys so don't worry about me for I am all right. I saw Ben Giggy the other day.

Harold A. Rasey
Co. K, Bar. 530, 5th Reg., Camp Perry, Great Lakes, Ill.
August 31, 1918

Dear Ones at Home:

Well as I had never had the mumps before entering camp, I am in the Isolation hospital with them and have been here for 12 days, so having lots of spare time I will try and describe my work and navy life as thoroughly as I can, although it is my first attempt.

I will start when we first entered camp, which was July 26. When we arrived at the gate, the Jackies began to shout, "Have you any cigarettes or chewing gum?" Those that had it threw it away because they were not allowed in camp at that time, although the order has been repealed since. As we entered we were greeted from all sides by "You'll Like It," which we found out later to be the camp slogan.

We marched into Camp Farragut and piled our baggage in a large pile and then marched to "chow". It was a novel meal to us, consisting of cabbage salad, beef, bread and coffee. After cleaning the barrack where we ate we were assembled at a large hall and had to sign a lot of papers and then were given a mattress cover to fill with straw. Next we were issued two towels and a pair of army blankets. We were then marched to Camp Decatur and assigned to our barracks which were 847 South.

At five o'clock the next morning we were awakened by the bugle and took a cold shower. It sure was cold by the way some got out from under it. Had chow at six and at eight took our "first shot". It was a great thing; some fainted from the excitement and we were all vaccinated at the same time. Five days later we got our second shot and second vaccination for those it did not work on, and in seven days more we got our third shot and I got my third vaccination.

August second we got orders to pack and we soon were on our way to Camp Perry. The third day after entering camp we were issued our uniforms. We stripped and entered a large store with a bag under our arm. The clerks asked us the size of our hats and shoes only. For trouser measure, you stepped on a box so the clerk could see your waist and he threw four pair at me. They did likewise with all of our clothing, glanced at you for your size and threw it. In about two minutes I was outside with four uniforms, (two blue and two white), one blue pancake hat, two white hats, peacoat, jersey, watch cap, shoes, six pairs socks, four suits underwear, and handkerchiefs, button, needles and thread, besides a knife, brushes for clothes and shoes, and a neckerchief.

Our barracks have to be scrubbed each morning before six, which is chow and roll call at eight. Then we get eight hours of army drill with the Springfield rifle.

Each Saturday and Sunday are shore leave days. We get 12 hours leave each week, after we have been here three weeks. My detention was up on Friday and so I got twelve hours Saturday and Sunday both. Saturday I went to Aurora when my folks came from Michigan and Sunday after they had visited Camp and started home, I went to a city north of camp, Waukegan, the last town in Illinois.

Our chow hours are six, eleven and five. We get fruit every morning, meat nearly every meal, and bread, coffee, butter, potatoes, salads and vegetables.

Reveille is sounded at five on all mornings save Saturday and Friday, which is 4:30. Taps sound at nine o'clock. My only disappointment since entering camp is that my company left yesterday for Camp Luce and will leave there before one o'clock Monday for sea and unknown destination.

Will Dawe
337th Inf. Supply Co., Am. P.O. 789, Am. E. F., Cosne, France
Sept, 14, 1918

Dear Chad and Edna:

I'll wager this is the first letter you have ever received from France. I had intended to write you for some time but kept putting it off. I wrote you a letter when I was in England. I hope you have it by this time.

Well, I have been in France over a month now and am getting used to the run of things. Things seemed mighty queer when I was in England, but it is different here. To all the queer French customs is added the French babble, commonly known as the most beautiful language in existence. I can't make much headway in using the stuff. A mighty few words are all I have added to my vocabulary.

I am working in Sales Commissary now. It is sort of a store to furnish the boys with a few extras, such as cigars, cigarettes, tobacco, candy and other such stuff. It is a good job and I take interest in it. Kind of keeps me on the jump, but I do not mind that. I am getting so I know the French money system quite well. We are paid off over here in the French money, and of course all the goods we sell are paid for in French money. It is peculiar to get used to but it will be natural soon. When I was going to school I never supposed I'd ever have a chance to use the French money table that I used to think was useless to spend so much time on, but one never knows what is apt to happen.

We have mighty nice quarters (billets) and also good stuff to eat, so I can't see that there is any great need to worry. Of course I'd much rather be back on good old American soil, but this life isn't too bad so far and I am going to make the best of it as long as I am here. Talk about a feed—we sure did have it here the other night. Our (Supply) Co. celebrated its first anniversary. Our supper compared to one of Mother's good Christmas dinners, so I'll just leave it to your imagination as to what we had. Our company is very fortunate I think in having a fine bunch of cooks. All our food is well cooked and is clean.

How are the kids? I suppose Bernard is going to school every day. Gee, I sure think lots about them all. Tell them I'll have lots of funny things to tell them when I get back.

I have had one letter from you since being here. It was one that you wrote to me at Camp Mills, wishing me a successful trip over the ocean, but it was "did' when I got your letter.

Are you going to have much of a crop this year? I hope everything is the best ever. Have you ever been to Hesperia to see how my bushel and peck proposition is coming along? Don't forget to look after that, will you?

We are having lots of rain over here. I hope that it clears up soon, so we can have some of France's summer weather again before winter. Ray is still in the Company. He has a job guarding. He has a good job and like me is contented as long as he must be here. Did you know that he was married before he left Camp Custer.

Well must get to work as it is almost time to open up, so will bid your adieu for this time and will promise you another letter before long.

Lieut. Darrel D. Alton
Theoretical Bombing Office, Instructor's Room 17
Ellington Field, Houston, Texas
September 15, 1918

Dear Folks:

It dawned on me yesterday that I didn't write last Sunday or Monday as usual and so I am going to do it now before I do another thing. We had new flying hours go into effect on Monday and maybe we were busy in our department making out a class schedule that would be free from conflicts, give the night flyers sufficient sleep, assure reasonable meal hours, etc.

One group now flies from 7-11 a.m. with classes from 12:30-3:00 and the other group of day flyers have classes from 7:30 a m. and fly from 11:00-3:00. One group of night flyers fly from 7:00-12:00 p.m. and the other from 12:00-3:00 a.m., both sections having classes in the afternoon and all men having recreational games from 4:00-5:00 p.m. each day. You can easily see that it took considerable juggling to get a schedule that would be fair to everyone concerned.

Up to the present there has been two of us instructing in Aerial Navigation, each of us having four lectures a day, the course consisting of four weeks' theoretical work. As soon as all our instruments arrive we are going to have practical application of this work added to three of the flying stages.

Another man arrived from Washington to help on this work, yesterday, and this week we will plan out the division of the work, both theoretical and practical. The officer in charge of Night Bomb Raiding, the most advanced course on the field, is Navigation Officer of the Post and is responsible to the C. O. for the proper instruction in the subject. He might be compared to the Superintendent of Schools in civil life. He appoints the instructors and sees that they are qualified and give the work that Washington wants given, but does not bother himself with any of the details of the work at all. He told me yesterday that he was making me Head Instructor and that I am to be in charge of the theoretical work and also be Navigation Officer on the Night Bomb Raiding stage at this field. This means that the other two instructors will be under me and our work won't be much different as we shall divide the interior work equally and one of them will have charge of the Day Bomb Raiding stage navigation work and the other in the same capacity in the advance Night Flying stage.

An English major that has been around inspecting for this government visited one of my classes and also one of Wachtell's (the other fellow on the job) and it was on his report that I got put in as Chief Instructor. It means that I will be tied up in Texas for some time to come, but it put me in a good line for promotion at some future date because there are only six fields in the country that will give this complete course, and it is an important branch too, and now there is only one man above me here.

It will mean however that when I do get into where it actually looks as if I was really doing something to end this affair that I will be more or less of a specialist and near the top in one line at least.

I think that this will have to be about all for this me.

Pvt. Vernon B. Gilbert
H'dquarters Co., Det. 337th Inf., Am. E. F., France, Am P. O. 789
September, 1918

(The first page of this letter is missing from microfilm leaving it to pick up in the middle.)

We all knew the thing was coming off could read the signs from back here, but dared not refer to it until now. The Huns used everything they ever heard of to stop them I guess, but nothing in the German category of frightfulness was sufficient.

I sincerely believe there is something in the American's environment, be it the climate of sunshine, cold winds, storms of rain or snow, which combine to produce a distinct American type regardless of his parentage, and he becomes a Yank. They have revived the traditions of "Yank" over here, no one wants to be called Sammy or Amex. They are cheap, flimsy nick names, cheap efforts for something great, and so far our boys up front have earned the right to this virile title. They have lived up to the standard which the name implies; it was born in struggle for freedom, christened and baptized in the blood of those who were the first champions of freedom. I think every American soldier is thrilled and proud to be called just YANK in a foreign land, and it strikes terror into the hearts of their enemy who dare to violate the traditions which gave it birth.

To illustrate one incident described by an officer who was there on this last Yankee push at St. Mihiel. The Germans had held on stubbornly to a little patch of woods until they discovered Yanks coming straight at them with fixed bayonets through a hail of machine gun bullets. Their surprise at being thus confronted by Yanks completely demoralized them. One Hun was to shout, "They are Yanks, here come the Yanks!" wherewith he with several others, dropped their guns and beat it, while the rest stretched up their arms high as they could and called "Kamerade." So over here even the enemy knows what Yank means and what he stands for. We fellows back here sleeping in houses and getting fat on good American beef, French turkey, geese and eggs have not yet earned the title.

Was over to the R. R. station last night and a big long train of British soldiers pulled in along the platform. They spotted my big campaign hat and one called to me, "Lo Yank." They were coming from a land far away and were hungry for news of the western front. "What news of the front, Lad?" I answered "British attack on a 16 miles front and penetrate 12 miles." "Bless me listen that," and bandaged heads and arms poked out of the windows all along the cars. But they nearly fell out the windows when I told them how the Yanks had straightened out St. Mihiel's salient and were now dropping shells into Metz.

September 19, 1918

I am still driving the car for my Colonel and I can sit here and write until he comes, then I have to drop this instantly and go, then resume where I happen to be, sometimes it is in the court yard of a beautiful old chateau, along side of the road or out in the middle of a big field. At present am out east of town just inside the hedge in a stubble field. It is the highest point around here for miles and the view is grand. Can see far down a broad river valley and the far gently sloping heights across the river with little villages here and there with their white walls and low tiled roofs gleaming in the sunshine. Everything is still, save a few birds scolding along the hedge rows. Farther down the hill some rooks are getting h_ell licked out of them by a pair of magpies. By the way, they are both thieves and robbers though the magpie is one of the sharpest birds I ever saw.

Away to the south west is a round mountain-like peak on the top of which is a beautiful and very old castle which stands out against the sky and is very beautiful in the morning sunshine. Far down the valley is a plowman with his horses hitched tandem and he walks beside his team, pops his whip and cries, "a'llee, a'llee." He wears wooden shoes and what looks like a woman's apron with sleeves in it, and though he is a mile away, his voice comes clear, I am so far above him, and the air is very clear although it rained all night last night. Can't you imagine such a fresh beautiful morning?

To my left and down on the highway is an old peasant woman herding her geese and goats. She sits in the shade of a gnarled and bent old tree on a little stool with her knitting, while her geese catch frogs and grasshoppers in the wheat stubble. The goats browse along an ancient stone wall all grown to briers and hedge. One old goat can nearly climb the wall and the silver tinkle of their little bells comes up to me so plainly, yet they are quite a distance away.

One could never believe this peaceful little world about one here had ever even heard of a war and yet within the area of this view is our whole division (the 85th) billeted in hamlets and farm houses. If it were not for one thing and that seems to come from deep down in the bowels of the earth, a constant rumble and growl. One can hear it only from these high places, sometimes so faint then again distinct like distant thunder. One can hardly believe it is from the front because we are so far away but I was never up here that I did not hear it as soon as I shut off my motor. It may be an artillery range, nevertheless it is big guns and they are eternally at it.

Here comes the old Colonel. He wants this field for drill grounds and he has walked around and across it a hundred times, more or less. I suppose he will track about a yard of this nice dirt for me to clean off the car rug.

September 22, 1918

Well guess I had better close this thing and get it censored and mailed or you will not get it by Christmas. We get newspapers every day now. They are branches of the New York Herald, Chicago Tribune and a paper called the Stars and Stripes, printed in Paris. Will send you a copy of the Stars and Stripes. Am feeling fine and am consternated. From the looks of things here now this will all be over about the first of the year.

Pvt. Harold B. Kempf
Co. F, 340th Inf., A. P. O. 798, Am. E. F., Somewhere in France
September 19, 1918

Dear Folks at home:

I received your letter on August 11th a couple of days ago and it seems odd to get a letter a month old but it seems to take a long time to get mail over here.

You wrote that you had everything harvested and had threshed some in around home. By the time you get this letter you perhaps will be preparing for Thanksgiving day or maybe Christmas, so you see it makes it rather hard for me to write. It was very dry here up until about a week ago, since then we have had lots of rain, really more than we needed. The climate here is very much like it is in the States as far as I can see and the seasons are about the same. They raise lots of grain here but I haven't seen a field of corn or anything that looks like a silo since I've been here in France.

This country looks rather strange to us as everything looks old, such as buildings, which are made of stone, practically all of them, and some of them look as if they had stood for years. Instead of using wagons like ours they use big wheeled carts and one horse. If they need more than one horse they hook another on in front. I have seen them hauling loads with three and four horses on a cart, one in front of the other.

The roads are mostly all gravel or stone and they never run straight, always turning and winding, with hedge fences on each side. The country itself is rather hilly and rolling. This perhaps will give you some idea of how it looks over here.

Suppose you have noticed that the Yanks are still going over here. Everything looks promising now and hope it is nearing some decisive answer. I sure can't complain myself for I don't know what it is to be sick in the army. I have lost in weight quite a bit as I now weigh about 160 pounds, but my muscles are strong and I really feel better than I did when I weighed 200 pounds. By the time I get back I will be ready for hard work again. Don't you think so? Most likely I will be ready for a rest. So you know what to expect. I'll do nothing but visit relations for a month or so. There is nothing like looking ahead and having it all figured out.

Well I have written about all I can for this time. Tell every one of the kiddies hello for me, and I'll tell you lots of things when I get back that I would be unable to write as it would take too long.

**Floyd Tinney
118 Field Art., Bat. B., Camp Jackson, Columbia, S.C.
September 19, 1918
Monday—out in the brush.**

Dear Mother:

Your letter reached me out on the range this morning, and while I am waiting for data to come down to fire, I will write you and will try and get it finished to send in tonight. I guess about the only news I can write is to tell you about this battle they are having here. We left Camp Jackson last Wednesday night at 10 o'clock, Battery A. B. C. D. E and F., each battery having two big guns to the battery. A. B. and C. have the six inch Howitzer, D. E. and F. have the four point seven Howitzer. This composed the firing battery of the 118 Reg.

Of course attached to us are the Medical Corps, truck drivers, machinists, telephone men, signal men, wireless men, cooks and so forth, each having their own particular duty. There are the 116 and 117 Regiment and the French Motor company which have same amount of guns and equipment as we have. We left with this equipment, while dark as could be, started out on this range which is a mighty big range about 17 miles long, 10 miles wide, with a second growth of pine, oak and hickory all over it.

Now you know how dark it is in the woods at night and there was not even a moon. Not a man was allowed to speak except in a whisper and not a person allowed to smoke until daylight. After we got out about five miles on the range, at a signal we pulled the guns into position, the men pitching their tents without a light. The ditch shoveling gang was put to work digging trenches and the gun emplacements. The wires were strung for telephones up to the front line trenches where the supposed Germans were. The wireless station put, ----well all I can say is, it's like a big circus.

Everyone has his own work to do. As it began to get daybreak such places as were exposed to the sky were camouflaged. Our tracks we made coming in were covered. Then the aeroplanes began to fly over the range trying to locate us. These of course were supposed to be German planes. Well everything remained quiet all the fore noon. In the afternoon hell broke loose for about two hours. This was supposed to be a barrage we laid down on the Germans. The noise all the guns made was great. The night was quiet and calm, only a few shots being fired in the early part of the evening.

The next day was hell. My shift is from 6 a.m. until 6 p.m. We fired steady all day. At noon a slow rain began to fall and of course my legs soon got wet. It rained all night, all the next day and the next night. Wet and dirty is no name for it. Talk about the "Cooties!" They have what they call red bugs here in the woods. They are about as large as the head of a pin. They get on you, eat a little hole in your skin, which you don't mind so much, until they get deep in, then it itches terribly. Well, they've nearly made me crazy.

About three o'clock this morning all the guns opened again and it certainly was some sight, the whole sky was lighted up.

Well, here it is four o'clock in the afternoon. Just got through firing, at least for a few minutes. During that time have been in a gas attack; we had the gas masks on about two hours. Tonight we make an advance. We are supposed to drive the Germans back, then in a few days they drive us back, but in the last attack we win the battle.

I don't know how long this will take but I suppose about two weeks yet. I haven't had my clothes off since last Wednesday. They'll be stuck on me with dirt by that time.

I must close now. Best regards to all.

HERALD COMMENDS SOLDIER

September 19, 1918
Fremont times-Indicator

That the American soldiers would be braggards and boasters when on foreign soil was a fear common in this country when America entered the conflict. That this fear is now dispelled is the essence of an editorial in Monday's *Grand Rapids Herald* which comments on a letter written by Dan Gerber of this city who is now at the front.

The editorial follows:

Dan Gerber of Fremont, who went to war with the National Guardsmen from Michigan and who helped crack the crack Prussian Guard, has written a letter home that is a gem of soldierly modesty.

When the United States went into this war and started sending soldiers across, our Allies were a wee bit skeptical of our men. They were worried chiefly for one cause; they expected the American soldier to be a loud-mouthed braggard who would expound the prowess of the Yankees from Calais to the Swiss border. Pershing's soldiers surprised the British and the French. The Manchester Guardian, for instance, is astounded because American soldiers actually ask Britishers how to do the things of war and concede their immaturity as fighting men.

But, as we were saying, Dan Gerber of Fremont has written a letter home. It was published in the Herald last Friday. Maybe you didn't read it, because it started off with a lot of stuff about the price of pork and beans in France. But down in the third paragraph, Soldier Gerber says; "I forgot to tell you the last time I wrote that I have been decorated with a Croix de Guerre by the French." He forgot to write home about the Croix de Guerre, given by the French only to those fighting men who display exceptional Heroism! And he writes as though nothing were of less importance. No need to worry about American boastfulness.

Most men would have raced for the nearest cable station immediately after receiving the Croix de Guerre on their expanded chests.

And then there's Sergeant Myron F. Beals of Plymouth, Mich., who writes home, "My left leg is gone, but otherwise I am all O. K." And he adds, "You folks have nothing to worry about."

Doomed to travel life's thorny path, a cripple, he glories in the happiness of being otherwise "all O. K."

There are sermons in these letters from France!

Pvt. David T. Hopkins
Co. C., 104th Inf., Am. E. F., Somewhere in France

Dear Folks at home:

I will write you a few lines to let you know I am still among the living and am feeling fine and I hope when this reaches home it will find you all in the best of health and enjoying yourselves.

Well I have seen a little fighting already, I have been "over the top" and believe me, we captured some Germans and Austrians and we got all kinds of beer, wine, bread and jam that they left in their dugouts. We surely had some feeds.

September 31, 1918

I received your first letter since I have been in France today and I was surely glad to get it. I thought I wasn't going to get any anymore mail as I hadn't received any for so long. I am all o.k. only have a little cold but not a bad one.

We are taking a rest now. We have dandy barracks to sleep in. The beds are made of chicken wire and we have straw ticks to sleep on and have a stove in our barracks. It rained here last night and is raining this morning and it is quite cool here. There are twenty men in the barracks with me and we certainly have the fun.

Believe me, we gave the Germans H___ while we were after them. They are giving up all along the lines and I think it is the best thing for them to do. They are afraid of the Yanks when they get after them. When they see us coming they turn and run like the devil. This is surely some war. If a man only gets wounded he is lucky and if he comes out without a scratch he is darned lucky, and that was me, but then we ran the Germans ragged just the same. The Germans are good fighters all right, to get off 300 or 400 yards and fire at you, but when they see the khaki clad boys coming "over the top" right after them the first thing they do is to throw up their hands and shout Kamerade, but we couldn't understand that at all. Either that or the boys let their fingers slip. Lots of accidents happen at times like that. I think they will get enough of it after a while.

I wish I could drop in at home and spend Sunday with you and see all my friends and have a good talk once more, but what's the use of thinking of it? We have this job to do over here and then "America bound." And I believe the boys can sing America" pretty strong. It may not be long and it may be another year.

Well, the boys from Camp Custer will soon be coming over here and I guess in time there will be enough of us to walk over to the city in Germany and we are mighty anxious to be on our way.

Well I had a piece of candy today that tasted just like you used to make. It was the first piece I have had in two months. It was from French people. They are certainly good to us. The government furnishes us with tobacco and cigarettes and sometimes we have cookies. This is what we had for dinner today: beefsteak, carrot stew, bread and coffee and you know I like beefsteak. Well I have got to pick "cooties" before long. I would send you one in this letter but the darned thing would eat its way out.

Yes, some of the boys are with me yet and I have found a lot of good friends over here. Walter Robbins is still with me. He is well and looks fine and he said Hello to you all. He is in the same company but in platoon three and I am in platoon two.

I am O.K. so don't worry about me and I am right there when the "chow" is ready and it is mighty good. Give my regards to all my friends and tell them Hello for me.

Bugler Carl Felber
Hdq. Troop, 1st Div., Am. E. F. France
October 1, 1918

Dearest Mother:

Just a few lines to let you know that I am still fine and O.K. and feeling real happy. It may not be long now and this war will be over and we can all come home again and live in peace and comfort.

I am writing this letter in a French Y. M. C. A. in a little historic town of an ancient war. I sure have seen a lot of France.

I told you, did I not, that I saw Mason Brace, another Fremont boy? That makes two that I have seen here in France.

Well mother, I could write a whole story book of what is going on over here in France, but as you know, censorship won't permit it, but after this war is over I can do better.

I must close now and say good-by. Tell Mrs. Hoad I said "Hello."

John Frens
Somewhere in France
October 2, 1918

I suppose you folks think I have forgotten you altogether but that is not the case at all. I could have written a week ago but we could not get the mail out, so you don't want to worry if you don't hear from me for quite a while because there is always some little reason.

I am sure feeling fine and I am in the best of health and hope you folks are all the same.

Well we have seen some of the real stuff by this time. We were at the front for about eighteen days. Got along fine. Do you folks ever hear from Ed? I suppose he is over here some place, but where I don't know. But no doubt he is getting along fine also. Is he still in the Artillery? I don't know if I wrote it before, but we were transferred into the 42nd Division quite a while ago. Ed may have been transferred also. It would not surprise me any if he was.

I have not had any mail yet but expect some most any day, as some of the boys that came over here with me have received some already.

I suppose by the time you get this letter the fall work will be about done. I do hope you are getting along well with it. Is Dick going to school again? Well, father, you have got it pretty hard this year, but I hope and pray that things will be different next year. From the way things look now, I think they will be too.

SERGEANT DAN GERBER GIVEN ROYAL WELCOME

October 3, 1918
Fremont Times-Indicator

Sergeant Dan Gerber, son of Mr. and Mrs. Frank Gerber of this city, who has just returned from the front in France, was accorded a big ovation yesterday morning when he alighted from the train after his long trip from the front in France. The Fremont Home Guard, Clark's band and 600 children from the public schools lined up on Main St. and marched to the depot to meet the sergeant.

After returning to the Main-Division corners Mayor Tinney presented Prosecuting Attorney W. J. Branstrom and Sergeant Geo. E. Nightingale who made short addresses briefly responded to by the returning soldier.

Sergeant Gerber has been in the thickest of the fighting at the front and was decorated by the French for bravery. He will remain in Fremont for ten days and will then leave for Alexandria, La. where he will be engaged in the government's military service at Camp Beauregard.

Pvte. David T. Hopkins
Somewhere in France
October 3, 1918

Well, I arrived safely overseas and am well and having a good time. Hope this finds the folks in and around Fremont all well.

France is surely some place. It is quite hot here now. The buildings are all old fashion. The houses are all made of stone, even the roofs. The houses and barns are all built together. Cattle, horses, sheep, pigs and people are all living under the same roof.

We are staying with the French people in their houses until we get settled. They all live in town, and go back and forth to their farms. They surely have got some nice horses and cattle here. The cattle are most all Jerseys. They have strange harnesses, just the harness and tugs and the collar and hames are all together. They have only two wheels on their wagons and that surely looks strange to me.

The French women will do all they can for us. They say the American boys are going to save them.

There was one old lady that had a son killed in the army and she invited us boys in the other night and cooked us thirty eggs and made us some coffee and we had some bread. Another lady gave us some milk. We offered to pay her but she would not take anything and would only point at her son's picture on the wall. There is a lady thirty years old that had a husband killed in the army that does our washing for us. She is certainly a nice lady.

Well, I just got through eating and I feel better and will try and finish up my letter. We had beans, bread and butter and water to drink.

Charles Sanborn
Battery F, 42 Reg. F. A., Camp Custer, Mich.
October 3, 1918

Dear Friends and Readers of the Fremont Times Indicator:

I have now been in the training camp at Camp Custer better than seven weeks. Of course I have not had any great experiences but have seen a lot of sights at that, and more men I believe in that time than I had seen all together before I came to camp. When I came here the first thing we heard was "wait until you get that shot", and so I will explain what they meant by that. Everyone who comes into the army is vaccinated and gets an injection in the arm for typhoid fever. And when they get shot one of the three will make a man sick. There are three of those shots about a week apart and if the first vaccination doesn't work they will give you as many as three, and if they don't work you don't get any more. Well, it was the first shot that got me. About two o'clock in the morning the fire alarm was given and while we were out in line I began to feel faint and fell over and they carried me in. But that soon leaves a fellow.

Well, most of the boys that were in the infantry with me were transferred to the artillery at the same time I was. But part of them are in the heavy artillery and some in the light. I am in the heavy.

The guns we will use are a little larger than six inch and we are motorized, but the light use horses and three inch guns. The gun we will use will shoot about eight miles. I like the artillery much better than the infantry. It is much more lively.

There is one thing about the army. We get all the good substantial food we need. I only weighed 129 pounds the day I came here and now I weigh 150 pounds. We have about as nice officers here as you could find. Our day's drilling now consists of an hour of physical exercises, an hour regular drilling, an hour's lecture, and hour tieing knots, an hour signaling and an hour with the big guns. Out of this we have ten minutes each hour to rest. We are off at 4 o'clock so we can take a bath, shave, get our shoes shined and clothes changed. We have inspection all over Saturday. We have to put our clothes out on our bunks so they can see what kind of shape they are in and we have to have clean clothes on as well. I surely get lots of mail here. It is awful nice to get lots of letters. It helps to pass away the time.

There are different kinds of work around the camp to be done and we all have to take our turn at it. But if some one does not do about as they are supposed to they have the worst part of it to do, such as working in the kitchen and washing the greasy pans or scrubbing the floor. I have had two passes and went home since I have been here, but I don't know when I will get home again as we can't get but a 24 hour pass at a time now. I know no reason for that unless they expect to get an order to send us to some other camp and want us to be sure and be near. But I have not heard any such thing, it is just my own idea. We will soon get our woolen clothes now. We should get them tomorrow but a new bunch of boys came into our regiment today so we won't get ours until they get theirs.

The property is protected here by the guards. They take guards all out of one Battery one night and out of another the next night. I have been pretty lucky about getting on guard so far. I have been up for guard just twice and once I got out of that. They picked out two of the neatest boys for orderlies and I was lucky enough to be one of them. That night and day it rained but I was in the dry and didn't have to do anything that night. The next morning at seven o'clock I had to report at Regimental Headquarters and the two of us swept the office and dusted and all we had to do the rest of the day was to run out to some of the barracks with some orders and were not out long enough to get wet.

The most of us neighbor boys that came to camp together are still together one of them having his bunk...*

(*Unfortunately the rest of this letter is missing from microfilm.)

Vern Gilbert
Headquarters Co. Det. 337th Inf., Am. P.O. No. 789, Am. E.F., France
October 9, 1918

Dear Folks;

Received your two letters dated Sept. 2nd yesterday morning and was mighty glad to get them. Had received only one letter from you previous to this, and one from Paul Merrifield who is over here and not far from me, but I can't tell where. He told me in his letter that he was attending an artillery school and the reason I know it is not far away is that when I am driving north of town up in the hills and rolling country, any time I stop my motor I can hear his guns, their steady distant growl and once in a while a "heavy" emits a more distinct grunt. On one or more occasions I have heard it plain like an approaching thunder storm. Burt Cathcart, Van Aiken, Peets, Chas. Marshall, Roy Parker, the two Henry brothers, Ellis Emmons, G. Deeters, Will Dawe are all here in this regiment yet but it don't look much like the organization that landed here, as the personnel has changed considerably.

Yesterday we lost our colonel, the finest representative of American military manhood that ever followed the Stars and Stripes on foreign soil. He is six feet tall, clean cut as a Greek statue; his features are too masculine to be handsome, weather beaten into a heavy leather tan, with grim lines about the mouth, heavy jaws, big nose, full lips, and set under dark heavy brows were a pair of cold steel gray eyes that were as bright and carried the luster of youth and radiating from the outer corners were many tiny wrinkles which grew long and deep or short and light according to his moods; an expert horseman, and on his breast the highest award for marksmanship given in the U.S Armies and which is worn only by a very few men.

Always stern, always sober, he went about among his men with a quiet dignity that compelled respect and the highest esteem from everyone, with no effort on his part. His was a personality which dominated every individual, when he spoke his voice had a deep resonance that trembled deep down in his heavy chest. Always distinct and short spoken, he never had very much to say but what he did say meant a whole lot. A natural born leader of men with a big future.

On the station platform that afternoon was a little group of officers and the Reg. Band and most of us of the Headquarters Detachment. The band played our Regt. Song and as it finished the train pulled in drawn by a huge American locomotive with a big Yankee campaign hat in the cab window. The Colonel shook hands all around, with "good bye, good luck," and as he mounted the steps the band struck up "Auld Lang Syne." We all stood at salute, the band continued to play there in the drizzling rain as the train rolled slowly out of the station. The old Colonel stood there in an answering statue of farewell, his face drawn and gray, as were many others. The cords on my eyeballs ached and pulled and I had a chunk in my throat big as a barrel, and I think there were many others, as each singularly avoided looking at the other and there wasn't much to say as we left the station. We didn't realize the hold he had on our affections 'til the time came for the parting. He was too valuable a man to be kept back here and will be put in command of a more active regiment.

Was just handed a letter from Geo. Rosewarne. He came over here with the first troops to sail for France. Gee! But I was glad to get it and he is only about three hours auto drive from me. Wish I could get the chance to go and see him.

October 10, 1918

This is a h-ll of a place to be at a time like this. All my training is being wasted back here. I can't shoot at any Boches and they are licking the deuce out of them up on the line. I asked to be taken along with the Colonel and he told me he would see what he could do, and I think he did try to have me transferred as his driver but he was allowed only one man and he took his personal orderly. While I have one of the best jobs in the Regt., I would gladly jump at a chance to drive up front or even shoulder a gun; I wouldn't care, but it is beginning to look as though the thing would all be over before our turn comes to go in.

The slogan over here is ---Hell, Heaven or Hoboken by Christmas and it sure will be Hoboken for we have them beaten already. Yes, two weeks ago they were decisively beaten, it only depends upon how long it will take it to soak into their thick heads. They are still thinking that every day we will be obliged to relax our terrible pressure, but if they knew what I know, if they could see the unlimited resources of materials and power that we haven't begun to use yet. Our pressure will continue to become more terrible until if they continue to struggle or to resist they will be crushed so utterly they can't even survive as a nation. We have a new weapon as yet unused which gives us the power to annihilate the whole damnable race.

A Yanks life over here takes many funny turns. Along with their fine percheron horses over here they work many of these little Spanish burros or donkey hitched to two wheeled carts. Every day I pass Yankee soldiers perched on one of these carts driving one of these diminutive animals to town for supplies.

Their table trucks were rather scarce around here just before the big push up front, but we have plenty now.

One day I was coasting down a long hill with the motor cut off and had slowed down to make a sharp turn. It is well I did so, for there just around the corner was a big two wheeled cart to which was hitched a little black and white burro, crossways of the narrow road, with a Yankee soldier facing him and pulling on both reins. The little cuss had his front feet planted firmly well ahead of him and sitting back on his haunches he refused to budge, despite the warning he was taking from the driver of a huge ten ton American truck which was coming up the hill and could not pass with its load for the front because of a 400 pound jackass. Right here I got a firsthand opinion of what a doughboy and a truck driver think of French jackass. They tried English and French on him, but nothing doing. They finally got him and the cart square with the road, but he still refused to travel—guess he thought it was his birthday or something, but he was doomed to an awakening, for as soon as he was headed straight up the hill they run up behind the cart with the truck and I nearly died laughing at them. The doughboy perched up on the cart flailing the donkey and being pushed from behind by a huge motor truck with a grinning Yank at the wheel. So much for Yankee methods. Had that burrow realized what he was up against he wouldn't never have started anything. A doughboy and a truck driver are a hard combination to combat, even for a jackass.

These doughboys over here can put a gas mask on a Missouri mule despite their reputation for kicking with all four feet at once.

Am wondering how long it took for you to get my cablegram. Everything is o.k. so far as I am concerned, plenty of everything we could wish for, a comfortable place to sleep and plenty to eat. Am afraid I won't get a hand in at the finish even if they don't send me up front pretty soon. Everything is all over now but the shouting, one or two more big drives and we will have the Huns whipped to a standstill. They are squealing pretty hard now.

Well I guess I'll close this and get it started on its journey—it is not so bad is it, when I can cable you at any time for a little over a dollar of American money? Give my best regards to my friends and tell them it is not my fault that I haven't had a shot at a Hun yet.

Paul E. Steffe Gives Life for His Country
Son of Rev. and Mrs. J. W. Steffe
Was Killed in Action in France*

Corporal Paul Ellis Steffe of Co. F. 126 Inf., 32d Div. F. F., son of Rev. Jacob W. and Julia A. Steffe, was born at Perrington, Mich., December 4, 1892 and died in France, August 30, 1918 from the effects of wounds received in action.

The first of July, 1917, he enlisted at Jackson, Mich., and was a member of Co. L, 31st Michigan, until the National Guard was disbanded and merged into Co. F, 126th Inf. From Jackson he went to Grayling, from there to Waco, Texas. The middle of January they were sent to Camp Merritt, N. J., where they remained in barracks until February 16, at which time they sailed for France, arriving at a port of France March 4, 1918. Their first training was received at Champlette, and from there they were sent to Alsace, and then moved farther north to Lorraine.

When he came out of action after the battle of Chateau Thierry, which was his third offensive, his captain had been killed in action and only 28 out of his company were left. The 32nd Division was known as the "Iron Jaw Division" and was used as shock troops. Paul wore his sharp-shooter's medal which he had received for accuracy.

After the battle at Chauteau Thierry the 126th went back into the woods for a much needed and well deserved rest, but they soon received their orders to move on to St. Mihiel, his fourth offensive, where he was wounded so severely that he died August 30th.

Paul was of a very bright and cheerful disposition and never during the past year has there been a complaint of any kind in any of his letters home, nothing but hope and cheer and always the word that he wanted to stay by it all until the end.

Paul's death is the first death in a family of ten, and while it is a crushing blow to them all, it is with pride they can know and feel that never was there a cleaner, better or braver life ever given for its country and humanity than his. It can be truthfully said of him, "Greater love hath no man than this, that a man lay down his life for his friends." John 15:13

(*Reprinted in the *Fremont Times-Indicator* October 10, 1918 from the *Newaygo Republican*)

Corporal Howard Hines
Co. 10, M. T. D. Group, M. G. T. C., Camp Hancock, Augusta, Ga.
October 12, 1918

Dear Folks at Home:

Saturday afternoon and I have quite a bunch of letters to write. As you may or may not happen to know, I am writing the first one to you, as I almost always do. Will admit I am a poor letter writer but so far I have managed to get by without any trouble.

Did a big washing this afternoon. Took two hours to wash all the handkerchiefs, sox, pants, underclothes, towels and leggings that had accumulated.

What do you think of what the papers have to say of the war? Sounds pretty good and I only hope it really is as good as it sounds. Am figuring that the Kaiser will wish a good many times that he was through with the mess before America gets through with him. Wish I had my way with him.

We are drilling at machine gun work again. All of the drilling is done with open formation a yard interval being kept between men all of the time. Quite true it is not as easy to work that way, but so far it has been effective. A couple of days ago some officers were found in the Base hospital who were accused of being German agents. They were regular Army doctors and according to report, had managed to do away with over a hundred of the sick men (some not very sick either) by giving them the wrong medicine purposely. They were found out by a patient who was a druggist in civil life and knew the medicine that should be given. They went to give him the wrong stuff, not knowing that he knew. It was then he noticed and refused to take the dope. The Doctors didn't even get a chance to get away. Would like to get a crack at them with the machine guns. Eh? Well yes.

Passed the inspection this morning without any fault finding. My machine gun had received two hours of solid work and my rifle had gotten 1½ hours. As for myself I don't remember. Only know that with my clean pants on for inspection I came in for breakfast this morning and sat down on some corn syrup carelessly spilled there by a waiter. Was the only clean pair I had so I kept them on. Luckily for me they passed inspection, though I don't know how it happened.

Am sending you a little sample of the South in a separate box. Don't know as you have ever seen any before, or very much at least. We see it here by acre on acre, the same as a corn or potato crop in the North.

Have not had any more hikes since the one of which I told you.

October 22, 1918

Dear Folks:

Tuesday evening and have just gotten in from drill. The company is standing retreat just at present. Have about three minutes before supper and then we go out to drill some more.

I get up at 5:30, shave, shine shoes, make up bunk and am dressed when we go out for reveille at 6:10. By 6:30 we are through and go into mess. Get through by 6:45 and then have a half hour to clean guns, sweep out the tent, etc. etc., wash up, etc.

Drill until 11:30 when we come in to dinner and don't go out until 1:15. Also polish shoes and clean up in general during this time. Drill then until 5:00 when we come in and wash, take bath maybe, or sit down for ten minutes. Have mess and when we get through it is 6:00. At 6:15 we go out to drill field for another session and return by 7:30 or 7:45. Then clean guns which we finish by 8:15 probably. Then wash clothes and maybe take a bath if we didn't before supper. We are through by nine o'clock after which time we can do some writing in the mess hall if we have the time and inclination. This enumeration of duties is just to let you know that I am not spoiling for want of something to do.

For supper we had stew—the best known and most cussed article of food in the army ration—which is made of pieces of beef, spuds, onions, thin juice or gravy. Had bread, lima beans, sweet potatoes and tea. Usual breakfast is something like this —bread, coffee, oatmeal or rice or corn flakes and maybe stew or "dogs" left from night before, and sometimes syrup for bread. Twice we have had bacon and eggs, when the company is small. Beans is another staple article of food.

Was called before the Major tonight to give evidence against one of the prisoners from our company. In the army, you know, there is as much penalty for talking back to or disobeying a non-com. as to a commissioned officer.

Cpl. Dallas L. Darling
139th Aero Squad., Verdun Front, France, A. E.F., via New York
October 15, 1918

Dear Folks at home:

It is almost 7:00 a.m. and I am at the hangars ready for work. We have to walk ½ mile from our barracks to the hangars. It's chilly here mornings so we have two blow torches in a big pipe and it makes an improvised stove hard to beat. We are on

Letters and Related Articles 1918

"alert" now and can't leave the hangars only at calling distance for our planes might be needed at a few moments warning.

I just finished reading an August *Times-Indicator* and glad of the home news too.

This cold rainy weather is like the fall weather at home. We are provided with high rubber boots and have all our knitted goods that you sent us last winter while in Texas. All are nice and new yet. We have lots of clean straw to fill ticks so we sleep warm and dry. We can hear the big guns at the front all the while and by the looks of things this job won't last long. Many are betting when it ends and the general bet is "no fighting after Jan. 1st" but some think it ends sooner.

We have been through towns and cities that had been through shell fire and it surely plays hob with everything. One city has been torn up and a company of Austrian war prisoners had been put to work cleaning up the city.

Today our squad, No. 139 put 11 Boche machines out of commission and no losses for us. One of our pilots brought down four alone. Not so bad for a day's record. When a pilot brings down five enemy machines he is called an "ace." Lieut. Putman was the U. S. "ace of aces" but he was killed in the Toul drive. He was one of our squad. He had 14 planes to his credit. Lieut. Fouck is the "ace of aces" for France. Up to date he has 64 planes. It's fine to hear the pilots tell of the fights they have in the air and it makes one proud to know the machine you have worked on for hours has brought down a

Hun machine. Mine got one the other day and I felt then that I had helped a little and was paid for working all night and all day Sunday to get my motor in shape for the flight on Monday.

The plane I call mine is No. 4. They all have names painted on them in large letters. Most of them are named for the pilot's wife or sweetheart. Mine is "Little Joe." The Lieutenant who flies this machine is the youngest flyer and I am the youngest motor mechanic in the squadron.

One plane here has a Michigan University pennant on it. The pilot is from Battle Creek and a dandy fellow. We two are all the Michigan boys in our squad. At present we have four squadrons working on the "alert." Our machines are the fastest on the Front.

A few days ago our group got 24 Hun planes without the loss of a pilot. I have lately had a nice ride of 60 kilometers in a touring car to carry gas to a pilot who had landed that far from the hangars. We went through cities that were torn and deserted and other places where the "building up" had begun. The names of these places I am not allowed to tell you now but it won't be long 'till you can know where I have been and some of the things I have seen.

I was made 1st class in August and Corporal the 1st of October. You asked me if there was any chance for a furlough. Gee! No! we don't want a furlough now. We want to see the end of course and the way to get it is for everybody to work until it comes. I am well, although working extra hours and harder than usual, but the time is surely getting short now until we will see a complete surrender of enemy.

**Herman Schuiteman
Care of Reg. Off., A.P.O. 712, Am. E. F.
October 15, 1918**

Charlie Andrews and family,

Dear Friends: I often think of you folks and as I have some time this morning I thought I'd let you know that I am feeling fine and having a good time. I got my first mail from home day before yesterday, five letters and two cards of which two letters were not from home. The letters from the folks were dated July 22nd, 26th and Aug 10th. It certainly seemed good to get them and now I'm longing for some more.

I don't know how long it will last but I'm having an easy time of it at present. I am billeted comfortably and get excellent food. I spend my spare time reading the works of long winded authors and poets which I never had time to read in civilian life. The country hereabouts is like our native hills and lakes only the hills are regular young mountains whose tops are covered with pine forest and big rocks, the sides being divided into small farms the boundaries of which are marked by hedges and stone fences. With the red tile roofed farm houses it makes pretty scenery. But I'll be glad to see the First lake and the little hills around it again. By the looks of things now it won't be so very long.

Give my regards to your mother and father and Vera, and write me some time.

FRED HOAD MAKES SUPREME SACRIFICE

Son of Mr. and Mrs. Chas. Hoad
Killed in Active Service in France Sept. 4
October 17, 1918
Fremont-Times Indicator

Mr. and Mrs. Chas. Hoad of this city (Fremont) received a letter from England October 12 conveying the sad news of the death of their son, Fred, who died September 4 in France while in the service of the British government. Fred served with the British forces in Palestine and while there wrote the interesting letter which appeared in the Times-Indicator last April. After serving in the Holy Lands he was sent to France for army service. He leaves a wife and six children. In his last letter to Mr. and Mrs. Hoad he wrote:

Dear Mother and Father:

I received your letter while I was holding the firing line but the thought of your prayers on my behalf and for the sake of my loved ones and being in the position I was at the time when reading it, brought tears to my eyes. But thank God He has spared me once more and I am having a little rest at the back of the line, but I still put my trust in God and I thank Him every day not only for my safety but for my mates and I often try and show them their sins they are living in, to bring them out of darkness into light. Now goodbye and may God bless and help you all for many years to come.

Fred.

James Tiesinga
October, 24, 1918
Fremont Times-Indicator

James Tiesinga, son of Andrew Tiesinga, died at Camp Custer of pneumonia Sunday, Oct. 20, at the age of 26 years. The body was brought here (Fremont) October 22 and the funeral service held from his home yesterday noon. Interment in Maple Grove cemetery.

Glenn Taylor
October 24, 1918
Fremont Times-Indicator

Glenn Taylor, son of Mrs. Rosa Taylor, was born March 9, 1896, in Sherman township, Newaygo county, and died at Camp Custer of pneumonia following Spanish Influenza, Oct. 16, 1918, at the age of 22 years, 7 months and 6 days.

The body was brought here Thursday and interment took place Friday afternoon in Maple Grove cemetery, Rev. J. W. Esveld conducting a short service at the grave

Ralph L. Hilton
M. G. Co., 167th V. S. Inf., Am. E. F., via New York
October 24, 1918

Sirs:

Not having much to do this afternoon, will try and write you a few lines to let the people at home know I am still alive and not hanging on a wire fence somewhere in No Man's Land.

Our division left Camp Custer on the _____of July and landed somewhere in France on the _____of August. The weather was fine when the division crossed. I have been transferred to another division since my arrival, I am now with the 42nd division, or what is better known as The Rainbow Division. It was one of the first to cross the ocean after United States declared war on Germany. There are six young men from Fremont in this division with me.

It is a wonderful thing that Uncle Sam has done over here since he declared war. You could not make the people at home believe it. The people in France are very peculiar. Their living apartment and the barn, also the pig pen and chicken coop are all in one large stone building. They call these places billets. The French people are very accommodating, they do everything in their power for the American soldiers for they realize what the America soldiers are doing for them. The great wonder of all, to the German prisoner in France, is how did the United States get those large railroad engines over to France. They can't just understand it. I would like to tell the people at home a great deal more but I will have to wait until I get back, which I hope won't be very long. You see the government is very strict about what we write in our letters so you see one has to be pretty careful what he says.

I hope that everything is getting along nicely in Fremont as everything is going very smoothly over here.

Corporal J. M. Leslie
October 31, 1918

The following letter was written to the parents of Don M. Dickinson by a fellow soldier. Unfortunately the first page is missing from microfilm, so the letter picks up in the middle.

...until 4:00 on the 15th. The French on both sides of them fell back without informing our boys. The consequence was that the Huns flanked Companies B and C on both sides, and surrounded them, with the inevitable results. Company C, Don M's Company went into the fight with 228 men; ___ managed to escape unhurt, 25 were killed, 15 wounded and found in hospitals of the Allies, 160 were missing. The boys of our Company who were missing have nearly all been located.

The last I saw of Don and my brother was about 9 o'clock Sunday night. My brother had placed your son along with another of the boys in charge of one of the guns. It was there, during the heavy shelling from the German lines, that your son was missed, and the other boy was wounded, and it was this boy who told me about your son. This boy died before he got to the hospital, after lying in the woods with several others of us from Monday morning until Saturday evening when we were found by the French Red Cross and taken to the hospital.

The orders of B and C Companies were to hold the lines, and they did, as is shown by the Hun retreat from that date.

I guess this is about all I can say in regard to the battle. Your son was a splendid soldier, always took great delight in his work and was well thought of among all the boys of our Company. If alive, he is a prisoner in Germany. If not, you may know that he died bravely fighting for his Country.

Author's note:

Donald M. Dickinson was working as a farm laborer in West Chicago when he registered for the draft on June 5th, 1917. On May 3, 1918, he left New York on the ship, City of Calcutta. He was listed as Don M. Dickinson PVT 110 INF 28 DIV, died in France July 15, 1918, aged 20, buried in Woodlawn Cemetery, Marine City, St. Clair County, Michigan, USA, by U.S. Find a Grave Index.

Pvt. Roy C. Gardenour
34th Amb. Co., Sanitary Training, 7th Div. A. D. F.
November 1, 1918

Dear sister:

Received your letter of Oct. 13. Glad to hear you are all well. Hope you have received some of my letters by this time. Guess I won't need to tell you anything about the war, as you will see all about it in the papers. But believe me, everyone is feeling gay.

They have quit talking about when the war will end and are now figuring how long it will take to get home, which route, ship, etc. they prefer.

It certainly is nice to roll up in our blankets and sleep all night long without being awakened by the speeding up of the already brisk pounding of our guns and the whiz bang of shells that usually follow. It would be hard for me to explain what it is like to be between our artillery and the enemy's during a barrage with shells going both ways. Some of them whistling the last long strain of America or star Spangled Banner, the lightning-like flashes and the roar that makes the ground tremble, with now and then a signal rocket and maybe an air squadron flying over head with powerful search lights directing the fire from the anti-aircraft guns, whose shells burst high in the air. All those things are best observed while on guard. It's simply grand. It would take a find display of fireworks to beat it.

Well, I am office orderly at present, and will try and write once or twice a week if convenient. It is now chow time so will close. Hope to hear from you again soon.

November 15, 1918

Dear brother:

Will write you a few lines this morning to let you know that everything is o.k. with us over here. How are you all by now? Hope you haven't got the Flu in your neighborhood, yet.

Received Letha's letter of Oct. 26. She wanted to know what country we were in. I know my few letters did not give much information as to where we were located but I suppose you have received letters from me by now that give you a good idea as to where we are located.

We may be allowed to write more in a few weeks. But if I don't write much I can tell you some good tales when I come home.

Anyway there are a few things that I won't forget for some time. Our company certainly did some good work, staying with it to the finish. Don't know when we will get to the U.S.A., but think we will spend the winter overseas alright.

Will bring you a souvenir when I come home. Most anything is a souvenir that comes from over here, you know. Such as a little bean shaped pebble which I picked up on the bank of the Neuse river, or a little door knob from an old castle which is claimed to have been built in the year of 1101. It is said Joan of Arc lived in it for a time.

Suppose you have some snow by this time. It has not snowed here yet.

John Scott
St. Nazarre (sp), France
November 2, 1918

Dearest sister, father and mother:

Well I am in the best of health and expect you are in the same condition. I am going to write you a letter and this one won't be censored because they wanted every boy to write a letter to his father and he could write anything he wanted in the letter and seal it. This is the only day and we can write but one letter.

The weather is fine. We had two weeks of sunshine but had a little shower this afternoon. We don't see any snow out here at all, and it does not freeze much, some nights a little frost. I suppose you are having some pretty cold weather there now and have snow. We won't see any here.

We worked today and it does not seem much like Sunday here. They are in a hurry to get this camp cleared up because we have to have it cleared up before the new year as the French take it over then. We have lots of trucks to set up and clean up. I don't know what we will have to do when we get this camp cleared, but I suppose move to another one. I hope we can go home, but it is hard to say. Some of the officers think we will be ready to go home about January or February, and others say that we won't be home until the fourth of July. So that is about all we know about it. We have it good here, have good barracks to sleep in, and good stuff to eat and all we want of it. Part of the time we get butter on our bread. We have French women here for cooks. They can be hired cheap. Don't worry, I am getting along fine. Of course I would like to go home but will have to wait patiently.

Joe is getting along fine. We were together in the same barracks but he had to move to another camp last night about one mile away. But we can visit back and forth just the same. He was back to see me today. He is working in the blacksmith shop and I am still working in the warehouse handling tires and canned goods of all kinds. We can do the work easy because we look out and don't hurt ourselves.

Well I received two letters Thursday and then Friday so I had something to do. Some were written from the 13 to the 21 of October, over a month old, but I was glad to get them.

Well how is the flu coming along? We don't have any here at all.

I suppose we will have to eat our Thanksgiving dinner in France this year, and probably our Christmas dinner too. I wish we could eat them at home, that would be the happiest dinner I ever ate. But we will have to wait patiently and have faith in the Lord and Savior and he will bring us safely home again.

It certainly takes money to buy things here. They charge 10c for an apple. We can buy all the beer and whiskey we want here, but I don't care for that stuff.

Write as often as you can. Best wishes to all. Merry Christmas and Happy New Year to you all.

George Baars
Field Hosp. 121, 106 San. Tr., Bordeaux, France
November ?, 1918

My Dearest Mother and All:

We have moved again and instead of being at Brest, France, we are at Bordeaux. Bordeaux is in the southern part of France, and the weather is quite mild and the roses are in bloom. This is a nice camp and not much mud for it's a nice loam sand. We are in good tile barracks with good warm quarters and a good place to eat and plenty of it.

I don't know what we will do, for our part of the war is over with. We might be transferred but of course nobody knows yet what we will do. I hope we stay here until we are ready to come home, which will probably be some time yet.

In Time of War

We came across the sea on one of Holland's big ships called the Rijndam. This ship was 650 feet long and carried nearly 3000 passengers besides a big cargo. We got on the ship at 2 o'clock Sunday afternoon, Oct. 27th and arrived in France Saturday, Nov. 9th. This is a long time to be on the water and we were all glad to see land. We could see the outline of the rocky coast of Brest for miles, perhaps 10 or 15 miles. We watched the outline grow and grow and finally could see some trees, then some buildings and finally passed in single file into the harbor and anchored. There were ten other transports that came with us and we were guarded by several sub-destroyers and a large battleship. It's a real sight, Mother, and I wish you could have seen us on the ocean. Most of the trip was fine but we had one stormy day and night which I will long remember. I'll tell you all about it when I come home. We saw the big Vaterland ship loaded with troops and that was surely a sight. I think it carried 12,000 troops.

On our way from Brest to our present camp we came through Lorient, Mantes, LaRochelle, Maran, and Bordeaux.

Yesterday was Thanksgiving day and I went to one of the best services I have ever been to. We surely have a lot to be thankful for, Mother dear, if we will only realize it. It will soon be Christmas and I hope you will get this before that time. Don't worry about us while we stay at Bordeaux for we are well cared for.

For breakfast we had good rice and gravy, good beef steak, good white bread, stewed prunes and good hot coffee. For dinner we had roast beef, brown gravy, mashed potatoes and good bread and apple sauce. That's plenty good for anyone.

Well Mother I must close for this time and wish you all a Merry Christmas and Happy New Year.

Glen Smith
Co. B, 104th Engrs., A. E. F., Am. P. O. 765, France
November 3, 1918

Dear Mother:

We are back in rest camp now and pretty comfortably quartered again, and it surely seems good. Maybe I won't have to go back again with all this peace talk that is floating around. I hope not anyway. I saw Darwin Ross two days after the big drive started but haven't seen him since. But one can't always tell by that. Maybe he is all right yet. You know he is in the 115 Inf., the same division, but in a regiment over on the Alsace-Leraine front. I used to see him quite often but don't know where they are quartered now. We have been upon the Verdun front which you probably saw by the papers. Some front too, but we did not have it so bad. Most everybody got away all o.k.

I heard from Ray the other day and he is still at the same place.

Later—

Well I have been over here a little over four months now and have done two tricks at the front, and have still a good hide. So you see it isn't so bad. We are in a rest camp now about 60 miles from the front, and Gee, it seems good too. We have just come from the Verdun Front, the "hardest boiled" lines in the whole section. Some time, believe me.

Saw Darwin Ross the second day after the great drive started but haven't seen him since. He is in the 115th Inf. They certainly did some good work up there.

This is the best country we have been in since we came to France and it is certainly fine. The village we are in has five gin mills, four stores, a large church and probably 2000 inhabitants in peace times. It falls considerably short of that now. It isn't such a bad little place. We are not over 7 or 8 kilometers from a large city, if you know how far that is.

GOLD STAR ADDED TO LOCAL SERVICE FLAG

Wm. Hutchinson, Aged 22, Died in France
November 7, 1918
Fremont Times-Indicator

Fremont added another gold star to its service flag last Saturday night when a telegram from the war department was received by Otis Hutchinson, who lives 5 ½ miles south and 1 ¾ miles west of this city, conveying the sad news of the death of his son, Wm. Hutchinson, which occurred in France October 20 following an attack of pneumonia. The young man was 22 years of age.

Mr. Hutchinson has been in the military service of his country since the 29th day of last April, when impatient to await his turn in the draft order, he enlisted and was sent to Camp Custer for training. In July he was sent to Long Island and after a short stay there he embarked with the 85th division to join the American Expeditionary Forces on French soil. He was a member of the Company A of the 337th Infantry. He is the first of Fremont boys who joined the colors to die on foreign soil.

Mr. Hutchinson is survived by his parents, Mr. and Mrs. Otis Hutchinson, five sisters, Mrs. Mattie Whitman, Mrs. Lizzie Maxson and Alice, Maggie and Anna Hutchinson and two brothers, Ora and Peter Hutchinson.

Wag. Juell J. Hewitt
Co. F, 2nd Engrs. Am. E. F., Luxembourg
November 13, 1918

Dear Parents and All:

I will try and drop you a few lines to let you know that I am still on earth and in the best of health and I surely hope you are all the same. From looks of present situation, I am living in hopes of seeing you all again, and all my friends of course. No one knows how soon that will be but here's hoping, the sooner the better. They won't find me lagging when they say go.

The boys over here are surely a happy bunch, so if I get this all upside down, don't blame me, or think anything about it, as one of my pals is singing everything he knows and reciting all the poetry that we ever heard tell of. He is certainly a queer fellow, although he is nearly old enough to be my father. He thinks I'm his boy.

I have to stop and turn over a few cooties. We all have them and plenty too. I haven't seen any one who hasn't got them. I sure will be glad when I can get some place and get cleaned up once more. I can't tell when I have had my clothes changed or even off. We never know when we go to bed where we will be when daylight comes. Just a little incident that happened to me a short time ago. I thought I had stopped for the night and was spreading out my blankets. I had my bed all made and was just about to go to bed. You know we sleep wherever we happen to stop. I was just ready to crawl in (heavy marching orders) when I heard my name ring out through the air. In responding to the call I found that I was to go to the front (right now) although I was already close enough, so that the Huns had been all day dropping those big ones awfully close. There was nothing for me to do but take up my bed and prepare to go as dark as it was. In a reasonable length of time I had four teams lined up and ready to start with my guide. I started. Things went fine all the way up, other than the roads. Because of the traffic, traveling was some slower than I could have gone and I guess Huns had lost track of me, for they had not bothered me for a few hours, and I knew something was wrong. I arrived at my destination fine and dandy, got my wagons loaded and received my orders to await further orders. So wait I did. But I can tell you that it was not because I wanted to, it was there the Huns got me located again. Things were going fine when a whistling noise was heard and the explosion came just a few yards away. Well you should have seen us scatter. We just went all directions, as things were rather warm.

In due time it quieted down a little. As we had already had blankets spread out on the ground we went back and climbed in to wait for orders, hoping they would come to start. The Huns had lost track of us or they had something else in view because they continued to shell but a little distance away so we thought it safe to go to bed. The funny part of it was we would lay there in bed and when one would light up the sky with its explosion we would duck our heads under the blankets to await the falling pieces of dirt and shell. One of the boys who was there said, "I'll be darned if I will lay here listening for those pieces to fall," as some were coming mighty close to us. So he left us to seek shelter—and he found his last one. And so it went on until we pulled out. It surely sounded good to us when the order came to leave. It didn't take us very long to get out.

I got the papers and two letters from you and one from Esther last night dated October 14. Well I suppose you know I am 21 now, the last day of fighting, just as throngs were finished up. You would have died with laughter if you could have seen me. Can you imagine me with a mustache, it was too funny to keep. Oh, yes, if you want to see my picture, it is in the Saturday Evening Post of Sept 14. I am standing on the left with my shirt unbuttoned. I don't suppose you would recognize me in it. I just saw the picture today. It was taken on the bank of the Marne river. I can tell you more about it if I ever get back, which I am in hopes will be soon.

I just got a letter from you dated Sept. 30 and also two Fremont papers which I was very glad to get. I can say that I am pretty well satisfied myself and I am not intending to make a profession of army life so care very little about wearing stripes, as stripes are no honor now days. In my travels I find that stripes are of no particular benefit. I also believe as my pal says, it takes a private to make the guns talk. Although I am not a private, I don't figure myself any higher and want to come back to my friends as the boy I left. This war has made a man of me, as I suppose I am now anyway seeing I can vote to help my country.

Now Mother, I owe so many letters that I have been unable to write and we could not get them censored so I will leave it for you to keep them posted on my behalf and whereabouts.

I remain your son and friend to all over in good U.S.A.

In Time of War

PROCLAMATION

The tragic war, which for fifty-one months has rocked the foundations of the earth is over. Forty millions of men have been under arms and more than eight million human lives have been sacrificed.

But now peace has come to calm the world and it is fitting, while we mourn for those who have yielded up their lives in the cause of Democracy, that we should rejoice and give thanks for peace with victory.

Therefore, I, Erwin Tinney, Mayor of the city of Fremont, do hereby designate and proclaim Sunday, November 17th, next, VICTORY SUNDAY, and I call upon the people of the city of Fremont to gather on that day in their accustomed places of worship and there by prayer and praise to render thanks to Almighty God for the triumph of our cause and the restoration of peace on earth.

Given under my hand this 14th day of November in the year of our Lord, 1918.

Erwin Tinney

Mayor of City of Fremont

Harry Dursema
Motor Ambulance Co. 34, A.P.O. 793, Am E. F., France
November 14, 1918

Dear Mother:

I am well and having a fine time now that the war is at an end. We heard a few days before the firing ceased that it was going to take place but didn't believe it.

We were sure glad when eleven o'clock came and all the guns ceased to their thundering. I am glad that I have seen active service at the front although I had some close calls and have gone out in shell fire when I never expected to come back. I drove my ambulance at night when the shells were dropping all around me and so dark I couldn't see the road. The flash of guns would blind me, but had to keep on going. Some experience though and I shall have something to talk about for some time to come.

Glenn Mathews is a few miles from where our station is and I am going to try to find him. I saw John Nyhoff of Fremont a couple of days ago and had a fine visit with him. He is the first boy from home that I have seen although there are a lot of Michigan boys close to us. I also met a nurse that had been in the Hackley hospital in Muskegon for a couple of years. It seems good to meet people from around home.

We are all anxious to start back now but of course we know that it will take some time to transport all of our boys home.

We won't be the first to go although I think we shall be home by the first of February.

The weather here is getting better since the heavy gun fire has ceased, and the sun is shining. It makes us feel better and I hope it stays this way all of the time I am here.

We have lots of fun running around the trenches and dugouts the Germans left, and picking up souvenirs. I could get a car full of them but haven't the ambition to carry them around. I have some papers that were dropped from an aeroplane a couple of weeks ago, some buttons and such articles as that. I also have some pieces of shrapnel which struck my car and will bring them home to show you what the men here had to stand when under shell fire. We were up in front 33 days and believe me, I have seen all I care to see of it. It certainly is terrible. I started to change a tire one day and the shells started whistling and dropping so close I had to drop on my stomach and when I thought I had a good chance I ran for a dugout. The way we saved ourselves a good many times was by dropping just as quickly as we could. In that way the pieces are not so liable to hit you as when standing up, but when we were on the ambulance we couldn't hear them coming and had to trust in God to bring us through.

Well, I hope I can get home soon as I am sick of France now and want to get back and start my electrical business going in good shape.

I suppose the snow will be falling again soon and cold weather will set in for a few months. That is one thing I dread as we shall probably cross the deep blue when it is rough so we will have to stay inside and get seasick.

Well, Mother, I hope you are feeling happy now and will write all the news from home and I shall let you know what I am doing as often as I can.

Milan Jackson
France
November 15, 1918

Dear Grandfather and All:

I have now a few moments to write you a line and let you know that I am still alive and healthy and sincerely hope you are the same.

During the past several months we have been on the lines most of the time and of course had no chance to write.

Of course you know by this time that Fritz has given up and is turning his back on what little of France and Belgium he still holds while the Americans with our division included, are following up the retreat to the Rhine where we will establish the lines. Of course this will be a long march, but knowing that we will soon have peace it won't be so bad. Most of the hardship is past, as we will probably billet in towns along the way, which will be much better than out of doors in pup tents, even though the towns are a great deal in ruins.

Of course it will be slow going, and the Boches have to move out ahead of us and their moving facilities are very poor. The French prisoners coming back across the lines say that they have no motor trucks and most of their horses are gone. This is certainly a fact for there is no end to the dead horses found along the road which have been killed by the American artillery. They certainly make a nice mess to march in all day, especially when they have been there about a week.

Well, I certainly hope that peace terms will be agreed upon and that we can get back by the first of March anyway. I would hate to see any more fighting now that I have gotten through this all O. K. I was certainly lucky, for there are only a few of the old men that got through without a wound. In the last battle I was hit twice by machine gun bullets but they were only light flesh wounds and I never even went for first aid.

Well, I am going to run short of paper so must close. Hoping this finds you both in good health.

Letters and Related Articles 1918

**Mech. Lawrence B. Henry
Am. E. F., France
November 17, 1918**

Dear Folks at Home:

We have moved around considerably lately and I have not received any mail for some time. There is no use to write war news as you get it before or as soon as we do. I am glad it is over and hope everything is settled soon, as it will be before you receive this letter. I haven't seen Frank for a few days. He is about five miles from here. I was over to see him a while ago. He had made a long hike and was rather tired. I am thinking of riding a wheel over where he is and see if there is any mail for me.

Well, I expect to be on my way home before long, in not more than two months at the longest. We are working on casuals now, who are men who have been up to the front and lost all their belongings. Several thousand come here to be fitted out every day.

We are allowed to tell where we are now, what we belong to and what we are doing. I am just a few kilometers from Toul. I don't know where Ellis is now but I think he is driving a truck. Clyde Britton and Walter Wolford are with me now. Wherever I go to write there are two or three hundred soldiers making all kinds of noise and it is hard to write when some one is bothering.

France is a beautiful country. It is like a garden compared to the States; the fields are so small. Our stay in France is not very long now from all report. I hope they send us home in time to start work in the spring. We have had good weather here for several days but it looks like a change tonight. It sprinkles and is warmer.

I received your letters the other day and was sure glad to get them. It takes a long time for mail to get here but when it does come it seems good. Well I must close, hoping this finds you all as well and good natured as I am.

S. A. Colman
Colonel of Inf. Chief of Staff
Headquarters 20th, Div. Am. E. F.
November 18, 1918

Now that its part in the action north of Verdun is finished, the Division Commander wishes to take occasion to express his deep appreciation of the skill, endurance and courage shown by the officers and men of the division including both staff and line, in a most difficult and prolonged fight. Everything was opposed to our success. We had a most determined enemy in our front and one skilled by four years of warfare, whereas this was the first real fight of our division. On most days the weather was bad and the ground difficult, added to the fact that the fighting was largely in woods. On account of the woods, ravines and dampness, gassing of our troops was easily accomplished and full advantage of this fact was taken by the enemy to whom the use of gas was an old story.

Without exception the organizations of the division and their commanders responded heroically to every call upon them and at the end of the fight we had not only gained our objectives, but we held them and turned them over to our successors. We advanced some eight kilometers through the enemy's trenches, and captured over 2100 prisoners, seven cannon, about 200 machine guns and a large quantity of miscellaneous military property. We had the pleasure of seeing two hostile divisions withdrawn from our front, one of which was composed of some of the best troops of the German army. On many occasions captured prisoners stated that our attack was so rapid and our fire so effective that they were overwhelmed and had nothing to do but to retire or surrender.

In this brief summing up the results of its first fight the Division commander feels that every officer and man participating, whether in planning or in executing, should feel a just pride in what has been accomplished. This is but repeating the praise that has been bestowed upon the division by both American and French superior commanders.

**Harold Zerlaut
Chanute Field (Champaign County, Illinois)
November 18, 1918 (from family archives)**

Dear Neva:

I have received a couple letters from you and one from ma today. I have not written sooner because we did not know what was going to happen next. The shipment that was to go out has been called off on account of the peace terms.

Everything here in camp is going about the same as ever except that we are not working quite as hard as we were. The cadets were to quit flying last Friday but they are still flying same as ever.

I have put in another application to fly and am to be examined tomorrow or the next day. There are several that has put in for it. We do not have to go to ground school and may start in in a few days if we get through all right. I am not so very particular as to whether we get through now or not. If we do it probably will take us till spring to get through the course.

We do not know anything about getting out of this army. It may be soon for those that they do not need and it may be quite a while. I do not look to get out before spring.

You were saying something about the folks getting a lot of questions to answer. A lot of the fellows have been saying that their folks got the same thing. I think maybe that they are going to stop sending money home. A lot of the fellows are getting their full pay now that used to get it sent home.

I am writing this letter at the barracks to-night. It is the first that I have written with a pen in quite a while. I doubt if you can read it. Well I must close. Will write if anything new turns up.

Pvt. Chauncey A. Warren
Bat. E., 328th Field Art., 85th Division, Am. E. F., France
November 18, 1918

Dear Folks:

Well, I guess the war is over as I haven't heard a gun for about a week. Yes, I was up to the front. Had the opportunity of seeing the Germans shell some of the trenches, but our guns let out a fire and the Huns quit. I can now say I have slept and eaten in dugouts. The influenza isn't as bad here as in America. Quite a lot of Newaygo county fellows are in my company. About four weeks ago we got an issue of woolen underwear—three suits—also five pairs of woolen socks. Have plenty of gloves and mittens.

In Time of War

November 24, 1918
Pont A Mousson, France

Dear Folks:

Have just been to breakfast; had mush, bacon, syrup, bread, coffee. Yesterday received your Nov. 3, Oct 27 and 30 letters and the day before a bunch of Presses and Indicators. By the dates I am receiving all the papers you are sending. Back a while ago I hadn't begun to get them but am now, also your letters. I guess I have received those 27 letters alright for some would only be two or three days apart. There are two Y.M.C.A.'s here, but really only places where one can buy things to eat. They haven't had time to fix up places yet, for only about two weeks ago hardly anyone was in this town as it was subject to air raids. Every day there are many Red Cross autos traveling by. I think they must be going to Metz, which is about 30 kilometers away (north about 18 miles). The clocks here were set back one hour about a month ago, making a difference of about seven hours in time. When it is 7 p.m. here it is noon in Michigan. Someone bought eggs here for seven francs ($1.30) per dozen.

The days now are clear and sunny, but frosty nights. I have been in this town about 12 days. It used to have a pre-war population of 75,000. It was only evacuated about three or four months ago. The Germans lived here, that is their army, a part of the old Hindenburg army. The old Hindenburg line went through here.* Some of the houses are shelled quite badly and others hardly any. The buildings we are in (three) are not damaged much. Just a few minutes ago the owner came in. Of course we can't understand him. I have a spring tick to sleep on. Am in a room with two other fellows from the 23rd engineers. All rooms have fire-places, but give me a stove. From appearances this used to be a smelting town factory.

Every day there are French prisoners returning dressed in all kinds of clothes, with all their belongings in a pack on their back. Some old and some young. They look around to see what has happened, just as we do. Some live here and others live in Paris and Marselis. Some have been prisoners for six months, one year, two years, etc. Have talked with some. There are also English prisoners and now and then some French women. There have been once upon a time some nice homes here. The streets are in good condition. The town is in a valley, with a river, the Moselle, through it. On one of the rests is a memorial for Joan of Arc, where she made her last stand. That has never been bombed. Until about 12 days ago no trains had been through here for four years. It wasn't because the track was all gone, but they didn't dare go through. A company of Italians and negroes are fixing it up between here and Metz. I saw some American engines and boxcars which are somewhat different than those we saw in France.

A great many negroes are located here; they were in infantry and were in real fighting so have interesting stories to tell. The sidewalks are not very wide. I believe they used the streets to walk in. Of course the buildings are of stone or brick. There is one big church, Catholic. It used to be elegant but has been shelled quite badly. You see the Germans thought the Red Cross might be located there. Had Protestant church there last Sunday. During that time some French Catholics came to see what was left of it. They are nearly as much strangers here as we are. There are some nice streets with well lined heavy top oak trees. It is a city of activity now, whereas two weeks ago silence prevailed. We have fed some of the returning prisoners.

Well I guess I will quit. Everything is O.K.

*The Hindenburg Line, named after Paul von Hindenburg, replaced the old front line in hopes of delaying a spring offensive by resuming the Battle of Somme in 1917.

Don M. Dickinson
November 20, 1918
Fremont Times-Indicator

Mrs. C. A. Dickinson writes of her son Don M. Dickinson, the soldier who was reported missing, as follows: "I have at last heard the truth of my dear boy's death and of his bravery on the battlefield. Gen. Pershing has honored him with a citation which he sent to me. They found his rings, bible, day book and letters, which were very moldy, and sent them also.

Wag. Edwin N. Brown
Amb. Co. 34, 7th Div., San. Train, A.P.O. 793, Vievelle En Huye, France
November 24, 1918

Dear Mr. Puff,

Just a few lines to let you know I am still alive and feeling fine. It has always been a job for me to write since I have been here. We couldn't tell all we wanted to as you know. But I understand the censorship has been lifted.

I want to tell you of my experiences in France since we landed at Brest, France August 27. They made us stay at the boat three days to unload, which wasn't a very pleasant job. From there we hiked four miles to rest camp, as they called it. We were there at least three hours. Some rest! That night, August 30, we hiked to the train and to side-door Pullman's to Pimells, a small town in central France. Here we stayed for six weeks for intensive training, when one morning the Wagoners were called out to go to Marseilles to get our cars. We rode first class to Lyon and then had to take second class. The trains are nothing like ours.

We drove our cars to the Lorraine Front, a distance of five hundred and fifty miles. We had forty-one cars in the convoy and all new ones. That is the only good time I have had in France. Our trouble started as soon as we got to the Front. I drove three days and nights without a wink of sleep and not very much to eat. We had to do all our driving without lights, which made it all the worse for us. My car has three holes through it and I got knocked down once. I have the piece, going to bring it home for a souvenir.

We are now living in a German dugout which the Germans built in 1915. It is 15 feet deep, 30 feet long and 15 feet wide. It is bomb proof, but I must confess that a few of the big six inch shells sure shook us up a little. I must say that I was a lucky boy to get out of this thing alive as we were called out all times of night to go to the trenches to get a load of wounded. The shells and shrapnel bursting around us sure made us think of home. Some of the time I thought I would never see the old dugout again, but good luck was with me.

It took six years to win this war but it will take thirty-six years to take up the barbed wire and fill up the shell holes. There are towns along this Front that haven't even a building standing. You can now see the French coming back looking for their homes. It is very hard to try to explain the condition of the country—I wish I had a camera.

You probably remember that eight of us boys left Fremont together. Harry Dursema and I are the only ones together now. Hope to be home soon. Will close for this time.

Mason Bacon
Troop B, 15th Cav., A. P. O. 205, Am. E.F., Bordeaux, France

November 24, 1918

Dearest Dad:

Well, Dad, last May I honored Mother with a letter, but today is set aside for our Dads, just like that day was for our mother. We can tell anything we want to in this letter.

You will have to excuse this writing because I am laying flat on my stomach on my blanket writing on a magazine. Gosh, but a fellow will get in some awful shapes to do anything. Our evenings go fast, here it is 8:30 already and it seems as if I just got through supper.

Well Dad, I am going to tell you a little about what we are doing and where we are. This is a liberty they gave us to write this letter, so I will try and take advantage of it but I won't tell you all because that would spoil all the fun for me when I got home. I am now at a little town called Carbon Blanc, just a little way from Bordeaux. Bordeaux is a darn big city and a very interesting place. Everything is so old fashioned. We are at a Remount Depot and there is more darn work here than there is in all Muskegon. A Remount Depot is a place where they keep horses and a few days ago there were over 3300 horses here, but now there are not so many because a large shipment went yesterday and we expect them all to be out next week some time. As I heard they are going to make the stables into barracks for soldiers and they will be used as an embarkation camp. I have changed my mind about being home and there isn't a one but what thinks we will be home by

March. Sounds pretty good, eh? It sure does to me. When we landed in Brest the Regiment split up and I haven't seen Leslie since. I sure would like to see him. Maybe I will soon.

Oh, yes, I won't tell you the main things that have happened to me but I got a scar that I will bring home with me though and of course it is right on the fore head over the left eye. Now don't ball me out for not saying anything about it at the time when it happened, but I thought it better not to. I will tell you all about it when I get home.

Well, I hope I won't have to go on any more horse trips now because it is too cold to ride in a box car with eight in it. We have been taking them up to the front to the artillery. But the Cavalry as a whole has not seen a great deal of action. The 9th and 10th Cavalry were blown up pretty bad but none of the rest. That is, the U. S. Cavalry. The English Cavalry was pretty badly blown up.

By golly, there were an awful lot of fellows laid down their lives to see this thing done and there are many more who would have willingly done the same. I myself would have had it been necessary. But, thank God, it wasn't and I am alive, well and happy and able to return home to the ones I love and want to be with. Could God do any more for anyone than he has for me. I should say not.

Well, Dad, I must commence to quit now as it is almost time for lights out and my bunk is not made yet and I want to make it before it is dark in here. I was sorry a while ago; they gave us slips to send home so we could have a package sent to us for Xmas. But the same noon they gave them to us I left with a shipment of horses for the front and when I got back it was too late, because the package had to be at Hoboken by November 20 and it wouldn't have had time to get home. But you think of me all day Xmas and wish I could be with you and that will be just as good as a present. You know that I will think of home all that day and certainly wish I could be with you so I could make up for what I spoiled last year. There is just one thing that I am sorry for since I enlisted and that is because I enlisted just before Xmas. You know it never entered my mind what I was spoiling until I got in Douglas and then I surely was sorry and would have given anything to have undone it.

Well Dad, Merry Xmas and Happy New Year to you. "Good luck and May God Bless you." Tell everybody Hello from me and I wish them Merry Xmas and a Happy New Year.

John B. Brookhuis
Near St. Agnan, France
November 24, 1918

Dear Folks at home:

Well I am going to write you another letter today as I read in the paper this forenoon that every soldier in the army had to write a letter to his "dad" on the 24th of this month and tell what kind of stuff he had been through. Guess this will be the longest letter I have written to you while over here. Will write about this camp first. If you have a map of France you can find some of the places I will write about. This is what they call a replacement camp. They send everybody down here when they are well and then send them to their company from here. It is just outside a town called St. Agnan. I arrived here last Monday night and got all of my equipment on Tuesday. Went to a dentist yesterday and had these roots taken out which hurt worse than being shot.

The weather is fine out here at present only it freezes pretty hard at night. Guess I will stop writing for now and go to see the ball game between the Marines and Infantry.

Well this is Sunday morning and as I can't do anything else will finish this letter. Will tell you a little of how I passed the summer. The first time we went in the lines was July 18. I didn't believe it until the boches began shooting at us. I could hear the bullets hitting the trees. Before we could get at them we had to wade a creek with about three feet of water in it. That afternoon we chased them out of the woods, which we were supposed to do, and slept in some of their dugouts, and in a few days we were covered with cooties. This was on the Chateau Thierry drive. They took us away from there and put us on the Vesle river, which was a pretty tight place for us. We were relieved on the 12th day of August and thought we were going back for a six weeks' rest, but we had quite a few new men so we went away back and drilled every day until the 25th of September when they took us on the Verdun front. When the artillery began there certainly was some noise. All kinds of guns, from three inch to fifteen inch. It was a moonlight night, but the sky was red for miles around. The Boches did certainly run for their dugouts and they didn't come out before the doughboys called them out of their dugouts. We could walk right through the barb wire entanglements, the shells had torn them all up.

On the afternoon of the 26th, a sniper spotted me. There were ten of us in a shell hole; guess they knew that it was full as they kept picking the dirt right above our heads. Three of us made up our mind to get in a better place. Well I was about a half minute too slow. I knew something hit my ankle but didn't think I was shot. I looked and saw two holes in my shoe. Had to walk about a mile to the first aid station. Then four German planes came over and shot at us and not long after sent a few shells over. I decided it was about time for me to get out of that place so I walked about three more miles to get to an ambulance. I laid out doors all that night and the next day and rode all the next night. It was just 48 hours before I had the wound dressed. There they gave us a good feed, cigarettes and chocolate, which certainly did taste good.

Guess I will stop writing about my experiences or I won't have any news to tell you when I get home. Am going back to my company soon and I think it will be next spring before I get back for they are on the march to the Rhine. I might be able to see Germany after a while. Guess all the boys from there will be home before me. You had better keep writing for a while yet. It's just six months since I landed in France and it seems like a year to me. We landed way up in the northern part at a place called Brest.

Will have to close for this time, hoping that this finds you people in good health, and that I may get some mail soon.

**Bill Dobben
Soissons, France
November 26, 1918**

Dear Folks at Home:

Today we may write without the aid of the censors. It has been requested that everyone write home today and we are allowed to seal our own letters.

The nearest we were to the lines was about six hundred meters, that is with our big naval gun, usually about 20 miles when we operated the big rifle. While we were at Soissons we fired upon a town named Laon, one of or shells hit a place where the Germans were having a moving picture show and forty were killed and 61 wounded. Papers the next day said the Germans made a record for fast moving after that shell landed. But they fired at us too and put over a few which made us go for the dugouts. But no one was hurt because we were just eating supper. That sure was great sport.

Last night our Admiral spoke to all the Railroad Batteries. It was sort of a party in his honor. He gave the history of the Batteries until the present time. All the Batteries presented him with a silver cup and he sure acted like he appreciated it. There also was a big army band of fifty pieces, and that sure was the music. I met some of the men that I had been in training with and who had been assigned to different batteries.

We have been intending to leave for the last three days but are still here and no telling how much longer. From here we go to Paris and expect a few days' liberty and then back again to St. Nazarre and from there I don't know where. Maybe I'll be home by May or near that time.

J. B. (Bart) Simmonds
Hdq. Amb. Co., 316 SanTrain, Audewarde, Belguim
November 26, 1918

Dear Mother Reddy:

Will write you tonight after such a long delay. I was so pleased to hear from you and I should have written sooner but some days were so crowded with work and at night I have been usually too tired or too much company in.

Well mother, it looks as though we might be coming home soon as I guess the war is finished for us and the results highly pleasing to all the nations. We have been in Belgium for the past month and the city we are now living in is west of

Brussels on the river Schelde, so you can see just where we are. This town has many historical places of interest and the Town Hall is three centuries old, a very fine example of Flemish art in building; one room we visited had paintings dating back to 1535 and a big carved door done in the 15th century and which took three years to finish. It's very beautiful. I have several very good post card views.

We expect to entrain within a few days for a four day railroad trip to some part of southern France. How long we will remain in camp do not know but hope we will soon be on our way home. If we are mustered out in some eastern camp will try and stop off in Detroit and also to see you for a visit. Of course know nothing of what the plans are but we are rather making some conclusions of our own.

Have never heard anything of the regiment or division that Harry was in but presume I have been close to him in some of the drives. I asked many times when new divisions were moving up to the front preceding the big battle in the Argonne. Then when we left the Verdun sector and came to Belgium we were supporting the French for awhile. It seems mighty quiet now to what it was three weeks ago; the air raids at night by the Huns and the big guns day and night. But it's all over now and the poor Germans will have to be taxed for years to pay for all the destruction they have made; the millions of lives lost that they have been the cause of; the women and children who have died from hunger, and the best pick of the French people wo have died. There is no amount of money that could replace the loss. The pitiful sights now are to see the peasants returning to their homes with their little belongings loaded on wagons with the men pulling them and the poor old women walking behind barefooted and hardly enough clothing on to keep them warm. The children are hungry, as the Huns took all the money, stock and provisions with them.

No one knows as we do the suffering and indignities the Germans inflicted upon them and stories you have heard you may be sure were not lies. I have found some very fine people who are kind and very hospitable and I have never regretted coming over here.

I must close for tonight. Love to all.

Walter Hindes
Nuderdouven, Luxembourg
November 26, 1918

Dear Father, Mother and Girls:

I wrote a letter the other day in accordance with the A.E.F. "Daddy Day" program but the Stars and Stripes of which I received a copy just a few minutes ago say that censorship is off now except on casualty reports, so guess I will tell a few more experiences.

We sailed from the North river docks of New York city on April 6th, the anniversary of the beginning of the war. About 4 p.m. that day we passed by "Miss Liberty" and haven't seen her since. We sailed for two days and reached Halifax on the night of the second day and anchored just outside the harbor. The next morning we pulled into the river and went up beyond the town which as you remember was all blown to pieces when an ammunition ship exploded in the harbor. Some wrecked town! The ship marked Belgian Relief which rammed the ammunition ship was partly submerged where it was blown to on the opposite side of the river.

We stayed in harbor all day while our convoy was making up. About 5 p.m. we sailed out, eight ships in the convoy, five shiploads of Americans, one of Australians, one of Canadians and one ship load of nurses. As we sailed out of the harbor a bunch of battleships, British and American, lay along the channel. Each one had its ship's band out on the forward deck playing for us as we went by. And believe me it made every Yankee in the outfit grow a bit taller as we sailed by the first battleship, British, playing "The Star Spangled Banner." It never meant so much before—as we started on what was known as "the great adventure." The next battleship we passed, also British, was playing the other most popular piece, "Over There." Then we came to the Yankee ships, who true to Yankee sense of humor, serenaded us first with "Hot Time" and then "Where Do We Go From Here Boys'—and we sure didn't know! We had wonderful weather for our trip and being a 1st Sgt. and so eating in the Officer' dining hall, we sure had wonderful chow and a stateroom to sleep in.

We were compelled to wear life belts all the time and had life boat drills each day. On the fifteenth, although quite a distance from the regular submarine zone, a submarine was sighted off to our right rear, which I suppose was on our starboard side and astern and right there and then I heard the first guns talk for business. The guns from all the ships let loose and also fired smoke shells so as to screen the convoy from the sub and the cruiser that accompanied us headed for that direction, but we never heard any results and all was well from there on.

On the 18th we went through that section of the zone, just off the south coast of Ireland, known as the "Kaiser Graveyard." A submarine got a French collier ship just a little way ahead of us but they didn't take a pop at us and all was quiet. On the afternoon of the 19th we sailed into Liverpool and if you think that there is any danger of a submarine or an enemy ship entering the harbor, just forget it. I guess we cut figure S's and S's and everything else for nearly four hours dodging mine fields so as to get into the harbor and we had a Liverpool harbor pilot too.

The next day we disembarked and crawled into one of their dinky little British trains, and riding all night we landed at Dover just across the channel from Calais. We stay in Dover most of the day, Sunday, (roaming over the fields of Dover and the Lime Cliffs of Albior) and crossed the channel in a little over an hour, and believe me we went some. I never saw a boat go so fast before in my life and don't hope to see a faster until it comes my turn to come home.

We went to Casual Camp, (British) known as Rest Camp No. 6 and put up for the night and then and there we got acquainted with the wonderful tea, marmalade and cheese of England, and also saw the first German prisoners. The next day we were equipped with gas masks and helmets and sent down in front of St. Omer (between St. Omer and Ypres) as a Division in reserve in case the Germans should break through which they were attempting to do at the time, and to complete our training in the meantime. Although we were out of range of most of the field guns, we could hear the terrify barrages the Germans were laying down in their efforts to reach Ypres and thence Calais.

We had been there exactly one week when I broke out with the measles and was sent to a New Zeeland hospital just in the outskirts of St. Omer. I sure was treated fine while there but they kept me there a whole month. I thought I'd die waiting for them to send me back. I guess I must have caught the measles on the boat coming over as several fellows came down with them on the boat—didn't think one could have them twice.

While I was there at the hospital I got my first taste of what "Jerry" aviators could do. They came on several occasions and dropped a few bombs but on this particular night they apparently decided to make a good job of it. The planes started coming about 3:30—one would fly over the town, dump its load of bombs and then leave, then the next and so on until over 50 planes had tried a crack at us and dropped nearly 300 bombs. Of course our airplane, that is the British planes were getting by as much as they could with anti-aircraft guns in action. It sure was one pretty sight to see 30-40 powerful search lights playing back and forth across the sky until suddenly they would locate a plane and then all lights would converge on this one plane and the anti-aircraft batteries would let loose. You could see hundreds of shrapnel shells bursting around the planes and streams of tracer bullets form machine guns and allied planes but always luck seemed to be with the "Jerry" and we didn't down a single plane that night. This was especially exciting as Jerry managed to hit an "oil drum" and set fire to large kerosene reservoirs so that it lit up the whole town making it easy to see. Yet the dense smoke from the oil helped to hide the planes above. The last Jerry pulled out about 3:00 a.m. having made a combined visit of about 5½ hours. That was when Jerry was running the air.

When I got out of the hospital my regiment had moved to Warluzel just back of Arras and there each non-com. did a three day trick in the trenches and then came out so that all of the non-com's. would learn a wee bit about the actual conditions in the line before the out-fit went in. I did my trick there too, just opposite Neuvel—about three miles south of Arras and there during my stay I found out what a barrage was like.

The British had enough guns to have plowed every inch of the front line in 30 seconds had they needed to and Jerry had a few too, and every time the Germans would open up the British would think the Germans were going to come over and so they would lay down a barrage and both sides would more than got at it and you never heard such a noise in your life as when a few thousand cannon start talking. Just as we were about to take over the sector there the Hq. A. E. F. decided they wanted us elsewhere so they pulled us out and we started hiking, hiking, hiking and then we rode and rode on trains around south of Amiens around Paris and then east beyond Toul and Nancy out the Lorraine sector in the Vosges Mts. We relieved the 42nd Division in the trenches up in front of Baccarot. I guess the whole division was holding about five miles in the trenches of front, when the second night we were in the line a Hindenburg circus hit us, and left us sadly dilapidated. It was supposed to be a "quiet sector" but naturally all of the Yankees wanted revenge and so we kept up constant patrolling and started raiding them. They didn't have very many heavy guns up there and so we only had an occasional interchange of artillery, but Jerry sure was there with his planes and we weren't.

We occupied the trenches by reliefs for nearly two months and the last part of July we pulled out for a place north of Chateau Thierry but I never got there as I was selected to go to Officer training school and went to Longres where I stayed in school for two months. After the school I was assigned to the 1st Division, went to my outfit via Paris and it sure is some place, but a good place to stay away from. I joined the first Division in the Argonne forest, just at the northern edge near the Romange woods and west and north of Montfancon. Shortly afterwards we were relieved and went back for a few days, got replacements and equipment and then started into this last push along the west bank of the Meuse.

The 2nd Div. "jumped off" or "went over" just north of the Romange woods on Nov. 1st. They were to go about 8 or 10 kilometers in the next two days and the third day we were to "leap frog" them and carry on the push, but they got to going and drove so fast that we didn't jump them until the morning of the fifth and they had gone clear to Beaumont which to have been our Divisions' objective. After pushing all day we pulled out at dusk and made our little dash for Sedan. The Germans had pulled out everything but a few machine guns north of Beaumont but we found more than machine guns en route to Sedan. We got nearly to Sedan and the French wanted to take if for some reason or other so they jumped us during the night and we pulled out.

Now we are en route to Coblentz as part of the Army of Occupation. Just at present we are holding up a few days on our hike on the west bank of the Moselle river, right on the border of the bridge heads that we are to guard I understand.

Have been in some rather warm places at times, but all's well that ends well. Hope I will be able to forget some things I've seen.

If you really want to see something worth while you ought to see the reception we are getting now wherever we go. It sure is grand.

Will ring off for this time. The best o'luck and wishes to you all.

Private Harold Kempf

**Co. I, 139th Inf., Am. E. F., near St. Mihiel, France
November 27, 1918**

Dear Folks at home:

The day before Thanksgiving and a wet, nasty, rainy day; the mud is getting to be quite bad here again. It was cold enough here last week to keep the ground frozen but since it has started to rain again, it has thawed everything into mud.

As it is most too nasty to be outside today we were given the afternoon off to sew buttons on our uniforms and fix our clothes up the best we can under the circumstances, so I am going to try and give you some idea of my trip over here, as we now have that permission.

You have often asked me questions that were impossible for me to answer at that time and I know that you have wondered just what part of the world I traveled over. Leaving Camp Custer on the 15th of July we started east passing through Detroit and through the tunnel under the Detroit river which brought us into Canada. We went by Niagara Falls about 1:30 on the morning of July 16. We passed through the state of New York and down through the Lehigh Valley in Pennsylvania, then into the state of New Jersey, stayed in Jersey City one night and went from there to Camp Mills, I., where we stayed for a few days.

We sailed from New York on the 23th of July, going up along the coast of Maine and landing again in the Halifax harbor where we saw what was left of that city after that terrible explosion which you well remember when those two ships collided in the harbor and blowing up shook the houses to the ground. We were there a couple of days and then started across for France or England, we knew not where. We sailed up close to the coast of Ireland, then south down around the south coast of England, coming back up the English Channel, then up the Thames river where we landed and got off the boat for the first time since we left on the 23rd of July. We landed on August 8th, making 17 days for us on the ocean. We were in sight of London. We stayed in England until the 12th of August when we started for France.

We crossed the channel and landed in France on the 13th of August in the port called LaHarve. We were there for a couple of days before we started on a three day train ride towards southern France where we were billeted about 150 miles south of Paris where we stayed until the 8th of October when I was transferred to this Company in the 35th Division. Since that time I have been near the front lines most of the time and I was only in the front line trenches once. But it is practically over now and I am looking ahead to the day when we will be sailing home again. I think I have told you enough of my trip so that if you will look on the atlas of mine you will be able to see just where I have been. We are located near St. Mihiel at the present time. I am sure you can find it on the map.

Tomorrow being Thanksgiving day I wonder what we will get for eats. Nothing extra I suppose. But just wait, I will be home next Thanksgiving and I am going to make up for this year, believe me. Well I must close, hoping you are all well when you receive this letter. There isn't a thing wrong with me so don't worry. Please write.

Austin Olney
U. S. Jenkins
November 28, 1918

Dear Mother:

Well, at last the war is over. The censorship has been lifted. I expect to be home for a short time within the next three months at the outside.

To-night we are tied up (meaning the ship of course) beside the U. S. S. Dixie (supply and repair ship) at No. 14 buoy, in Cork harbor, Queenstown, Monkstown, Aghadda (where we have a large seaplane base), and several other small towns that are on the harbor. As you likely know it is the old Irish river Lee which empties into this harbor.

We are putting new boilers in the forward fireroom. Will likely finish in another week. Then it is either a pleasure cruise in the Irish Sea, visiting different points or a start for the U. S. A. Don't know which it will be yet. Bet it is mighty cold over there now. Gee makes me shiver to think of it. All we get here is a very slight temperature drop and lots of wind and rain.

Have been following the censor's rules so long that scarcely know what to say, now that I am allowed to say it. Of course you know about the subs and German fleet.

I have been on messenger watch all day. I get it once in four days. We radio girls, as we are called, don't have much to do in port except keep our shack in good condition. There are six of us in the gang, so you see we are not overworked. However, when we were going to sea regularly it was a different story.

I have been hunting subs for over a year and in all that time I undressed just two or three times while at sea. I mean that we always slept with our clothes on. Our hat and life belt for a pillow and my shoes stuck in the side of my bunk. And sometimes I slept with one foot hanging out of my bunk ready to jump, and more than a few times we jumped, too.

Well, it seems now that some of us may be given a chance to leave the outfit when the row is all settled. They won't see me for dust if I get out of here once. Ha! Weigh 168 pounds.

In Time of War

Benjamin Lambers
November 28, 1918
Fremont Times-Indicator

Benjamin Lambers passed away at Ann Arbor Monday October 28 with pneumonia following Influenza. He leaves to mourn their loss, a twin brother (Lambert Lambers), four sisters. There was a short service at the grave, the remains being laid to rest in Maple Grove cemetery. The family has the sympathy of the community

Mason Brace
Walfedinge, Luxembourg
November 28, 1918

Dear Sis:

Well, sis, it is thanksgiving and the war is finished, for which we are all thankful. We are in the army of occupation and I hope will soon be in Germany. France was a nice country but you should see Luxembourg. Everything so clean and neat. We are billeted or rather have our depot in one of the palaces of the Grand duchess. The people sure treat us royally although prices are way out of sight.

I saw yesterday's paper and it had a grand headline in it, "One Million Men to Leave for the Good Old U. S. A." We may not be there so quickly but it can't be long now. We enjoyed a fine dinner today although we all of course wished we were home where talks with our friends and people would make it a real day for us. We are nearly sure of eating Christmas or at least New Years dinner at home.

Did Chester ever get across? He's lucky if he didn't for the paper says, "Men at home and in England first." I was down to Luxembourg city the other night and went to a regular old German Rathskeller. It sure was some place although I couldn't understand the lingo. Pretty nice for us. We just got so we could make the French understand us a little and now we have to learn a new lingo. I'm progressing slow, as usual. I can say "Ja" and "Nein" and a few words besides, which is wonderful for me.

I haven't received many letters from you but suppose you're real busy, so it's all O.K. Really I haven't had time to write as much as I would have liked to but I have had to keep up as near as I could with Mamo, for if I didn't she would worry, so the rest of you had to suffer. Will try and write more often now that everything but moving is done.

This is German stationery. Does it give you a thrill?

"Deek"

**Chas. M. Coburn
December 1, 1918**

Dear ones All:

I wrote a letter to you a day or two ago but find that I can tell where we are and where we have been so will write again.

We left New London, Conn. March 32, Easter Sunday, and went to Bermuda, stayed there a few days and went to St. Michel Island in the Azores. Stopped there a week or so and then went to Gibraltar. From there we went to Malta and after a few days went to Corfu Island and established a sub chaser base. There is where we have been all summer. We formed a line of chasers across the Adriatic sea and would drift around for four days at a time, then go back into the base for supplies and repairs and stay four days. Four days in port and four days out. When we _____ old Fritzy boy in his under sea craft we would locate him and drop a few depth charges on him and for some reason or other he would stop and nothing but oil on the surface of the water would mark the place he stopped at never to go again. We stopped several of them and now that we are up where they had their base we find that we stopped more subs than we really though we had.

I told you of our raid on Durrazo. We got four subs there also. Shortly after that the armistice was signed and now we are just sticking around going from place to place and waiting for a settlement to be made. These Jugo Slavs seem to be very nice people and very friendly towards the Americans. There is a lot more I would like to write but can't yet.

We think we will visit several ports that were once Austrian ports before we leave here. We stopped at Valona and Cattaro on our way up. The weather is something like March in the states so that explains that part of it.

I will close for this time. I am well and hope you are better than that.

John G. Frens
Red Cross Mobile Hospital No. 2, A. E. F.
December 5, 1918
Written by Rose Peabody, October 15, 1918

Just a line to let you know that I have been wounded and am getting along fine. There is nothing to worry about and will write very soon myself.

I will be sent to a base hospital in a few days and will write you as soon as I can from there.

Best love to all. Your loving son,

John

JOHN G. FRENS

DIES OF WOUNDS IN FRANCE

December 5, 1918
Fremont Times-Indicator

John E. Frens who lives two miles west of Fremont received a telegram from the War Department Friday conveying the sad news of the death of his son, John G. Frens, who died in France November 12 of wounds received in action October 15. He was 22 years, nine months and 25 days old. Mr. Frens is the first Fremont boy to have given his life as a direct result of contact with the enemy.

That Mr. Frens did not believe his wounds would prove fatal is evident from a letter dictated by him to a Red Cross nurse.

John G. Frens was born on the farm where his father still lives west of the city and grew to manhood in this community. In August of 1917 he went to Platte, So. Dakota, for his health and remained there about three months. After spending a few weeks at home he went west again in January of this year and remained there until called into service May 29 when he went to Camp Custer. He remained at Custer until July when he sailed for France with the 85th Division.

Mr. Frens was one of the fine young men of this community. He was always especially solicitous for the welfare of his parents and his one ambition was to alleviate their burden.

BERT JONES REPORTED DEAD BY RED CROSS

Letter from Washington States Death Was Result of Wounds Received in Action
December 12, 1918
Fremont Times-Indicator

Mrs. Corniel Klootwyk is in receipt of a letter from the American Red Cross in Washington, D. C., conveying the news of the death of her brother, Bert M. Jones, who was with the American Expeditionary Forces in France. No detailed information could be given by the bureau of communication of the Red Cross.

The letter follows:

December 4, 1918

My dear Mrs. Klootwyk:

It is with deepest sympathy and with a feeling of reverence for the sacrifice you have made that we write you of the official report in our files of the death of your brother, from wounds received in action.

No other lesson has come to America than that of the courage in living and in dying of her young manhood. May she prove herself worthy to have borne such sons as these.

We are today sending to our Paris representative for particulars of your brother's death and shall try to get just that information which we hope will bring some measure of comfort to you. Due to the congested condition of the foreign mails and the time necessary for an investigation in France, it will be some six weeks before we shall hear. We shall then forward the information promptly to you.

We feel it a privilege to be of any service to you.

Very sincerely yours,

W. R. Castle Jr

Ralph Hilton
Rainbow Division, M. G. Co., 167th Inf., American E. F.,
Drisis, Germany
December 12, 1918

Times Indicator:

As it is raining this afternoon and I am not going out for drill I will drop you a few lines to let you know I am still alive and in Germany. The 42nd Division or better known as the Rainbow Division entered Germany on Dec. 3, 1918.*

I know that the people in Fremont will be surprised to know that American soldiers are in this country but such is the case. They are very good to us. They do everything they can for the Americans.

I was in the St. Michel drive and the Argonne Forest drive and they were something to remember. The Americans put over a barrage that will go down in history. There was quite a lot of Newaygo county boys in those drives. The 42nd Division has made a name for itself in this war and I am satisfied that I was transferred to that organization. The division has traveled over 100 miles in the last three weeks and I have been in four different countries. The countries are France, Belgium, Luxemburg and Germany and I guess you will say that is traveling some for three weeks trip. I don't know how much longer they will keep us over here but I hope not much longer, as this country is all right for those who like it, but not for mine. The U.S.A. is good enough for me and I think you will find a lot who feel the same way over here.

Well, I hope to get home before long and then I will tell you all about it.

(*Colonel Douglas MacArthur nicknamed the 42nd Division made up of National Guard units from 26 states the Rainbow Division because it stretched from end to end across the country.)

Ralph Beisel
U. S. S. Orizaba
December 16, 1918

Dear Folks and All:

Well we are just returning to France from our first trip to Rotterdam, Holland. We are at the present time along that part of the English coast where the noted chalk cliffs are. It is just 5:30 p.m. and is almost dark but we can see these cliffs very plainly as they are so white and then the moon is shining right on them, which helps some to make them visible.

Say I was surprised to see Holland, the country, that it is. The dykes are wonderful and the city of Rotterdam is as clean as any town I ever saw in the United States and cleaner than many of them. Everything is as clean as a pin and it is really a modern and up to date country. It is cleaner and more up to date than any country I have been in on this side of the Atlantic ocean. I didn't think that I was going to like Holland so well at first for when we went there, there was an awful heavy fog and the weather was very disagreeable, but when the weather cleared up the next morning, I soon changed my mind. The Holland people really think a great deal of the American people and were very glad to see us as this was the first U.S. ship that had been in there since the U.S. got into the war. It seemed as though the whole town turned out at the docks to see us. The police had to come and keep them away. I really didn't know that I was so much of a Dutchman but found that I could talk to them and get along very good.

The next trip I make to Rotterdam I am going to try to get liberty long enough to take a trip up to Hague, Holland, to see the noted "Peace Palace". It is only about thirty minutes ride on the electric car from Rotterdam.

Now that the German submarines are done away with our main difficulty is the many mine fields and mines that these submarines have laid during the war, and believe me, they are sure plentiful in the English Channel and the North Sea where we go. It is nothing to hear some ship sending out a notice by wireless, giving the position of a floating mine. Of course when we see one we try to explode it by shooting at it with machine guns. We saw one this forenoon and came very close to it before we saw it. We circled around and shot at it until we sank it. I have spent almost a year now sailing around in the Atlantic and most of that time was spent on this side and have only experienced one attack by an enemy submarine, but am sure getting my share of experience with mines, but then they are not so dangerous, at least we don't fear them.

We have aboard three thousand French soldiers who have been prisoners in Germany. Most of them have been prisoners for about four years. Many of them have souvenirs which they have picked up in Germany and I have managed to purchase from them which I will send home at my first opportunity. They will give you most anything for a package of tobacco. It is very interesting to hear them tell of how they were treated in Germany. Of course I am not much of a Frenchman and they are not very good at talking English, but I manage to get along with them about as good as I do with the people in Holland.

If everything goes well during the night we expect to land at Cherbourg, France, tomorrow morning at eight o'clock where we will unload the prisoners. They are sure a happy bunch of fellows now that they are going home.

I have some newspapers that I am going to send home one of these days that are published aboard the ship every day.

Well I guess I will close for tonight as I have the four to eight watch in the morning which means that I must get up early.

Harry C. Fox
Co. B, 4th Inf., Plaidt, Germany
December 18, 1918

Dear folks:

I now am living in Germany for a time, don't know how long. The other day we were in town by the name of Oberwesel, on the Rhine river. We made some hiking to get there. Have seen some pretty good sights. The German people use us all right.

Haven't heard from you folks over there for quite a while. The last one I got from home was dated August 18th, so if you folks don't get my mail it isn't my fault, for I have written as often as I could.

On the hike I carried two blankets, one shelter, half raincoat; bayonet rifle, one hundred rounds of ammunition, gas mask, over coat and helmet.

The weather over here so far has not been very cold and I hope it doesn't get cold while we stay here. By the looks of things I will spend my Xmas in Germany. Hope you folks are all well over there. I am feeling fine only a little bit stiff from hiking so long.

In Time of War

Pvt. George Baars
Field Hosp. 121, 106 San. Train, Am. E. F., Bodeauz, France
December 19, 1918

Friends at home:

A brief sketch of my six months' experience of army life from the 15th of last June to the present time might be of interest to you, so I will tell a few of the sights I've seen and a bit of my six months of army experience.

It was a brisk and beautiful June morning when my brother and the yellow car took me for a twenty mile ride to the County Seat where I met four other young men who were to don the O.D. uniform shortly. They were Fay Burnes, Walter Christenson, Frank Scott and Steve McDonald. We left White Cloud for Grand Rapids at 9 a.m. and there we met Ben Lanning, another one of the (young men) to be Sammies. At this place we took dinner and then left for the place of training, passing through, and stopping at Kalamazoo, and reaching Ann Arbor at about 6 o'clock in the evening. We were checked up in strict military manner by a first Lieutenant. After this we went to supper, which they called mess, and finally at about 9 p.m. we were given our empty straw ticks to be filled and taken to our barracks, where we made our own bed from the bottom to top for the first time in our life. We were not bothered with insomnia that evening, for we were tired out and the rest was welcome.

Next morning was Sunday and instead of sleeping as long as we wished, we were routed out by the bugler at 5:45, went to mess, came back and drilled some and then came our examinations by 10 or 15 doctors who gave us an almost microscopic inspection and finally our vaccination for smallpox and our inoculation for typhoid fever. The day's work was over at 7:45 and the evening was spent by attending a chorus of singing.

The next day was nearly as bad, for they got us up again at 5:45 and after mess and calisthenics we were taken out for our first hike which of course was the beginning of sore feet. The next day we began our study in auto mechanics and of course started in on the Ford, the universal car. (The only place I haven't seen the Ford was on the ocean.) Then came the first letters from home and they surely were welcome, this being nearly a week at camp.

Next day was Saturday, or inspection day, when everyone had to be eagerly dressed, cleanly shaven, hair combed, shoes polished, bed well made and the following articles out on our bunks for inspection: towel, tooth brush, tooth paste, comb, shaving cream, shaving brush, razor, toilet soap and drinking cup. These of course had to be scrupulously clean or we would be confined to quarters or something similar. Well this was the first week here and the following seven weeks were similar only more interesting.

At this place we had a palace to live in and waiters at the table and a university training besides being paid $1.00 per day and being close to our homes. After spending eight weeks here 77 of us started for somewhere. We did not know where, but after riding for two days and two nights in passenger cars we came to Camp Wheeler in central Georgia. This was both a pleasant and interesting trip for we passed through Toledo, Troy and Cincinnati, Ohio and then into Kentucky where the beautiful scenery began.

We passed through the Cumberland mountains which were mostly covered with green grass and cut with many riverlets and large valleys with the sun visible only at times. The sun became warmer and we passed through Atlanta during the night and reached camp at 1:30 the next day the sun at its hottest and the sand at its deepest, while we were hungry and loaded with full pack of barrack's bag and suit cases with a mile and a half walk ahead of us. We stayed at this detention camp for six days and they were the hottest and most sultry days I have ever gone through. After six days here I was fortunate in being assigned to the Medical Corps which was located in another part of camp and much better than our previous place.

After a month and two days of training at this camp in the Medical line we entrained for Camp Mills, N. Y., to embark for France. Our trip to New York was a pleasant one and we passed through many cities, arriving finally at Long Island from where we had a 20 mile ride to the camp. After being here for eight days an epidemic of influenza broke out and we were called on to help out at the Base hospital. This epidemic lasted for over a week and just as the cases were recovering nicely we got orders to entrain for England and stayed up all night and early the next morning took the 20 mile ride to Long island.

Just before the ferry started with us we got orders to unload and go back to camp. After we got back to camp we were told that the ship had sunk so we awaited our next call which came 12 days afterwards. It was 650 foot Holland ship called the Rijndam, which brought us safely to Brest France.

Leaving Hoboken we went south for some time and clung near the coast, but out of sight of land as far south as the Carolinas and then east across the great Atlantic for 12 long days. Everything was going fine and we were enjoying ourselves until the ninth day out when we ran into a large storm so that the waves were estimated by the sailors to be 20 to 150 feet high. It reminded me of a Michigan snow storm blizzard but of course made me feel quite different. The ship was rocking so much that it touched the sea from side to side. Two of the life boats were washed off the top deck and one of the life rafts was smashed to pieces, which happened to be the one that 28 men of our company, including myself, were assigned to, while the waves were rolling over the deck and injuring several soldiers and sailors.

Many of us tasted salt water during the storm while some took their first salt bath. This was an exciting time but very dangerous and I hope we don't have one on our return trip. One of the sailors was washed overboard but luckily caught a rope that was hanging along side the ship. This storm lasted from 10 o'clock one night until 6 o'clock the next evening.

It was interesting to watch the sub destroyers during the storm, for you'd see them one minute and then maybe you wouldn't see them for a while and you'd really think they were going under.

When we got off the ship we gave it a cheer and started for our four mile hike over hilly country to the rest camp where we were supposed to stay for from three to five days and then go to the front, but the armistice being signed a few days after our arrival kept us here for 12 days and then we entrained for Bordeaux in box cars. This was a dreadful trip for 40 of us were packed in a box car about half the size of the American box car. This trip lasted for two days and two nights.

While at Brest I had the opportunity of seeing most of the city besides the old fort or Chateau which was started 50 years B.C. and finally finished by Napoleon. While here at Camp DeSouge I've seen the city of Bordeaux which is a very pretty city and show the better class of people and the better side of France. At this place I saw many sights of interest one of the first being the Girondins monument which is the most beautiful piece of art I have ever seen. Then I went to one of the big Catholic churches called the Saint Andre. This is a large massive building with beautiful interior decorations with a magnificent pipe organ in one end.

Then I went up the Per Berland tower which is 600 years old and 30 feet high and of course has a stationary elevator, it being winding stone steps which were worn down by the many footsteps that have gone up and down in the past 600 years. From this tower one can look all over the city and it reminds one of being on top of the Woolworth building and looking down on New York city and its harbor. After this I went to the Saint Michiel pier where I saw 74 mummies which were 400 years old. They were buried without coffins and had lain in the ground for 300 years and were in the pier for 100 years. I saw many sights besides these of which I intend to bring views with me as souvenirs.

Besides the sights and experiences I have seen and had I wish to make mention of three organizations which have been of great value to the boys in uniform. They are the Red Cross, Y.M.C.A. and the Knights of Columbus. Of these three we cannot speak too highly and the Red Cross comes first of all. In the thousands of miles I have traveled since entering the army, and the many stops we have made the Red Cross ladies were looking for us to give us good hot coffee, doughnuts, cookies, apples, cigarettes or post cards. If we did not stop while going through a town or city, the Red Cross ladies would be out to pick up our mail as we threw it out the windows. They were always on the job and every cent of money that was donated to the Red Cross associations was well spent and put to good use.

The Y.M.C.A. and the K. of C. organizations which are similar to each other have also played an important part in keeping up the morals and spirits of the boys in khaki. Being a Protestant myself I will speak of the Y.M.C.A., but what I say of the Y will in most cases be true of the K. of C. The Y.M.C.A. is the nearest like home of anything in the army. It has been with us in the States, it was with us on the transports and it is with us here. Over here the Y consists of quite a large wooden hut with three or four different rooms, one large room for the canteen, writing paper and game tables; another large room for lectures and the movies, and another room for the library and writing room. At the Y canteens we get articles at nearly cost and the Y men are always ready to give information on anything they can help us with. Sundays they have religious services in the forenoon and evening and some of the best sermons and lectures I have ever heard have been in one of these little wooden huts from me in the O.D. uniform.

These Chaplains and Y men talk to the soldiers as man to man as plain and simple language as possible. At these places we sing the old time songs such as our fathers and mothers used to sing which brings one near to God. Without the Y and K. of C. the army would not be complete. Words cannot express what these three organizations have done for the boys in khaki, and we surely appreciate their efforts.

Of course there are many morose things I could write about from my six months of army life but will not take up anymore of your time except that the boys in olive drab uniform want William the Second to get out of Holland and to have the peace conference held in the ex-emperor's previous place of business, and have him come as an ordinary murderer and plead for his life. I think I am voicing the sentiments of every true-blooded American by saying that we want him to be tried for the deeds he has done and to pay the just penalty that is due him.

We are all glad the war is over and hope that Kaiserism is done away with forever and all time. Many an American soldier has spilled his blood for this cause and many American homes have become saddened through the terrible World War, and as we were anxious to come over here to help our Allies so will we also be anxious to come to our homes as soon as peace is signed.

America is the land of the free where one and all can enjoy the blessings of life and appreciate the greatness of "Our Country" and we thank God for allowing us to call such a country our own.

Darrell H. Eppele
M. G. T. 12th Cav., Columbus, New Mexico
December 19, 1918

Dear Mother:

Received your most welcome letter some few days ago and was surely glad to get a letter from home.

Well I guess we will not get away from here for some time as we were expecting a raid here about a week ago. Villa and Caranza were fighting about 40 miles south of here and we expected trouble. We slept for three nights full pack ready for anything that might happen. We have mounted drill in the forenoon and drill with machine guns in the afternoon.

There is a fellow from Muskegon with me so I am not the only one from Michigan here.

Stanley Morrison
Co. H, 34th Inf., Am. E. F.
December 25, 1918

Dear Mother:

I will write you a line and let you know I am still well and hope everyone at home is the same. Everyone is happy over the way the war is ending and they haven't anything over me along that line.

Well, I was on the front line when the firing stopped, and believe me, everyone was glad. No doubt you have heard about it long before you get this. We are stationed in a town that was all torn to pieces by the Germans, but we have a good place to stay. I am sleeping on a feather bed and it surely goes good after being on the front for 32 days. I haven't heard anything about when we will go home. I don't think it will be very long. I hope not anyway.

Sergeant R. E. Bulger Thrills Big Audience

December 25, 1918
Fremont-Times Indicator

Sergeant Richard E. Bulger, bomber with the Canadian forces, delivered a thrilling address to an audience that filled the Methodist church Sunday evening. Sergeant Bugler was in the hottest of the fighting at Neuve Chapelle, Ypres and Messines Ridge and his descriptions of the battles and war maneuvers were vivid and intensely interesting.

The sergeant was born in Ireland and was raised in the United States. He went to Canada in 1914 and enlisted in the Royal Canadian Dragoons, later being transferred to the Toronto Rifles. In the famous charge following the blowing up of Messines Ridge he went down with a machine gun bullet through his left shoulder and another through his right arm. While being carried to a dressing tent both his stretcher bearers were instantly killed and he received numerous additional wounds. He was wounded 17 times in all. His story was enthralling and it combined humor, pathos, and inspiration most effectively.

Sergeant Bulger comes from a family of fighters. Six of these Bulger brothers have fought for democracy, two in the Canadian army, two in the English army, and two in the American navy. Two of them were killed and the remaining four wounded.

Pvt. Harry C. Reddy
M. G. Co., 56th Inf., Base Hosp. No. 210, Toul France
December 25, 1918

Dear Mother:

Today is again Xmas and what a change the year has brought forth. Last Xmas I wasn't home. And again this year I'm so far away I couldn't be home if I wished to, and you may be sure I wish I could be with you at this time. I wrote you the 22nd and again today so you will get two letters from me about the same time. You can be sure we boys all thought of home today and with our dinner and all the stuff we got from the Red Cross, there is still a strange something that makes us all a little sad. We have had a good dinner, in fact as good as we would have had at home but—the home spirit is lacking, and all of us were a little homesick even if our looks and actions did not show it.

There is one organization without which the boys would be so S.O.L and that is the American Red Cross. Tell the people at home that the Red Cross deserves every cent you can raise—that from me—for I've been where I've seen and observed the great work they are doing.

There is another but little spoken of party of people who have done more good than they have been given credit for, and the world will soon know it. That is the Salvation Army, and right now, Mother dear, I'll say they will always find me ready to donate.

This is a half way decent day, for a wonder. Last night it snowed pretty hard but it's all gone, in fact it didn't stay long, as it was damp and wet and only in the distant hills is it still visible.

Well, Mother dear and Dad, I've got to write another letter so will close for this time, wishing you a happy Christmas, which is now past, and a happy new Year, and hoping I'll soon be home with you once more.

**Harold Zerlaut
Americus, Georgia
December 27, 1918 (from family archives)**

Dear Neva,

I will try and write you a few lines today as there is not so very much to do just now. We have been quite busy for the last few days as there are so many away on furloughs for the holidays. I received the things that were sent all O. K. Many thanks for the candy and tell the folks the same for the ten dollar gold piece. That is the first ten dollar piece that I have ever saw. I received the candy a couple of days ago, but did not get the registered package until late last night. Mail has been so mixed up that it was hard to get anything.

I spend Xmas day at Andersonville, Ga. A lot of us fellows went up there to see the old civil War prison. It's quite a sight to see, but there is not so very much left except some of the old banks and gun walls around the sides and the holes that the prisoners dug for water. There is a big cemetery there where thirteen thousand nine hundred were buried. Nearly every state in the north has a fine monument there. Andersonville is just a small town and everything is run by negroes except one or two stores. We saw a fine scrap between a bunch of them just before we left. A bunch were drunk and they all went at it with knives about six or eight inches long. We fellows did not mix up with them very much but beat it.

I am working in the big warehouse here now. Am checking up air planes and motors and so on. It's a pretty good job and is inside where it's dry. I go to work about eight and quit at five. There is about everything imaginable in the warehouse here, all the DeHaviland planes and Liberty motors and Rhones that were to be shipped across. The warehouse covers five acres.

We had a fine dinner here Christmas day. All the turkey that we could eat, cake, pies and nuts and nearly everything imaginable. The 287th Squadron had about a thousand dollars in the mess fund when I was transferred into it and I guess we lowered it some Christmas. We ate our dinner out on the ground out of mess kits but it tasted just as good as if it were in some swell place.

We are moving today, that is, when we can get off to move. They are taking the hangar tents down and we are going into smaller ones. We hear that there is to be another squadron to come into this depot. If there is they will have to move or discharge some of us. When all the men get back from furloughs there will be about two or three hundred men here that they have no use for.

Well I will close for this time, wishing you a happy New Year.

Ralph Beisel
U. S. S. Orizaba
December 28, 1918

Dear Folks and All:

Well here we are under way and are well out into the North Sea on our way to France with a load of prisoners. We left Copenhagen yesterday about 3:15. We are having all kinds of excitement today. Early this morning we found a civilian that had got on the ship at Copenhagen and stowed himself away and when they found him he told the captain he wanted to go to the United States. He was only a kid about 15 or 16 years old. He was out of luck. He should have stayed hidden a few hours longer as we hadn't put the pilot off as yet, and when we did, we put him off with the pilot.

It is now three o'clock and since one o'clock we have sunk six floating mines by firing at them with our large guns. Believe me, the mines are some thick up here in the North Sea. Although this ship has only been attacked a couple of times by submarines, we are sure seeing action with these mines.

Well I guess if everything goes well we will be in France again by next Monday evening or Tuesday morning.

I will try to explain to you a little bit how we were greeted in Copenhagen. It was the first American ship that had been in there in more than three years, and believe me, they were sure some glad to see us, and more so when they saw that it was one of the transports that had been carrying troops to France. When we went ashore most of the people thought we were English sailors, but when they found out different, nothing was too good for us. I stayed aboard ship Xmas day and visitors were allowed aboard the ship so helped to entertain them by showing them over the ship. I met a Doctor who asked me out to dinner the next day, and believe me, he sure showed me a good time by showing me over the city, besides we had a fine feed. The Danish people think a great deal of American people and will do anything for them. There were thousands of people came down to see the ship every day.

The people of Copenhagen gave to each member of the crew of this ship a piece of candy (a bar of chocolate candy, I mean) and a package of cigarettes for Xmas, and that is more than they did for the British that were in there. The Y.M.C.A. at Copenhagen sent us this stationery. In one public hall in Copenhagen the orchestra played the "American National Anthem" when they saw that there were some American sailors there. There were also some British sailors there and they went up and asked the orchestra to play their national anthem and the orchestra refused to play it. Gee! But the British were sore. The Americans didn't even ask them to play our national anthem.

In Time of War

PART THREE

In Time of War

Victory Achieved
1919-1921

On the eleventh hour of the eleventh day of the eleventh month of 1918, the war ended—at least on paper. In reality the fighting still continued in other parts of the world. In March 1918, the Provisional Government of Russia forced the Tsar Nicholas to abdicate. The new government vowed to continue the fight against Germany. To support their efforts the United States and Britain supplied them with money and weapons. When the Provisional Government was later overthrown during the Bolshevik Revolution, the Bolsheviks agreed to an armistice with Germany. The Allies had worked hard to keep Russia in the fight, but the Brest-Litovisk Treaty dashed any plans they may have had. Thus, the Allies agreed to back any political force willing to stand up to the Germans. To that end, stockpiles of military weapons were delivered to Russian ports.

The Allies found themselves deep inside Russia's civil war as fighting escalated between the Bolsheviks, who had murdered Tsar Nicholas and his entire family to remove them as threats, and the forces of the Czech Republic. Those stockpiles took on more importance as it appeared possible they could be transferred into German hands using the Trans-Siberian Railroad. German troops along the western front were involved in intense fighting. To re-establish an eastern front, intervention seemed the only option Britain and France had. They began sending troops to Murmansk and Archangel in northern Russia near Finland to secure the area. It wasn't long before plans changed from protecting military supplies to overthrowing the Bolsheviks, which many believe was the true purpose of Britain and France all along. After pressure from France and Britain, President Wilson began sending troops to Russia in the summer of 1918.

Over five thousand American troops set foot on Russian soil. This included the 339th Infantry, of which seventy-five percent were Michigan-born soldiers. They were chosen in part because it was believed they could better handle the cold climate of Russia. They dubbed themselves the Polar Bears and became part of the Polar Bear Expedition.

This oft forgotten part of World War I was no less harrowing for them as it was for those who were still fighting in France. The men who thought they, too, were heading to battle in France suddenly found themselves on ships on the way to Russia. And, as it seems to happen too frequently when planning is everything, the British who were in command left the expedition totally unprepared. Though Britain was not responsible for the Spanish Flu, their lack of provisions for those under their charge was appalling. In September 1918 as the ships entered the Arctic waters and the cold temperatures of Russia, many aboard were dying. Their bodies were wrapped in sheets and left to the sea. Many others lay desperately ill on board. The ships had no heat. No warm

Victory Achieved 1919-1921

clothing was available, all having been stored in cargo holds. No blankets covered the ill. And medical supplies promised by the British never materialized.

Upon landing as they traveled miles to camps they continued to bury their dead in make-shift graves along the way. When they finally reached their destination it was revealed the Bolsheviks had already looted most of the military equipment, medical supplies, and food. A nearby village had been left to starve. A plan that had started out to be guard duty of military supplies and protectors of the Czech Legion soon turned into an all-out, long-term fight with the fierce Bolsheviks.

Before leaving England, the American soldiers were told to hand in their rifles and received inferior weapons in exchange. They were given Mosin-Nagant rifles made by Americans for the Russians. These rifles had low velocity and frequently jammed. The Browning machine guns they were accustomed to were replaced with Vicker guns that would freeze in arctic temperatures. The Bolsheviks who often outnumbered the Americans, fought with more up to date weapons putting the Americans in greater jeopardy.

Men suffered from severely cold temperatures, often dipping to sixty degrees below zero, where touching a weapon without gloves could cost a soldier his fingers. Making matters worse was the frequent shortage of ammunition, food, and warm clothes. Men struggled knee-deep in swamps, or dug deep snow trenches where they tried to sleep on frozen ground without blankets. The Bolsheviks were used to the climate and knew the area well. One of their more frightening tactics was to attack at night, often during a snowstorm approaching ghost-like on soundless snowshoes dressed entirely in white.

Months passed and the armistice with Germany was finally signed. While people celebrated in the streets of Paris, London, and elsewhere in the world, the Polar Bears were freezing and dying in Russia with absolutely nothing to cheer about. It seemed the only thing they had in their future was more suffering.

After seven long months of fighting in deplorable conditions the Allies began to withdraw. In April 1919, the French pulled out after mutiny took place in their ranks upon hearing the news of the German Armistice. The Czech Legion and the Bolsheviks eventually reached their own armistice in early 1920. The American troops and most of the other Allies left in 1920, leaving only the Japanese to remain until its withdrawal in 1922.

Ten years after the expedition veterans returned to reclaim the remains of the fallen. They were buried near a large polar bear monument erected at the White Chapel Cemetery in Troy, Michigan. More than two hundred Polar Bear soldiers died. Of those, most called Michigan home. Twenty-two bodies have never been found.

While those brave men fought the Bolsheviks, climate, and terrain of Russia, a conflict of a different sort, one with worldwide consequences, was taking place. The question remained as to what the Allies should do with Germany now that the Armistice had been signed. The Allies were fraught with disagreements. Premier George Clemenceau of France wanted the harshest punishment possible for Germany, whereas British Prime Minister David Lloyd George wanted Germany disarmed but not left so destitute it would fall into the hands of Russian communism.

President Wilson sought to find a way to avoid future wars. To this end he became the first president to leave American soil while still in office. He traveled to Peace Conferences in Paris where he worked diligently to promote The League of Nations. He traveled widely to other countries including the United Kingdom and Italy where he was well-received. Upon his return from his second trip to France he and former President Taft, a Democrat and a Republican, shared the stage at the New York Opera House to further promote acceptance of a League.

In the beginning thirty-nine U. S. senators, mostly Republicans, opposed the League, but after several weeks of debate, some modified their stance for a more limited acceptance. Constructive amendments were made by Mr. Taft and Secretary of State Elihu Root which were later adopted into the constitution of the League of Nations.

The war officially ended June 28, 1919 when Premier Clemenceau of France announced the signing of the Peace Treaty at Versailles. At first Germany had refused to sign the agreement. An ultimatum was given. Germany had five days in which to sign or the war would resume. Peace seemed the better option. However, back in the United States senators still argued whether they should accept and sign the League of Nations document as it stood or keep trying to modify it. President Wilson refused to accept any Republican compromises. Instead he toured the nation urging its signing by the U. S. Senate. On March 19, 1920 the Senate voted 49-35 against membership in the League. After his unflagging efforts for the United States to become a member, his campaign had failed.

The war, the fight for the League, and the general unrest of the country with strikes affecting coal, steel, and railroads took a toll on the president's health. He became chronically exhausted. He suffered from his long time ailment of asthma. Then in October 1919, he suffered a severe stroke. In January 1920, he contracted the Spanish flu. This was followed by yet another massive stroke in March 1920. What occurred next was a serious lack of judgment on the part of the president and others. For the next eighteen months his wife and physician took over the duties of the presidency. They did their best to keep the true nature of his health a secret. They decided which matters would be brought to the president's attention, screened his visitors and all correspondence, even filled out his papers for him. It was during this time the president was awarded the

Victory Achieved 1919-1921

1919 Nobel Peace Prize for his efforts to end the World War and create a League of Nations. However, the disabilities caused by his stroke kept the president from attending the award ceremony.

President Wilson lost re-election in November 1920. It was then the country took the necessary steps to add the 25th amendment to the Constitution. This amendment allows the replacement of a president or vice-president in event of death, removal, resignation, or incapacitation.

President Wilson died in 1924 due to a final massive stroke. Had his 14 Points for peace not been rejected by Allies more intent on punishment of Germany than pursuing future peace, it may have allowed the world to avoid WWII. Among his 14 Points was a call for reduction in arms, abolition of secret treaties, adjustments for colonial claims, and freedom of seas. Instead Germany was forced to pay billions in reparations to Allied nations. Unable to repay compensation for the war along with the depression of the 1930s, German citizens turned to Nazi leadership in the form of Adolph Hitler.

The end of the Great War was not the end of unrest as so many had hoped. On the heels of the women's vote and Prohibition, around the corner from the Great Depression, and in the shadow of the Second World War, World War I was never what it claimed to be, the war to end all wars.

Home Front
Newaygo County, 1919-1921

The Armistice had been signed. War weary soldiers began making their way back to home and family. Some of those who returned brought with them wounds and illnesses that would later claim their lives. People longed to return to their old lives, but too much had changed to simply go back to the way things had been. As we know from our own experiences with later wars or the aftermath of contentious political battles, resentment can run deep, even after the conflict is considered over.

Patriotism continued to be a hot button issue. Newaygo County failed to subscribe enough people to meet the quota for the fifth and final Liberty Bond, known as the Victory Loan. These bonds were issued to help the United States consolidate its debt accumulated during the war. On May 8, the *Fremont Times-Indicator* took to task the slackers who had yet to purchase their bonds, asking if it was too much to ask for help in paying for the cost of victory. Every red-blooded American was urged to do their duty and head directly to the bank and purchase their bonds.

By the fall of 1919, the newspaper often sounded much as it did when there was an active war. Under the title "No Hope for Alien Slackers" in its September 4 issue, it warned those who thought they had escaped retaliation for avoiding service.

Home Front Newaygo County, 1919-1921

It stressed "alien slackers will neither find peace nor comfort in this country if the proposed policy of the American Legion, the national organization of American veterans of the world war, is carried out. These individuals who failed to respond to the country's call during the great conflict may think their cause had been forgotten since an armistice was signed, but that is not the case." The Legion informed the public that it had "compiled a list of all alien slackers, was giving their names to the press for publication and making their existence uncomfortable generally. Foreigners who canceled their first papers (for citizenship to avoid service) at the outburst of the war are included in the list of slackers."

It was not just the alien slackers who were drawing attention, but their employers, as well, were being put under scrutiny. Calls followed for all those who had escaped military service to be immediately deported.

A new American Legion post, Post 91, was organized in Newaygo County in September 1919. Frank H. Raymond was elected Post Commander and Fred P. Reber as Vice-Commander. As part of a national organization for veterans of the World War they accepted anyone who served in the U.S. Army, Navy or Marine Corps between April 6, 1917 and November 11, 1918. It was said to be non-partisan, with no distinction for rank or service, and stood for "100% Americanism for the preservation of what you fought for, for mutual helpfulness and comradeship."

The new post needed a name and at its first meeting unanimously chose to honor C.C. Upton, a local young man who had died in France. This 26 year old man had seen it all. He was gassed, temporarily blinded, shot, hospitalized twice, and finally succumbed to pneumonia. The new Legion felt he had earned the honor which commemorated his name for his courage and fidelity.

In November the C.C. Upton Post held a Victory Day celebration. It was an all-day affair honoring the servicemen of Newaygo County. The men were asked to wear their uniforms for the parade of soldiers and sailors. Following the parade drill exercises were performed. The day included dancing in the street on Division Ave. to the music of the Clark's Band, an address by military personnel, and finished in grand style with music supplied by Fry's Orchestra for the military ball.

The American Legion was asked to help in the distribution of a memorial booklet for former soldiers of the American Expeditionary Forces in France. The memorial booklet was a gift from the French government in appreciation for the United States participation in the war. The tribute expressed their deep gratitude as follows:

"At the time when you entered the war, the French and British armies at their maximum strength, all efforts to dispossess the enemy from his firmly entrenched position in Belgium and France had failed. Your brilliant dash, your uncalculating spirit of sacrifice, checked the onward movement of the adversary.

Your great numbers made possible the final Allied offensive which forced the Germans first retreat and then to capitulate. France will ever remember you and your intrepid chief as the generous and heroic citizens of a great democracy, the Expeditionary Forces of a new hope and better world whose hope is in America." (*Fremont Times-Indicator* 12/25/1919)

During the first year after the war, activities honoring soldiers were frequent. Lieut. Selah M. Reber and "Big Bill" Dobben spoke at a packed Men's Club meeting specifically held to show respect and honor to all returning soldiers. The Congregational Church of Hart and the Methodist Church of Fremont held joint services on a Sunday designated as Memorial Sunday by Governor Sleeper, in memory of the honored dead. And as these smaller remembrances continued, a larger project was in the works.

In June 1921 a four day dedication took place at the newly built Soldiers Memorial Community Building. As Fremont had no auditorium for its citizens, it seemed a building dedicated to bringing people together would be a fitting way to honor the soldiers of the World War. Besides the assembly hall with a stage and seating area for two hundred and fifty people, the building also contained a bowling alley, billiards room, library and kitchen. The basement became the new home of the City Hall offices. The dedication honored over two hundred fifty-five men who had served in the war from the community.

We still continue to remember our veterans every year by observing Veteran's Day on November 11, but our veterans and their service can be reflected upon any time. In Fremont a quiet stroll through the beautifully landscaped Veterans Memorial Park allows for quiet reflection. Park benches placed in front of memorials honoring those from the Civil War, World War I and World War II, to more current wars allow one to sit and contemplate the many names engraved in stone in commemoration of those who served. It's a good reminder of the enormous sacrifices that have been made on our behalf. The amphitheater, playground, and picnic area along with family friendly events and festivals provide a place for people to gather in happier times, many who no doubt are descendants of the heroes honored there.

Letters and Related Articles
1919-1921

In Time of War

January 1, 1919

Dear Folks:

Well here it is New Years day and just had dinner. We sure had some feed too. Just about the same kind of feed that we had for Xmas. We were in port for Xmas but since we have been to Cherbourg, France and unloaded a load of prisoners and are now on our way back to Copenhagen. We are present off the coast of England, just at the mouth of the Thomas river. I was going to mail this letter from Cherbourg but we didn't stay in port long enough even for me to get ashore so I guess I will have to mail from Copenhagen. We are planning on getting some mail in Cherbourg this time but didn't get to because we weren't in port long enough. Gee! I wish that we could have had some mail.

As far as we know at the present time this is the last trip that we make for the French government and then we head for the U.S. once more. I hope that we won't be disappointed, but there is plenty of chance for us to be.

You see I am writing letters New Years day and so as to start the new year in right. Well I guess I will close for today but perhaps will be able to write more before I mail this.

January 4, 1919

Here we are in Copenhagen again and going on liberty in a hurry so guess I must bring this letter to a close in a hurry.

In Time of War

Dale DeVere Whitney
January 30, 1919
Fremont Times-Indicator

Dale DeVere Whitney, member of the old Muskegon Rifles and one of the boys who went with the company to Grayling, then to Waco and overseas, died of wounds in France Nov. 12, it has been learned. Whitney was in the motor truck service, was wounded in action and died November 12. The government dispatch to his relatives here does not state the date he was wounded. Mr. and Mrs. N E. Whitney, parents of the young man, now live near Grant. Previous to enlisting with the local company, Whitney drove the North Muskegon bus and also drove a private car for a Muskegon family, it is understood. Dale Whitney graduated from the Fremont high school about three years ago.

Corp. Harry C. Fox
Co. B, 4th Inf., 3rd Div., American E. F., Plaidt, Germany
January 25, 1919

Dear folks:

I don't know where my letters go if you don't get them, for I have written every week since we have been here, which is six weeks tomorrow night. Got three letters Friday, one from you folks, one from Fred and from Bernice.

I'd like to have been there and gone to the party you had for the boys. It won't be long before you can have one for Earl and the bunch that are in the 85th division. I heard they were on their way home. The way it looks now, the robins will be singing before I get back.

It is a little over six months now that I have been on this side of the pond and it is six months that I will never forget.

Last week I was in a Browning machine gun school. On the front I used one, so they wanted me to tell them what I knew about it. Guess we will go out on the range tomorrow and do some shooting with it. My finger is getting along fine.

Since we have been here I have been getting pretty good feed and am getting fat.

The weather is about like it is in November over there, the ground is frozen but no snow. This will be all for this time.

February 10, 1919

I haven't heard from you folks for over three weeks. I got a Fremont paper today and it seemed good to hear what was going on over there. I was out and watched a football game this afternoon between the 6th Eng. and the 4th Inf., the latter being beaten.

I was out drilling last week and my finger that had the felon* on it is too sore yet to handle a rifle. Was on the rifle range Friday, it was pretty cold to shoot very good.

Had a pass yesterday, a boat ride on the Rhine river from Andernach to Bonn. It was a nice trip and would have been great in the summer time. Left Andernach at 10 a.m., had dinner on the boat at Bonn, got back to Andernach about 3 p.m., had supper there and went to a boxing bout at night, so take it all around, it was a fine trip.

I haven't run across any one that I know from around home. I would like to see Adrian Ish but don't suppose I will over here.

The last week has been pretty cold but not much snow. Every day is the same so I haven't any news to write. Hope you folks are all right and don't worry about me as I am feeling good and eat my three meals every day. Don't know how long we are to stay here but I guess until after peace is signed anyway. It is time for retreat so will have to stop writing and hand in the letter.

Good bye

*Felon: infection of the fingertip.

Author's Note:

After January 30, 1919, several issues of the *Fremont Times-Indicator* are missing from microfilm and sadly many letters are presumed lost at this time.

Pvt. Otto W. Smith
Field Hosp. 331, Am. E. F., A.P.O. 901-C, Italy
February 2, 1919

Dear Mother:

Sunday forenoon and I am in Rome again. Left Treviso last Wednesday and since then have been taking in sights in Venice, Naples, Pompeii, Vesuvius and Rome. Have about six more days to spend in Rome and Florence, so you see I got my leave all right. There were ten of us when we started out. Only four are in Rome now, guess the rest are in Naples. We couldn't keep together.

Well Rome is a very nice place. We have sunny days here. These are the coldest days of winter and the fields are of a lovely green. The city is quite like an American town. There are many here and in Naples who speak English. We took in all the important places with Y.M.C.A. guides. The Knights of Columbus furnish us with rooms free, so we are pretty well cared for here. The U.S. pays car fare, otherwise I couldn't have taken the trip as everything is quite high here. The streets are lousy with street cars, fare three cents. That's one thing that is cheap.

Friday we climbed to the top of Mt. Vesuvius and gazed down into the still live crater. It has a very large crater, large enough to bury a small town. The clouds of vapors still roll from the summit. We could look down and see the molten mass with gushes of flames occasionally, with a roar of rushing air. We had a good view of Naples across the bay from the mountain. You see the mountain is several miles from Naples. Pompeii at the base was well covered with lava. The old ruins are quite interesting. It was quite a thrilling trip. I would not care to take it very often, the mountain might take a notion to talk. They were picking oranges and lemons at Pompeii. On top of Mt. Vesuvius the snow was a foot deep, as they had just had a snow up there. Walking through it made me think of home.

Well, I won't try to tell you all because it would take too long. I can tell you better when I get home. I ought to have some mail when I get back to my company again. The trains are so crowded that it's hard traveling. Will write soon.

French Girl Grateful for U.S. Assistance
March 13, 1919
Fremont Times-Indicator

Rev. and Mrs. F. W. Magdanz are in receipt of a letter from a French girl in which she expresses grateful appreciation to America and American soldiers for the part they played in the great world war. This girl is Gabrielle Vignon.

Among other things she said:

Poor France was a bit feeble. She stopped, but could not force back the enemy. If we have the victory now, it is thanks to the American soldiers and the brave heroes, who struggled well to the very end. Without them we would still be in the great scourge, which made so much misfortune and sadness and so many widows and orphans. Today we have peace, but we shall be still happier when all the brave men shall be home with their families. My own dear brother is now in Constantinople; it will be four years the 9th of April since he went to war. He was a mere boy of sixteen. Four years of suffering and moral tortures we have passed through, but we hope there will not be another terrible war like that which has just taken place the last four years, and we must resign ourselves with courage, for some day my brother will come back and we shall be united again. Receive best wishes from all my family and a devoted young French girl.

C. C. UPTON POST

September 8, 1919
Fremont Times-Indicator

In commemoration of the heroic deeds and the supreme sacrifice of a local son, the Fremont chapter of the American Legion, recently organized here, has taken the name "C.C. Upton Post." The action of these newly organized veterans will meet with general commendation. Mr. Upton was one of two local boys who died on foreign soil, the result of active service in the recent struggle for human liberty.

C. C. enlisted in the government service on June 28, 1917, and was a member of the 78th Co., 6th Regiment of Marines, and went overseas the latter part of January, 1918. The first battle in which he was actively engaged was on the Marne. He was gassed June 14 in the battle of Chateau Thierry and was confined to the hospital until October. For two weeks he was totally blind and after being in total darkness for six weeks his sight was restored. On October 31, 1918, he was shot through the left thigh and was again confined to the hospital but recovered sufficiently to start for the place of embarkation. He was taken ill with pneumonia, however, and from this siege he did not recover.

This is indeed a sad story of heroic sacrifice which tells volumes in patriotic devotion to our country. Almost from the time he placed foot on foreign soil the havoc of war began to exact its toll of sickness and death. He fought in battle with courage and fidelity, and has earned the honor which will commemorate his name.

Donald E. Crabb
January 15, 1920
Fremont Times-Indicator

Word has been received here that Donald E. Crabb, a former Fremont boy, sailed from London for the U. S. on January 9. He has been overseas since the 85th Division went over and is the last man to leave there who is entitled to wear the "Polar Bear." He has been, until about four months ago, in Russia where for some time he was clerk to the Vice Consul, and has held that position in London until he resigned last week. He is bringing his bride with him, as he was married at Christmas time. They will go direct to Detroit where they will be guests of Mr. and Mrs. Fred Hall, 372 Leslie Avenue.

Carl H. Felber Is in Army Training School
February 19, 1920
Fremont Times-Indicator

Carl H. Felber, son of Mrs. Rudolph Zimmerman, 112 Gerber Avenue, who is a member of the headquarters detachment of the famous First Division, now stationed at Camp Zachary Taylor, near Louisville, Ky., is now studying the operation and repairing of motorcycles in the camp school, which he is attending by permission of Maj. Gen. Charles P. Summerall, commander of the First Division.

The purpose of the school, which is being developed along lines planned at a recent conference of high army officers at this city, is to train those serving in the army for trades and professions which they can enter after completing their terms of military service.

Those who have been admitted to the motorcycle an automobile departments consider themselves especially fortunate since they are not only qualifying for an attractive and important branch of military service but are also being prepared to take up one of the most progressive and remunerative trades when these return to civil life.

Body of Dick Deur Buried Yesterday
August 19, 1920
Fremont Times-Indicator

The body of Dick Deur, an American soldier who died in France, was brought here Tuesday from New Jersey for burial. Mr. Deur passed away October 22, 1918, following a short illness of pneumonia in the hospital at Camp Cortquiden. He had not entered active service to the time of his death.

Mr. Deur was the son of Henry Deur, who was a resident of East Saugatuck and Holland for many years but who recently moved to Fremont. His mother died while he was in infancy.

The deceased was born in East Saugatuck February 14, 1890, and spent his entire life there and in around Holland. He was taken into the service through the draft in May, 1918, going to Camp Custer for training. He was at Long Island for two weeks before sailing and went to France during August 1918. He was a wagoner in Supply Co. 328, Field Artillery.

Besides his father, Mr. Deur is survived by two brothers and two sisters, George and Raine Deur and Mrs. George Van Dyke of Fremont and Mrs. Dick Stegenga of North Holland.

The funeral service was held yesterday afternoons from the first Christian Reformed church, conducted by Rev. J. Mokma, pastor of the Second church. Interment in Maple Grove cemetery. The American Legion accompanied the body to the grave where the Legion's funeral rites were used.

Ralph Leroy Hilton Passed Away Friday
August 8, 1920
Fremont Times-Indicator

Ralph Leroy Hilton of Munising, Mich, son of Mr. and Mrs. Frank Hilton of this city, passed away at the home of his sister, Mrs. Inez Smith, of Grand Rapids, Friday, July 9, after a long illness of tuberculosis. He was 29 years of age.

Mr. Hilton was born in Fremont January 16, 1891, and spent his boyhood days here, receiving his education in the local high school. At the time of his death he was a foreman in the plant of the Michigan Tanning & Extract Co., in Munising.

He spent a year in the government service overseas during the World War and was in the 42nd division, machine gun company 167, infantry. At the close of the war he was honorably discharged.

On July 4, 1918, he married in Fremont Miss Myrtle Shall of Munising and to them was born one child.

Mr. Hilton was a member of Pilgrim Lodge, No. 180, F. & A. M., Fremont Chapter, and the Consistory and Shrine at Marquette, Mich.

Besides his parents, wife and baby, he is survived by three sisters, Mrs. Hiram David of Greenville, Mrs. Jay Yockey of Newaygo and Mrs. Inez Smith of Grand Rapids; also two brothers, Harold Hilton of Detroit and Elgin S. Hilton of Munising.

The funeral services were held from the Methodist Episcopal church Tuesday afternoon at 2 o'clock, conducted by Rev. J. Wesley Esveld, the pastor. The body was interred in Maple Grove cemetery where the Masonic rites were used. Members of the American Legion acted as escort at the funeral.

Albert Siems, American Soldier, Buried Friday
August 12, 1920
Fremont Times-Indicator

With military honors the body of Private Albert Siems who died in Coblenz, Germany February 2, 1919, while in the service of his country, was re-interred in American soil Friday afternoon. He was the second of the boys who died in Europe to be brought back to this city for burial.

The young man entered the service at White Cloud, May 28, 1918. He was first sent to Camp Custer and after six weeks training was sent to Camp Mills, New York, where he remained a few days before embarking for France.

He served with the Rainbow Division, in the Argonne Forest, Chateau Thierry and Verdun.

After signing the armistice, he was transferred to the Army of Occupation and was stationed at Sinzig, Germany, on the Rhine.

He was taken ill at Sinzig with pneumonia and was taken to the hospital at Coblenz, where he died February 2, 1919.

The body arrived in New York August 2, 1920, and arrived at Fremont Thursday morning, accompanied by a soldier.

Mr. Siems was born at Fremont, Mich., December 28, 1897, the son of Mr. and Mrs. Klass Siems. His mother still resides on a farm two and one half miles south of Fremont, his father has died about a year ago.

Besides his mother he is survived by four brothers, Ralph, Henry, John and Corniel, also two sisters, Mrs. Alta Sipkens of Caldwell, Idaho, and Jennie of LaFayette, Indiana.

The funeral service was held in the Church of Christ, Friday, at 2 p.m., conducted by Rev. J. W. Hofstra of Holland, Mich., pastor of the Seven Day Adventist church of that city.

The American Legion attended the service in a body and had charge of the service at the grave in Maple Grove cemetery.

The municipal and other flags floated at half staff the day of the funeral.

William Hutchinson Buried in Bridgeton
January 6, 1921
Fremont Times-Indicator

The body of William Hutchinson, a World War veteran, who died in France October 20, 1918, following an attack of influenza and pneumonia, was brought to this city last Friday and the funeral service was held at the Schenk school house, south of the city, Sunday afternoon conducted by Rev. Charles Curtice. The body was laid to rest in Bridgeton cemetery.

Letters and Related Articles 1919-1921

The young man was the son of Mr. and Mrs. Otis Hutchinson, who live 5 ½ miles south and 1¾ west of Fremont, and was born April 25, 1896. He was drafted into the service April 29, 1918, and was sent to Camp Custer. He remained there until August 10, 1918, when he was transferred to Long Island, N. Y. After remaining at Long Island for two weeks he embarked for France. In October, 1918, he contracted influenza and died October 20 at Camp Hospital No. 62, Saint La Sere, France, and was buried in Eighty-fifth-Division cemetery.

He is survived by his parents, five sisters and two brothers.

**Oley L. Gunderson Died at the Home of Emmett Eldred
May 5, 1921
Fremont Times-Indicator**

Oley Lamont Gunderson, an ex-serviceman, passed away at the home of his uncle, Emmett Eldred, two miles east and ¾ mile north of Fremont, last Wednesday, April 27. Mr. Gunderson served overseas during the world war and was gassed while gathering ammunition between the lines. As a result of this he contracted tuberculosis and was ill about 18 months. He was cared for in several of the government hospitals but came here about ten weeks ago to be with relatives and has since been at the home of Mr. Eldred.

Mr. Gunderson was born in Muskegon May 19, 1889. After the death of his mother in 1895, he made his home with the

Eldreds for about 18 years. He went to the western states where he was connected with several large shows as a slack wire performer.*

The funeral service was held from the Eldred home Friday afternoon conducted by Rev P. R. Norton, pastor of the Methodist church. The funeral service was in charge of the C. C. Upton Post, American Legion. Interment in Maple Grove cemetery.

*Slack wire is an acrobatic circus act that involves the balancing skills of moving along a flexible wire suspended in the air.

Honor the Memory of Dale Whitney
August 11, 1921
Grant Herald

The funeral of Pvt. Dale DeVere Whitney was held Sunday at 2:30 p.m. from the Grant Community church, Rev. Livingstone officiating. The church was crowded to the doors while two hundred people unable to even find standing room within stood outside. Approximatly 60 ex-servicemen were in uniform, attended in a body, representing Ensley, Newaygo, and Grant American Legion Posts with a firing squad from Kent City.

About 100 automobiles formed in the procession to the Shippy cemetery where, under the direction of Lieut. DeBoer, of the

Letters and Related Articles 1919-1921

Carl Johnson Post, Grand Rapids, the impressive military service was conducted. After the committal service was read the firing squad fired three volleys over the grave, then as a hush fell upon all, from far away the sad sweet notes of "Taps" and once more the brave wearer of the khaki was "at ease." Dale DeVere Whitney was born at Shelby, April 8th, 1898. He attended Grant public school in 1908. At the age of 13 Dale took the eighth grade examination and had the highest standing of any person in the county. He later attended Fremont high school, from which he graduated in 1915 at the age of 17. While in high school Dale was very much interested in athletics, being a member of both the football and the track teams. He was also a member of the glee club and by his cheery manner was a general favorite in the school and community.

On May 14, 1917, he enlisted in the Muskegon National Guards and left with Co. G for Grayling and from there to Waco, Texas, where he was assigned to Co. I, 128th infantry, Sept. 23, 1917. After reaching France he was transferred to Co. F. 107 supply train. Here he distinguished himself for daring as a truck driver, his officers stating that there was never a dangerous commission that he hesitated in taking and where other drivers failed to get thru he accomplished the task assigned him.

It was on the morning of the signing of the armistice, at ten o'clock that he was wounded by a bursting shell. He died the following day, Nov. 12, 1918.

Fall from Silo Was Fatal to Frank Henry
September 15, 1921
Fremont Times-Indicator

Frank B. Henry, Jr., son of Mr. and Mrs. Frank Henry of Dayton township, died suddenly last Friday as the result of a 20 foot fall from a silo on which he was working. Mr. Henry was rebuilding the silo on the farm of Duncan McCallum on the county line when the accident occurred. He was engaged in nailing the stay laths to the silo when the lath on which he was standing gave way. In an attempt to save himself from the fall, he struck the back of his head on one of the laths, thus sustaining the fatal injury. He was hurried by automobile to Hesperia but succumbed just before reaching the doctor's office.

Mr. Henry was born in Dayton township July 2, 1891, and with the exception of two years spent in the upper peninsula, has lived in Dayton all his life. He was unmarried. The deceased was a carpenter by trade.

Mr. Henry was in the United States military service for 21 months during the war, 11 months of which time was spent in France. He served in the 85th Division, 337th Infantry, Headquarters company.

Besides his parents, he is survived by four sisters, Mrs. Roy Parker, and Lucille Henry of Fremont, Mrs. Ellis Emmons of Big Rapids, and Mrs. Chas. Young of Rockford; also three brothers, Floyd Henry of Muskegon, Lawrence Henry of Fenton, and Ralph Henry of Howard City.

The funeral service was held Monday afternoon from the Congregational church here, Rev. M. Klerekoper, pastor of the Hesperia Presbyterian church, officiating. The Masonic rites under the direction of the Hesperia lodge, of which he was a member, were used at the grave. The American Legion furnished an escort to the cemetery.

**Saves Man's Life, Reber is Honored
December 15, 1921
Detroit Free Press**

Washington, Dec. 4—For saving the life of an unidentified man who had fallen into the Seine, the French government has forwarded, through the navy department, a bronze life saving medal and diploma, descriptive of the award to Frederick Paul Reber, a Fremont, Mich., ex-machinist's mate, second class, United States navy.

Reber was walking near the Seine on June 13, 1919, when he was approached by a group of people under the end of the Pont Royale. Attempts were being made to discover a means of pulling ashore the struggling body of a man who had either jumped from the bridge or fallen from the bank. Reber arrived on the scene when the man was considered by the crowd to have sunk but seeing a dark object about 15 meters from shore, he threw off his shoes and coat, struck out in the Seine and discovered it was the body.

With the assistance of a French surgeon the unknown (man) was brought back to life.

Reber enlisted April 28, 1917, and was honorably discharged August 9, 1919.

Letters and Related Articles 1919-1921

A time to tear and a time to mend,

A time to be silent and a time to speak,

A time to love and a time to hate,

A time for war and a time for peace.

Ecclesiastes 3:7-8

Note of Thanks

So many people have contributed to the success of this book. To my friends and acquaintances who often asked about the progress of my book, I thank you. Your support reminded me there was an audience out there waiting for *In Time of War*. When I got bogged down in my writing, I only had to think of the people who wished me well. That was all the encouragement I needed.

Much gratitude goes to Jerry Hagans, Scott McCormick, and Kathy Smith, teachers all, who took time out of their busy lives to read the manuscript and offer up their expertise. You rooted out mistakes and smoothed the rough spots. It's a better book because of you.

For Jim Johnson, who read through pages and pages of war-related material with the eyes of someone whose father was severely wounded in WWII, your insight into the consequences of war and your natural love of history made for some great discussions. Your enthusiasm for this work was truly contagious and I sincerely thank you.

Many thanks to Cyndi Sanders, librarian for the Local History Room, Fremont Public Library, who searched diligently through the files and books available on WWI., and also kept the old microfilm machine humming, ready to go on days I was expected to do research. That machine was a trial!

Note of Thanks

Without it, I would not have been able to obtain the letters for this book.

For Myrna Brenner, niece, friend, confidante, and teller of tales, thank you for your support, for listening when I wanted to throw up my hands, and for making me laugh. With all you've had going on in your life, taking time to read one of my manuscripts once again, I can't thank you enough.

And last, but not least, for Mark Worthing, who has made all my books incredibly better by his own experiences as an author and teacher of writing. No words can express how much your support has meant to me.

Bibliography

Bausum, Ann. The Battle for Democracy on the Home Front During World War I. Washington D.C. National Geographic, 2010.

Binyon, Laurence. "For the Fallen" at https://en.wikipedia.org (accessed Jan., 11, 2023)

Brittain, Vera. Testament of Youth. London: Victor Gollance Ltd., 1933."

Burnes, Elizabeth. Immigration and Naturalization Blog. National Archives Jul 1, 2022 at https://history hub.history/gov (accessed Nov. 28, 2023)

Daniels, Patricia E. "The History of Trench Warfare in World War I." ThoughtCo, Apr. 5, 2023 at thoughtco. com/trenches-in-world-war-i-1779981 (accessed Jan. 5, 2024)

Doak, Robin S. Assassination at Sarajevo. Minneapolis, Minnesota: Compass Point Books, 2009.

Freedman, Russell. The War to End All Wars, World War I. New York: Clarion Books, 2010.

Grant, R. G. World War I from Sarajevo to Versailles. New York: D. R. Publishing, 2014.

Bibliography

Herschell, William. "We'll All Go Broke if We Have To—But There's No One Busted Yet." Fremont-Times Indicator, Oct. 10, 1918.

Holihan, Kerrie Logan. In the Fields and Trenches. Chicago: Chicago Press Incorporated, 2016.

King, Susan Zerlaut. Out of the Wilderness, A History of Sitka, Michigan. Australia: Morning Star Publishing, 2018.

McCrae, John. "In Flanders Fields" at https://en.wikipedia.org/wiki/In_Flanders_Fields (accessed Jan. 11, 2024)

Miller, James and Confield, H.S. The People's War Book and Atlas History, Cyclopdia and Chronology of the Great War. Cleveland, Ohio: R.C. Barnum Co., 1920.

Nelson, James Carl. The Polar Bear Expedition, The Heroes of America's Forgotten Invasion of Russia 1918-1919. New York: Harper Collins Publishers, 2019.

Roos, David. "The Sedition and Espionage Acts Were Designed to Quash Dissent," August 25, 2023 at https://www.history.com/news/sedtion-espionage-acts-woodrow-wilson-wwi (accessed Nov. 28, 2023)

Tuchman, Barbara. The Guns of August, The outbreak of World War I. New York: Random House, 2014.

Unattributed Sources

"5 Reasons for the U S Entry into World War I" at https://historylists.org/events/5-reasons-for-the-us-entry-into – world-war-i. html (accessed Nov. 28, 2023)

"A Brief History of Chemical War" at https//sciencehistory.org/stories/magazines/a-brief-history-of-chemical-war (accessed Jan. 5, 2024)

"America Goes to War" at wwichangedus.org/all_resources/America-goes-to-war-prepraredness-v-peace-movement/ (accessed Nov. 28, 2023)

"Espionage Act of 1917" at https://en.wikipedia.org/wiki/Espionage_Act_of_1917 (accessed June 26, 2023)

"German Americans During World War I" at https://www.ancestery.com/contextux/historyicalinsights/wwi-united-states-german-americans (accessed June 26, 2023)

"German-Americans during World War I" at https://www.immigrantentrepreneurship.org/ (accessed June 26, 2023)

Home Guard Notes. No author. No date. On file with Terry Wantz Historical Research Center, Fremont, Michigan.

Unattributed Sources

"How the Shocking Use of Gas in World War I Led Nations to Ban It" at https:www.history.com/news/world-war-i-gas-chemical-weapons (accessed Jan. 5, 2024)

"How the use of Zepplins in WWI changed warfare forever" at https://www.historyskills. com/classroom/year-9/zepplins/ (accessed Jan, 10, 2024)

"Immigration Act of 1917" at https://en.wikipedia.org/wiki/Immigration_Act_of_1917 (accessed June 6, 2023)

"Immigration Act of 1918" at https://en.wikipedia.org/wiki/Immigration_Act_of_1918 (accessed June 26, 2023)

"Internment of German Americans" at https://en.wikipedia.org/wiki/Internment_of_German_Americans (accessed June 26,, 2023)

"Life in the Trenches of World War I" at https://history.com/news/life_in_the_trenches_of_world_war_i (accessed Jan. 5, 2024)

"M2 gas mask" at https://en.wikipedia.org/wiki/M2_gas_mask_(accessed Jan. 10, 2024)

"Mexican Border Duty Prepared Wisconsin Guard for WWI" at https//ng.wi.gov/news/16113 (accessed June 21, 2023)

"Michigan's World War One Centennial" at https://www.worldwar1centennial.org/index.php/Michigan-in-ww1-home-page.html (accessed June 21, 2023)

"On the Mexican Border, 1914 and 1916" at https://www.militarymuseum.org/MexBdr1916.html (accessed June 21, 2023)

"Pancho Villa" at https:en.wikipedia.org/wiki/Pancho_Villa (accessed Aug. 7, 2023)

"Pancho Villa Expedition" at https://en.wilipedia.org/wiki/Pancho_Villa_Expedidtion (accessed June 21, 2023)

"Preparedness Movement" at https://www.britannica.com/event/Preparedness-Movement (accessed Nov. 28, 2023)

"Preparing for War" at https://www.nps.gov/subjects/worldwari/preparing-for-war (accessed Nov. 28, 2023)

"Punitive Expedition in Mexico 1916-1917" at https://2001-2009.state.gov/r/pa/ho/time/wwi/108653 (accessed June 21, 2023)

"Second Battle of Ypres" at https://www.britannica.com/event/Second-Battle-of-Ypres (accessed Jan. 11, 2024)

Unattributed Sources

"Selective Service Act of 1917" at https://en.wikipedia.org/wiki/Selective_Service_Act_of_1917 (accessed June 26, 2023)

"Spanish Flu" at https://www.history.com/topics/world-war-i/1918-flu-pandemic (accessed Jan. 5, 2024)

"Spies Among Us" at https://www.nypl.org/blog/2014/10/07/spies-among-us-www-apl (accessed June 26, 2003)

"The American Expedition Forces" at https://www.loc.gov/collections/stars-and-stripes/articles-and-essays/a-world-at-war/american-expeditonary-forces/ (accessed Nov. 28, 2023)

"The History of the United States Military Draft" at https://newsomcontentknowledgeproject.weebly.com/world-war-1.html (accessed Nov. 28, 2023)

"The United States Prepares for War" at https://pressbooks-dev.oer.hawair.edu/ushistory/chapter/the-united-states-prepares-for-war/ (accessed Nov. 28, 2023)

"The Zimmerman Telegram" at https://www.archieves.gov Zimmerman (accessed Aug. 11; 2023)

This Fabulous Century, Volume II, Time-Life Books. New York: Time, Inc., 1969.

"United States Entry into World War I: A Documentary Chronology of World War I" at https://edsitement.neh.gov/lesson-plans/lesson-3-wilson-and-american-entry-world-war-1 (accessed Nov. 28, 2023)

U.S. President Woodrow Wilson Signs National Defense Act" at https://www.history.com/this-day-in-history/u-s-presidesnt-woodrow-wilson-signs-national-defense-act (accessed June 26, 2023)

"World War I" at https://www.michigan.gov/dmva/about/history/military-events/highlights/world-war-i (accessed June 21, 2023)

"World War I Packs" at https://www.history.com/topics/world-war-i/world-war-i-packs-video (accessed Jan. 18, 2024)

"World War I Enemy Alien Records" at https://www.archives.gov/research/immigration/enemy-aliens-ww1 (accessed June 26, 2023)

"World War One: How the German Zeppelin wrought terror" at https://www.bbc.com/uk-england-27517166 (accessed Jan. 10, 2024)

"World War Ones role in the worst ever flu pandemic" at https://theconversastion.com/world-war-ones-role-in-the-worst-flu-pandemic-29849 (accessed Jan. 5, 2024)

www.ingramcontent.com/pod-product-compliance
Lightning Source LLC
Chambersburg PA
CBHW020514080526
44583CB00013B/597